WE STRUGGLED FOR LIFE

The Hungarian Zionist Youth Resistance
During the Nazi Era

Rafi Benshalom

JERUSALEM ♦ NEW YORK

Copyright © Moreshet — Sifriat Poalim
The Society for Research of the History of the Zionist Youth Movement in Hungary
Copyright English edition © Gefen Publishing House
Jerusalem 2001/5761

All rights reserved. No part of this publication may be translated, reproduced, stored in a retrieval system or transmitted, in any form or by any means, electronic, mechanical, photocopying, recording or otherwise, without expressed written permission from the publishers.

Translated from Hebrew by Ora Cummings and Riva Rubin
Typesetting: Marzel A.S. – Jerusalem
Cover Design: Studio Paz

1 3 5 7 9 8 6 4 2

Gefen Publishing House
POB 36004, Jerusalem 91360, Israel
972-2-538-0247 • orders@gefenpublishing.com

Gefen Books
12 New Street Hewlett, NY 11557, USA
516-295-2805 • gefenbooks@compuserve.com

www.israelbooks.com

Printed in Israel

Send for our free catalogue

ISBN 965-229-235-4 (alk. paper)
Library of Congress Cataloging-in-Publication Data
Benshalom, Rafi.
[Neevaknu lemaan ha-hayim. English]
We struggled for life: Zionist youth movements in Budapest, 1944 / Rafi Benshalom.
1. Jews—Persecutions—Hungary—Budapest. 2. Holocaust, Jewish (1939-1945)—Hungary—Budapest. 3. World War, 1939-1945—Jewish resistance.
4. Benshalom, Rafi. 5. Budapest (Hungary)—History. I. Title.
DS135.H92B83213 2001 • 943.9'12004924—dc21 • 2001018184

Contents

Rafi Benshalom — Portrait of a Jewish Resistance Leader 5

Chapter One	A Democracy So-called	7
Chapter Two	Meetings With People and Politics	17
Chapter Three	March 19	24
Chapter Four	General Headquarters	29
Chapter Five	Jumping Borders	32
Chapter Six	Ups and Downs	54
Chapter Seven	Kastner's Grand Plan	59
Chapter Eight	The "Transport"	66
Chapter Nine	"Our Consulate"	71
Chapter Ten	October 15	79
Chapter Eleven	A Trick Known as a "Letter of Protection"	85
Chapter Twelve	Our Ties With the Underground Labor Movement	90
Chapter Thirteen	The Parachutists	97
Chapter Fourteen	52 Baross Street	103
Chapter Fifteen	Budapest Under Siege	108

Epilogue 111
Josef (Joshka) Meir's Testimony 115
Efra Teichmann-Agmon's Testimony 123
David Gur's Testimony 135
Cwi Erez Hungarian Jewry in World War II 160
Names of Cities and Streets in Hungary and in neighboring countries 175
Notes 179

> The lack of a homeland provides our freedom with a new significance. Those who have no attachment whatsoever owe no consideration to anything
>
> (Stefan Zweig)

Rafi Benshalom
Portrait of a Jewish Resistance Leader

The English translation of Rafi Benshalom's book "We struggled for Life" appears more than fifty years after the original was written and more than twenty years after it was first published in Hebrew. It is the only authentic document on the subject of Zionist resistance, written immediately after the liberation of Hungary from German occupation.

Having survived in Slovakia for several years as a "musician," Rafi became a "conductor" in Budapest, where he illegally arrived in 1944. No-one was more equipped than Rafi for this role. He spoke perfect German (having graduated from a German high school in Bratislava), as well as fluent Hungarian (from his childhood in Temesvár-Timisoara). With his deep blue eyes and blond hair, he looked as Aryan as any German. He also had personal courage, a sound Zionist education, a drive to be active, a profound sense of responsibility, an allegiance to his movement — Hashomer Hatza'ir — as well as a tremendous loyalty to his friends.

Rafi was a soft-spoken leader, with a naturally accepted authority. He never had to impose his leadership. A true fighter, he was totally void of all machoism. Rafi was a born negotiator and diplomat; in time he actually became one, on his appointment as first Israeli Consul in Prague and later, Ambassador in Mali, Cambodia and Romania.

When the movement decided to organize refugee rescue operations and prepare Hungary's Jews for the perils of German occupation, Rafi moved to Hungary in 1944 to oversee these activities. With his deep conviction that the only possible revenge and revolt against the Nazis could be achieved by rescuing Jews and helping them to survive, he took charge and responsibility almost immediately.

In Budapest, Rafi acted under several false names, mainly "Dr. Rafay" and "János Sampias." Although bearing false papers, he made frequent daring visits to the Swiss Consulate and many other official authorities.

The Red Army's thrust toward the West and the expected landing of the Allied Forces on the European continent, signaled the imminent collapse of the Nazi regime. It was clear in those days, that the main task of Jewish resistance was to prevent the liquidation of Jewish "substance." Saving Jewish lives became the prime objective of the Halutz movement. Indeed, in comparison with all the other countries under German occupation, the Hungarian Jewish resistance movement saved the most lives and, in these final stages of the war, prevented the Germans from carrying out their intent of leaving Europe "Judenrein."

In his report, in a very modest, almost self-effacing manner, Rafi describes some of his daring actions. In Budapest, he was very fortunate to meet Tamarka, who moved in with him and supported him, not only through her own courageous participation in underground activity, but also with her devotion, calm and balanced personality.

Rafi was a faithful and active member of Kibbutz Ha'ogen. When not abroad on his diplomatic duties, he worked (mostly manually) in the kibbutz plastics factory.

Rafi Benshalom passed away in 1996, leaving his wife, Tamarka, his sons, Dany and Alex, his grandchildren as well as many friends and admirers.

Moshe Alpan
2001

Chapter One

A Democracy So-called

We came to Hungary at the end of January 1944. We traveled through Košice[1] on a steam engine, illegally of course. After a few days this particular route was canceled, but for us, it still worked perfectly well. We arrived with Aaron[2] at ten o'clock in the morning, at the Eastern station,[3] and from there made our way to the Palestine Office[4] which was the only address we had in Budapest. Our eyes opened wide at the sight of crowds of people in front of the office, and as we were informed later these people visited the office often, hoping for a chance to emigrate to Palestine. At that time, our status in Slovakia was completely illegal. I had spent the last eighteen months under an Aryan pseudonym and Aaron had recently escaped from a labor camp in Nováky.[5] In Bratislava,[6] there was a "Jewish Office,"[7] which served as a means for liquidating the Jews, but as for Zionist activity or any kind of emigration, these had long ceased. My first impression of Budapest therefore, was that life was going on as usual.

Yoshko[8] used to write extensively to us about this and indeed, this was the main reason he called for the people of the Zionist youth movement — Hashomer Hatza'ir — to come to Budapest. It was a tune he would repeat in each of his letters: In Budapest, you can go to the cinema, theater and opera. The movement is operating on a legal basis, with its own clubs, and last but not least: emigration was continuing.[9] In Slovakia we had already forgotten there existed the freedom to emigrate or to carry out educational activity. Moreover, unhindered community activity of the Jews was so limited to us it was virtually impossible to describe, whereas here in Budapest, the reality was very different and indeed, all that our friends had written about, was actually happening.

In the evening, we were taken to a club,[10] where a group of young people had gathered for a party. They sang Hebrew songs with tremendous gusto. The walls were plastered with slogans and posters in Hebrew. The youngsters were in possession of the latest publications from the movement. For me, in Europe of 1944, this seemed like a fantasy. At the reception, I tried to express my shock. At that time, my Hungarian was pretty poor and anyway, I had a hard time trying to find the right words. What I was saying must have seemed quite strange, but the members of the Hungarian movement somehow managed to understand our amazement. Later on, they also experienced something similar when they escaped to Romania. One of them even wrote from the town Arad[11] that he what we had said on our first evening in Budapest.

All this was possible because of a very special political situation. The Kállay[12] Government was already in touch with the Allied Forces, and its Prime Minister wanted to hold these negotiations via the Jews. It had been a naive step to grant legal status to the Zionist youth movement[13] although it could have been considered a wink in the direction of London and Washington. Certain people in the Foreign Office carried out negotiations with Komoly[14] and Szilágyi.[15] Just a short while before, Szilágyi had written a detailed memo at the request of the Hungarian Government with regards to the Jewish problem in Hungary. He did not conceal the existence of antisemitism in Hungary, nor even the blood bath of Novi Sad.[16] Instead, he compared it with what was happening in other countries, which was relatively minor. Thus Hungary could claim to have been the last island of democracy in Europe and did not identify with the barbarian Nuremberg Laws.[17] The democratic press repeatedly reported these facts too. Incidentally, for someone who since 1939 was used to newspapers compatible with the German term "gleichgeschaltet,"[18] a review of the Hungarian press was something of an eye-opener. The editors of Magyar Nemzet[19] and others, frequently took the liberty of daring journalistic slip-ups and tended more to "write between the lines" than official reporting. Nonetheless, this layer of democratic ice was extremely thin and could have broken under the slightest pressure. Day-to-day life in Hungary was anything but democratic. After World War I, Hungary became the most reactionary country of all and remained so until 1944. It made no progress, but the surrounding countries became increasingly fascist.

There were many young people in the movement, under police surveillance and were unable to act openly. The Hashomer Hatza'ir movement was regularly outlawed, in the absence of any other "communist victims." The movement's history was littered with a chain of alternate breakdowns and recoveries.[20] The last numerous arrests decimated the movement at a time when its members were coming to the aid of the Slovakian refugees. At that time, almost the entire membership of the movement in Hungary was placed in concentration camps. The youngsters were retained for months in Garany[21] and released to constant police surveillance.[22]

At the beginning of 1944, the refugee issue quieted down somewhat. Its importance waned, since the thousands of refugees to whom Hungary had given rather dubious asylum, became another excuse and indication to the West. But the terrible experiences of our refugee friends during the war, did not abate their constant fear. The concentration camps at Garany and Csörgö,[23] the Budapest prisons in Szabolcs, Magdolna and Columbus Streets,[24] the sophisticated persecution on the part of the "KEOKH" detectives,[25] the constant search for foreigners, betrayals by house concierges, the enormous difficulty in obtaining food cards, especially cards for sugar, all these had sunk deep into the bones of each of the "Zenész."[26] Almost all the (movement) members who had arrived earlier in Budapest found themselves the victims of language difficulties, a total lack of experience and the complete indifference of Hungarian Jewry, many of whom were still imprisoned in concentration camps. Joel, Sender, Ruth, Paul, little Ruth, Yancho, Moshe and Feigi,[27] had all experienced the horrors of the Hungarian counter-intelligence services and Hungarian prisons. Yoel, who had been suffering from a serious injury to his spine for many months, would write to me from Garany, expressing a deep disappointment with life. Ruth was confused, as a result of severe torture, while "little" Ruth was completely apathetic. Those members of the movement who were still free felt that the ring was tightening around them. "Mimish"[28] shocked me deeply when "just for your information" he told me about some of his experiences at the hands of the counter intelligence services.

The Hungarian Jew was still an almost equal rights citizen. The first and second Jewish laws, compared with the Nuremberg Laws, which were already in effect all over Europe, were relatively mild.[29] It was still possible to find Jewish students.[30] Every second shop in Budapest belonged to Jews. Jews seeking entertainment could still visit coffee houses, cinemas and theaters. While in Poland, hundreds of thousands of Europe's Jews were being annihilated and the whole world lived in fear. The Jews of Hungary lived in the quiet belief that nothing would happen to them, and they were even unwilling to offer any kind of assistance. Since Feigi, one of the first Slovakian members to arrive in Budapest, was trying to organize the aid-operation for the others who were supposed to be following him, he applied to the offices of the "Jewish Welfare Office."[31] When he presented himself as a Slovakian refugee, they did not even wait to hear him out, they simply pointed to the door and threatened to call the police. Their subsequent "aid" consisted of calling him back later and giving him 5 Pengö.[32] Apart from several Zionists and brave orthodox Jews, no-one in Budapest was willing to stand by us. Thus we were obliged to rely on our own resources and befriend members of the underworld. Most of the first refugees were arrested and imprisoned in a transition camp for criminals, called "Toly."[33] Their encounter with the inmates was a unique experience, because these people were like something out of a fantasy world, thrown into Budapest by the terrible earthquake in Europe. Often, they became good friends, guided by the supreme law of "honor among thieves."[34] Naturally, we also met many criminals who took full advantage of our inexperience. Most of the refugees assumed the identity of Hungarian Jews who had died, or been recruited, or they would use various other kinds of forged documents. Those with better foresight were already living as Aryans.

We purchased our first documents at a high price from cunning forgers, who later turned out to have been irresponsible and plain greedy. Dependence on these people, together with the almost constant shortage of cash, cost us the freedom of Joel, Sander, Ruth, Yancho and others. During the years 1942-1943, pioneers from among our refugees tried to infiltrate the circles of document producers. Since these were mostly members of the underworld — an unreliable and anti-social group — we could hardly blame our colleagues for their lack of success. As refugees from Slovakia, ours was the harshest fate. The Poles and Yugoslavs enjoyed the option of being granted legal status, since Hungary was not in a state of war with Poland,[35] and Yugoslavia had an 'official' representative, by way of the Swiss attaché! But Czechoslovakia had disappeared from the map of Europe, and Slovakia the allied country, did not take us under its auspices. We were sentenced to death there as well.

In 1944 we found a sympathetic ear with the "KEOKH,"[36] — the foreigners' police — and arranged a kind of legal status for some of the refugees for a certain sum of money.[37] Some of our members, especially Dan, were opposed in principle to all forms of legal status, because we did not believe in it. They did not want to live within the law. They did not wish to be registered anywhere. The forged police documents, which were not registered anywhere, gave them a much greater sense of security than any legal documentation.

Indeed, the first days of the new year were completely paradoxical. More progressive voices began being heard in Hungarian policies.[38] The Social Democrats and the Independent Small Holders' Party were working in close cooperation and developed a whisper propaganda, which was actually well heard. Books began appearing, with a defiant tone. An unexpected wave of awakening flowed over the Hungarian Zionists.[39] Immigration followed immigration. The general feeling was one of optimism, security and comfort. We seemed to be the only ones refusing to be swept away by the general atmosphere. We were afraid, we were cautious. We warned, and we went on warning...!

At the beginning of February, I gave a lecture to the "Gordon Circle"[40] on "The Tragedy of European Jewry." I pointed out the open, blatantly cruel way in which the Nazi administration was dealing with the Jewish issue everywhere — down to the same tiniest detail — and that the same events were happening in many countries. Events even accelerated over recent years, and operations were following each other. But Jewish resistance was also on the increase. In Germany and Austria Jews reacted to the various forms of persecution with a wave of suicides. In the Czech states Jews organized themselves to fight the suffering. As animosity grew, so did Jewish awareness. At the beginning of the persecutions the Jews of Slovakia escaped en masse to Hungary. Thousands of young people assumed an Aryan identity. The Jews of Poland turned from passive to active opposition and organized their defense. And now — I said — the Jews of Hungary are having to come to terms with the fateful question: What do we do when the fascists take over here as well?

Our response was derived from the accumulated experience of the other countries:

1. We must create a situation of chaos;
2. We must take advantage of every opportunity to escape; everyone must leave the country. If not, then they must find somewhere inside the country, in the very middle of the nation's capital.

For God's sake, do not let yourselves become heavy of movement; do not insist on keeping your belongings! The lighter you are, the better; and you should all take as much initiative as possible.

There were various reactions to my speech. Some people were annoyed at me for putting ideas in Satan's mind. Others began dealing seriously with the issues. After a while, Haika[41] gave a lecture on the Warsaw Ghetto and the history of the defense in Poland. That evening left us thoroughly shaken. We had "walked past a million corpses," as Kolb[42] stated later, in an attempt to define his feeling of shock.

We made it our objective to cause panic among the complacent Jews of Hungary, who were deluding themselves.

We "refugees" (*plitim* as we defined ourselves in Hebrew), were different. In fact, we did not always understand each other. We were subject to daily problems of housing, food, clothing and employment. We were also especially keen to make it to Palestine as soon as possible. This might seem strange, since food was also a problem. But that's how it was. We longed for an ordinary domestic kitchen. We were familiar with hunger and to top it all, every meal we ate was accompanied by the fear of imminent arrest, because at that time most of the refugees were arrested in the cheap eating houses they frequented. When the storm subsided, people started eating at "Uncle Frisch's,"[43] a musicians' restaurant. Although visits to this eatery contradicted all logic, we couldn't resist it. Uncle Frisch's was not only cheap, some of the food was excellent too. Moreover, we did not need ration cards there. He knew most of us by name, was familiar with our problems, knew all about the movement and our plans for emigration. What surprises me to this day is the fact that nothing ever happened to Uncle Frisch.

In Hungary, the movement knew no such problems. It was too busy calmly preparing educational programs.

The movement had two "Kens" (clubs) in Budapest. Eleven emissaries operated in the suburbs on behalf of the movement. Following a long break, the movement began re-issuing pamphlets on its educational ideology. Naturally, the refugees did not take an active part, but still served as reinforcements. The movement's horizons widened; we had brought with us a distinguished consignment of Czech and Polish tradition and supplied ideas, as well as several new activists. The Hungarian movement was now enriched by the presence of a politician — Yoshko Baumer. He gave the movement a new status among the Hungarian Zionists, one which they had not known for a long time. Emigration certificates were given almost exclusively to refugees, who also needed most of the money being sent from abroad.[44] It was clear to us that we should have to dabble in "politics."

When the first of our members arrived in Hungary,[45] all Hashomer Hatza'ir's activity was controlled by Szilágyi, who also represented the movement. Yoshko gradually took over all this activity. At the beginning of 1944, when he was preparing to emigrate to Palestine, people started asking about his successor. His position was firm and irrevocable: Dan[46] and Mimish had been his only assistants — Dan handled our finances and Mimish was responsible for the welfare of fellow members who had been imprisoned. In time, more man-power was added. Before Yoshko's departure, we sat down to re-delegate and discuss responsibilities. The most innovative decision to come out of that meeting consisted of the task we entrusted to Dan.

From now on it would be Dan's responsibility to equip our members with identification papers. Until then, we had been unable to give our people anything more substantial than a birth certificate and in certain cases, an ID card. Dan's work had consisted of an occasional "drawing" of "the Police Residential Report Form." Now, he would go out to the residence of the apprentices at "Zöldmáli,"[47] where he was permitted to work undisturbed. We new arrivals, did not favor such a superficial attitude to the issue. (Yoshko, for example, had had no documents for a couple of years, a fact which had certainly hindered his ability to work. We spoke out freely against this.) Our objective was to perfect the documentation, to achieve constant Aryanization, especially

Pil,[48] who demanded more incentive in thought and action. It was Dan's job therefore, to "create papers."

Pil and Mimish undertook the task of dealing with the newly arrived refugees, an activity which required discretion and above all boundless understanding and love. People had to be taught about Budapest and all its complexities. We Slovaks were mostly provincials, this being our first time in the big city.[49] We thus had to teach the people how to be "street wise," such as the meaning of red and green traffic lights, in an attempt to bring them to a position where minor, unimportant issues would not result in their downfall. Each new member was given a map of Budapest and Mimish explained the city's logical building plan. But the problem was not simply the lay-out of the streets; the houses and apartments themselves posed an even greater problem. The people had to pay attention to the buildings' doormen,[50] learn the rudiments of the "ration card" and how the "tenants' roster" was managed.[51] Finally, everyone had to invent his or her new "life history" and learn it by heart.

We decided that greater attention had to be paid to the prisoners, to try to get them released. This decision was probably based on a sense of guilt. We learned only much later why we had been unable to save our fellow members at that time. It turned out, in order to make any headway in releasing our fellow-members, we would have had to have been extremely generous. We would have needed to expend huge sums of money — and we were extremely poor. Even the employment of four salaried activists posed a serious financial burden for us.

Haika wanted to clarify one issue: What would our position be in the event of a holocaust? Would it be one of defense, in other words, self-defense in the form of armed combat, or rescue — the use of every possible means in order to save lives? This was no simple matter and we tried to reach conclusions based on four bitter and horribly eventful years. At our meetings we were able to summarize what had happened in Germany, Slovakia, the Czech countries, Poland and Yugoslavia. Haika and Aaron supported a defense tactic. Haika was very enthusiastic about the Warsaw uprising, which she saw as one of the rays of light in our history. She had witnessed first the annihilation of thousands of Jews and, more than anything else, had been shocked by their surrender — the way they had gone "as cattle to the slaughter." Her conclusion was that there was no real way out anyway, the Germans were bent on murdering all the Jews slowly and systematically. Since we were still together, we had to start organizing an efficient defense program.

This tactic did not receive unanimous support. I for one, felt that a suitable rescue system would enable us to save lives. So many millions had already been lost, I claimed, and went on to stress the importance of saving each and every individual, if we wanted to maintain the existence of our nation. There was no justification for every "historical act of courage," nor should it be allowed. We reached no conclusive decision — this will probably remain forever an issue for which history will never reach a final verdict.

We thus began preparing our two-pronged operation. While Dan was working on the rescue issue, Mimish was establishing the preliminary stages of a defense tactic. In this, he was assisted by Avri[52] and Michael[53] — two young men from Bratislava, full of romantic energy and enthusiasm, pure of spirit and willing to follow any order. They had already proven that they were capable of carrying out even the most daring of operations. They had escaped three times from concentration camps. They had recently fitted a key to the main gate of the Magdolna Street camp,[54] escaping one misty night to freedom. They planned to build several shelters-bunkers, in which they could hide weapons and later people. After much searching, they decided that the cemetery most suited their purpose.

They spent a week reconnoitering the region, in the midst of snow-storms and cold February nights[55] — roads, traffic arrangements and the system used for guarding the Óbuda cemetery.[56] On one occasion they tried to enter one of the small churches, for warmth. Their "burglar's key" broke in the lock. They were unable to extricate the incriminating object and were thus forced to discard their plan of making a shelter in the Óbuda cemetery.

At the movement "Kens," they picked out some suitable youngsters and organized them into groups. These underwent military training in subjects such as topography, Morse code, navigation etc. The first romantic efforts in the cemetery proved to Mimish that we were probably incapable of putting together any kind of military operation. However, what we had learned in the attempt, might have turned out to be very useful in the event of a future need to escape. Still, it was quite clear to us that if we were ever in a situation from which there was no other way out, we would certainly fight. We had no real idea at the time, how difficult and what a huge responsibility it was to define such a situation. Michael and Avri discarded their romantic occupations and settled down to some practical work. They collected a large number of birth certificates, identity cards, "Levente" authorisations,[57] and other documents and went to work. The documents were washed, according to a novel invention of Mimish's. The idea was not to wash off individual words or lines from a larger block of words, but to place an entire document in a bath and erase its entire contents.[58] They soon discovered that this elicited good results. They copied a name off one of the house gates,[59] and recorded the precise details of its inhabitants. They then went to the census office and asked for the person's birth certificate, which they received without any trouble.[60] This document enabled them to obtain other documents, such as those pertaining to parents, wedding certificate, baptismal registry, etc.

Yohi[61] once visited the census office and the clerk very kindly handed her the census book and told her to search in it for herself. She forthwith copied out about fifty names. The others could then return later and request the documents relating to these people.

The other youth movements soon learned of this idea and one day the census office clerk sat at his desk, a bewildered look emanating from behind his spectacles. He was not clever enough to understand the meaning of this "attack" by all those young people.... After this incident we transferred our activity to other quarters of the city.[62] Later, we ceased this activity altogether. Anyway, by March 19, 1944, we were the owners of several dozen original documents.

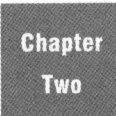

Chapter Two

Meetings With People and Politics

I have already mentioned Haika on several occasions. She came from Bendin,[1] having spent the previous months in a bunker. She had been a founder member of the movement in Shlezia and had maintained regular connections with the people in Warsaw. She was an eye witness to the tragedy of Auschwitz.[2] The Bendin group had opened the escape route to Slovakia through which Haika came to us. She was the kind of woman who knew exactly what she wanted, had a very determined outlook on life and a talent for organizing and educating. In Budapest all her latent femininity was reawakened. She enjoyed being a survivor, as well as the quiet, the concerts,[3] the colors of Budapest's streets, the Danube, the castle,[4] the people; in a word — the life — without which she had had to do for so long. She would often read to us from her journal, which was mostly devoted to the Warsaw Ghetto uprising. She had not been an eye witness to those events. Her writing was more in the style of a fascinating illusion. Everyone who landed in that bunker had been her friend, spent years with her in youth movement training, and together had built up the movement; her childhood sweetheart had been one of the last victims to go down fighting in the uprising.

Haika meant a great deal to us. She was a perfect representative of the Hashomer Hatza'ir mother-movement in Poland, from which all the other movements drew their traditions and experience.

Here in Budapest, Haika acted only as an observer, occasionally offering us advice. She was very enthusiastic in her preparations to emigrate to Palestine, notwithstanding certain trepidation. And indeed, complications arose prior to her departure, but after a two week delay, she took her place beside the window on a fast train to Bucharest. With tears in her eyes, she whispered to us, that she did have faith after all. She left behind her a world in flames and ruins and went to a new world, where hundreds of her friends were waiting for her with baited breath.[5]

"The Gordon Circle" was an interesting Hungarian offshoot of the Zionist movement. It consisted of Zionists with progressive views, close to those represented by Hashomer Hatza'ir. The "Gordon Circle" was more than a council of parents, the sort we had in other places. It was comprised of several serious and gifted Zionists, who identified with the uncompromising political line of Marxist Zionism. For us, the "Gordon Circle" had been a political necessity. Hungarian Zionism had never been a synthesis, but rather a permanent struggle among four political parties, each of which was required to supply several 'representatives' to the overall "Zionist policy," the Palestine office, the General Labor Federation (*Histadrut*) and various other committees. If the 'circle' had been part of reality at first, it had gradually developed into a serious political body. For us, it was a new concept. After all, the movement's strength had always been as a youth movement, not as a political party! For several years we had kept a distance from the adults — for fear of losing our independence. I was therefore surprised to find this group here in Budapest, and I studied it with interest.

One of the group's members, for example, was Uncle Federit.[6] He was as enthusiastic a representative of our interests in the Palestine Office as he was as manager of the VAC[7] in the sports league. He handled our affairs with all his heart and so much love and integrity, and we could always rely on him. To this day I am not sure what induced this pleasant and courageous man to join us, but it was good that he did. I gladly devoted time and effort to maintaining close ties with him, listening to his concerns and guiding him. We had to take special care with such people; a great deal of prestige was at stake here. Issues which to them seemed short of a tragedy, often caused us a mere shrug of the shoulder.

Of course, I shall not discuss all the members of the "Gordon Circle," but I feel duty bound to mention several of the more prominent ones. Moro (Moshe Rosenberg[8]) was most useful to us. He was an architect with an exceptional, razor-sharp brain. A socialist and an excellent Jew, he was very close to us from the very beginning. Finding us was a source of tremendous delight to him. We were later able to include him in the "overall policy," confident that he would never blunder or lose his head. When he took over the defense leadership later on, he proved himself courageous and daring in action, above and beyond any widespread concepts.

Kolb, who enjoyed a first class reputation in Hungarian literature at the time, was the "heart" of the operation. Even then, he served as senior editor with the large publishing house, "Singer-Wolfner."[9] He also had a good reputation among the progressive Hungarian policy-makers. But Kolb still did not feel completely at home with us. By the time he left he had still not given free reign to his personality. We were very pleased to have been able to rescue him from the horrors, and had great expectations of him, for the benefit of the movement.

And it is only right to mention another very pleasant and intelligent member of this group: Aunt Kudelka,[10] manager of the "Yavne"[11] publishing house. She knew almost half the population of Budapest and had excellent connections. She was as well-loved everywhere she went, as she was by us. When we had no place to work in, she broke all the rules by letting us use a desk in her own office! She even turned a blind eye when we used that same desk for creating our first forged documents.

There was not a night during that period when I got to bed any earlier than one o'clock in the morning. I sought out people, listened to them and absorbed my fair share of experience, kindly supplied by the city of Budapest. Only rarely did it occur to me that I was actually navigating — with dreadful uncertainty — through a mine-field. We were far from being safe. People like us had not yet been forgiven for "infiltrating" Hungary. I continued to live outside; in Kelenföld,[12] in a small room in the back yard of a beer factory. Yancho had lived there before and I had taken over the place from Yoshko. It had no window, and was bitterly cold. Nor was there any wardrobe. But there was one enormous advantage: the house had no concierge. The gate was open day and night. I could come and go at will. The landlady was not too concerned about me. In fact I only met her twice: once when I took possession of the apartment and again when I left. On the first of each month, I would put my rent on the shelf above the sink and the following day, I would find a receipt. By the standards of those days, this was absolutely the best accommodation conceivable.

On returning from a meeting with our friends one Saturday night, we got into a conversation with Szilágyi. Graduates of the movement made a habit of congregating at the Jewish National Fund offices on Saturday nights.[13] Szilágyi refused to be absent from any of those meetings, although he would never actually enter the hall. Once he said to me: "Those voices, that sound that comes from you youngsters when you are together, is like music to my ears, so holy and spiritual is it." This time Szilágyi opened the conversation, by pointing out yet again his dissatisfaction with us, with the world and with Judaism. In the Middle Ages, the rabbis could die for the glory of God, and with their last breath call out "Hear O Israel." Nowadays — he said — the rabbis are running away from their communities, and making a last break for freedom, dwarfed and terrified. They are no different from anyone else. Judaism has lost its greatness, even in the face of death.

That same evening, I was obliged to walk home, having missed the last tram, so I pondered at length on what he had said. How easily the Jews of Hungary could express themselves about the greatness of death. I doubted if they could feel even a smidgen of the unrest of a lone "musician," making his way on foot to Kelenföld, stopping under a street lamp in order to make sure that a certain Ipolyhegyi László István,[14] whose documents he had been carrying for the last three days, had indeed been born on 11 December....

All in all, we had quite a lot of trouble with Szilágyi. He was the kind of man who had his head in the clouds, while causing considerable aggravation "down on earth." He was no longer a movement member; moreover, he now seemed to be waging a war of reaction against the movement. He filled an important and even decisive role in Hashomer Hatza'ir in Hungary for many years [15] and his personality had left its mark on the entire movement. With great love, he had educated many young members and they had "hearts of gold," like him. He taught them to dabble in the Bible and in Spencer,[16] astronomy, Chinese culture, Plato and other fine things. I don't know what caused one particular group to rise against Szilágyi. The resulting rift had appeared shortly before my arrival, and Szilágyi was now going through life gravely injured, hiding within his own self and spreading prophesies of doom.

That Saturday evening, he showed me the "Young Man" painting by Georgeone,[17] which he said was how the Hashomer Hatza'ir had once been. I told him that Hashomer was still alive and kicking.

I had other such intellectual experiences, typical of the emotional atmosphere of the time. One evening, Yoshko took me to to a "communist saloon" at Weiner's,[18] where high level discussions were being held; dinner was not at all bad either. I told them a few stories and expanded on some thoughts similar to those I had heard at the "Gordon Group." A sharp debate followed. Our main opponent was Tibor Barabás,[19] a young communist with an impressive intellectual background. He made a political statement to the tune of: "The Kállay Government has realized that Germany has lost this war and from now on Hungary will slip, slowly but surely, out of the war. From today, the condition of Hungary's Jews is improving. If the Germans decide to occupy Hungary after all, which is unlikely, the issue will not be the "Jewish question," but the "Hungarian question." The army would take a firm stand against the Germans, the working classes will support the army, and he hoped that the Jews too, would lend a helping hand.

After a long time, I was once again hearing the words of an assimilated Jew, who, despite everything that had happened, continued to deny the Jewish issue. He himself of course, had not yet personally felt the effects of the Holocaust, but we all rose up with all our might against ideas as unrealistic and dogmatic as these. The debate was often very sharp and most of those present took a stand opposing to ours. I thought a lot about Barabas in days to come, but I never saw him again.

Szilágyi was a gifted politician and not uncourageous in presenting outspoken political positions. It was from this that what became known as the "Agreement with the Mizrahi" developed. I am not sure to this day why Zionist life in Hungary had to be so politically unruly, but perhaps it was because of the special character of the Hungarians. In any case, there was plenty of pettiness, back-biting and political intrigues. I must stress that the agreement with Mizrahi was not easily understood. In essence, it meant that Hashomer Hatza'ir (the Zionist left) and Mizrahi (the Zionist right) should cooperate with each other.

Zionist policy in Hungary operated on two axes and everything revolved around them — the Palestine Office and the Aid and Rescue Committee. The Palestine Office was headed by Krausz.[20] Back in Bratislava, I had already heard a lot about this man, not always good. In recent years, he had been responsible for all activity concerning emigration to Palestine from central Europe. Our displeasure with him in Bratislava was similar to that of our colleagues' in Zagreb.[21] I could now take a closer look at things. There were two rooms in the Palestine Office, one of which was permanently packed with hundreds of people. Krausz occupied the other room alone, taking care of things. He dealt with the authorities and the consulates, while negotiating with travel agencies and sorting out technical details. I soon realized that this was his way of working and that it had a very specific objective — not necessarily proof of his superlative work ethic. Indeed, Krausz had plenty of time, after all. He never let anyone disturb his beauty sleep. He never arrived at his office before ten o'clock in the morning. It never bothered him if a group of emigrants, which was supposed to leave on Tuesday, ultimately set off the following Sunday. Each of the youth movements had a permanent observer in the Palestine Office, whose job was to take an interest in what was going on there. How simple and logical it was to make them official representatives of the office! How simple it would have been to get some order out of all that chaos! But I learned soon enough that even this chaos did not lack some kind of system. I was naive enough to propose to Krausz a time-saving program and a system by which the Hehalutz representatives could deal efficiently with all current issues. Krausz told me that he was always at the disposal of the public, and would continue to be so for anyone who approached him individually. He stressed "individually."

Krausz was a Mizrahi man, and that is why the Mizrahi movement was in control of the emigration policy. Based on the 1939 elections to the Zionist Congress[22] the Palestine Committee consisted of four members from Mizrahi, three from General Zionists, three from Hashomer Hatza'ir and one single representative from Ha'ihud. It was this committee that followed the agreement reached between Hashomer Hatza'ir — under the auspices of Szilágyi — and Mizrahi. Yoshko, who adopted this line, explained to us that in Hungary there was no other way to conduct Zionist policy, so long as we want to ensure our rightful demands. We were unable to reach a dialogue with Ha'ihud, who were closest ideologically to the Hashomer Hatza'ir movement, because of their desire to take control of us, as Mapai (Israel Workers' Party) had done in Warsaw, Prague and Palestine.

I was soon aware of our many problems with Ha'ihud. The Aid and Rescue Committee was entirely in their hands. Brand[23] handled all the *"tiyul"* activity from Poland. Kastner[24] was in charge of connections with rescue committees in other countries and Springman[25] was responsible for currency exchange and couriers. They imparted an air of underworld romance to their work and allowed no-one to look at the rules and the committee's activity. Yet, notwithstanding their powerful position, they were unable to achieve a similarly influential position in the Palestine Office. At that time emigration was more important than money. No-one realized then that emigration could be achieved only by means of money, certainly emigration, which was not organized through the Palestine office. Those Ihud representatives did not always appear to act in a gentlemanly manner.[26] We admired one of them, Moshe Schweiger,[27] without reservation. It was certainly no coincidence that Moshe had grown up within the Yugoslav and not the Hungarian Zionist movement, and he brought his Yugoslav traditions with him. One of our Yugoslavian friends Ivo,[28] introduced him to me once at the "Bucsinsky" cafe.[29] I tried to find a way out of this political confusion. It was clear to us that in the final analysis Hashomer Hatza'ir and Ha'ihud belonged to each other. There was no problem with Ihud youth, but we did harbor suspicions about the Kastner faction and refused to surrender to them under any circumstances. The negotiations we held were difficult. None of us dared deviate from the accepted path, and no-one offered us guarantees.

But we did have several conversations with Schweiger, in which we managed to rise above day-to-day issues. Although not a statesman, he was a man of ideology, an idealist. Once he quoted Meir Ya'ari as saying: "What we must be is friends-enemies."

Later, Ernő Marton[30] from Cluj[31] was included in the negotiations, as a representative of the General Zionists. A democratic revolution was in the offing; it was necessary to clean out the Aegean stables[32] — to tidy up the mess of the Hungarian Zionist movement. But then came March 19 and we found ourselves suddenly having to face a host of new and far-reaching problems.

Chapter Three

March 19

It was a Sunday. As if in a nightmare, I was once again observing a terrible spectacle, the like of which had taken place in the streets of Prague exactly five years before.[1] The endless columns of gray tanks, the motorbikes, the vehicles in military camouflage, everything moving forward wordlessly with clockwork precision, spreading fear and terror across the snow-covered city. What we had so feared and had warned of so often, was now happening. In an act of spontaneity, we all met at the movement HQ. From there we made our way to the Jewish National Fund offices, knowing that this was where the entire local Zionist leadership would be. Indeed, they were all sitting there together. All those gentlemen, who had always been so sure of themselves — brewing up their own storms in a tea-cup — were now waiting for someone to offer words of encouragement, some suggestion for their next course of action. And now for the first time, these experienced men of authority, always demanding more than their share of respect, were confused, turning to us for assistance. Now they recalled our warnings and wanted to know how it was exactly and our precise proposals. We looked at each other — Leon Blatt[2] from Poland, Ivo Davidovitch from Yugoslavia, Eli Sajó[3] and I, from Slovakia — and we could not keep the bitter smiles off our faces.[4] The four of us agreed: those Zionists must not take responsibility for what would now occur, and they must not be given the position of leaders, since everything that was about to happen would take the form of annihilation and we must not give the executioners a helping hand. It was imperative that we take to the shadows, and conduct matters from there, quietly and without drawing attention to ourselves, in order to achieve whatever we could.

It was still necessary for some of our people to remain in the offices, to supply information and aid. Moreover, it was our job to engender panic, since only panic was capable of saving the Jews. The greater the chaos, the less attention would there be to details and registration. The greater the damage, the larger the number of souls would be saved.

It should be admitted that the movement too, was unprepared for the sudden changes, although these had been expected. Our first task was to obtain Christian documentation for all the movement's members. It seemed terribly hard work and entailed obtaining documents for the entire movement in Hungary. During the first few days there was a feeling of helplessness. Until this point, the Jews in Hungary had been law-abiding citizens. We too, were used to meeting at the movement's "Kens" and various Zionist offices. From now on, we decided we would give all these places a wide berth. It was necessary to carry out a decentralization of the entire movement and to revert to meetings in the streets. This was no easy matter of course and there was always the risk of being ambushed in the streets. We visited various places in the city and started hunting down people who looked Jewish. Incidentally, the city had become a paralyzed fortress. For many days, no publicity was given to recent events;[5] we had no idea what had become of Horthy,[6] or what the fate of the state would be.[7] Power was in the hands of the Gestapo. Leading liberals were arrested on the first day, including many well-known Jews — in accordance with lists.

(Two weeks later I came across a copy of the Swiss weekly "Schweitzer Illustrierte"[8] dated early February, with an article on Budapest. Among other events, the Swiss reporter mentioned that there was an outstanding number of German holidaymakers in Budapest. Evil tongues were claiming that this was a never ending stream of people with a specific objective. The democratic Swiss reporter rejected this innocent claim and said: these officers and soldiers were coming to Budapest to holiday beside the beautiful blue Danube and to feast on the exquisite Hungarian food....)

On March 21, representatives of the Jewish community were called for a meeting, at which they were told in a friendly manner that they had nothing to worry about, since no harm was to come to them. They were to go about their business in peace. It was clear that the Jews would have to curb some of their excess energy, but no-one need fear for their lives. This was when the Judenrat, or the Jewish Council[9] was born. The wise Budapest Jews accepted the Gestapo's primitive sleight of hand, and optimism ran high.[10] At that very moment, several Jews were already incarcerated in the Kistarcsa concentration camp[11] which had been reinstated. The Judenrat had no program and was helpless in face of the new situation. In sight of the suffering and the inability to supply answers to the Jewish man-in-the-street, the Zionists decided to establish an information department in the council building at 12 Sip Street. Most of the veteran Zionists worked in this building, but their work was Sisyphian.[12]

Krausz disappeared and it was much later that we discovered he had gone to the Swiss consulate which he refused to leave for weeks. Kastner and Brand began negotiations with the Germans, while we began our extensive work program. Meno[13] dealt with the first documents, including blank birth certificate forms. And we went into operation. Fortunately for us, we had just received a copying machine[14] from Slovakia, after a long wait. Since, together with the Shapiograph, our Slovakian friends sent us all the necessary types of ink, we were able to produce all the material we wanted. For the first few days after the occupation, Dan worked in various private apartments, but he soon moved to a workshop on Izabella Street.[15] We met every morning for breakfast, each time at a different place. At these meetings, we presented him with orders for documents and discussed the day's work schedule. Dan had plenty of work, which he proved capable of undertaking. He had nerves of steel. At that time it was still quite a big deal to be involved in the production of forged documents in some apartment, especially during the days when house to house searches were on the agenda.

Mimish and Pil were each in charge of a group of refugees. They made all the arrangements and especially the matter of tenant registration, without which it was impossible to move about. A day after receipt of the order, the necessary documents were handed over, and the people were supplied with money and advice. The people in the Hungarian movement who were involved in this activity were Avri,[16] Nesher,[17] Uri,[18] and the two Efra's.[19] At that time the movement in Budapest consisted of almost 500 members. In those early days we had to meet each member every day, just to ensure that no-one had been arrested, but people were keen to bring us even their tiniest of problems. I was responsible for contact with Kastner and his men in the Judenrat. No matter how hard I try, I cannot recall my daily schedule. I only know that I arrived home very late at night, my nerves frayed and my mind so full of troublesome thoughts it was impossible for me to sleep more than three or four hours at a time.

During the first few nights following March 19, we all learned anew the meaning of fear. We did not pretend, we were gripped by terror. We were well aware that this was no game to be played. We knew the Germans and it was quite clear that the Germans knew us. Our programs for defense had long ago appeared in their own operations plans. If we had experience, so did they. The mere thought that we were destined to perish was unbearable to us. When we thought it through, it was terrible. We had only just survived the deportations from Slovakia; with superhuman effort and heavy losses, we had managed to save the lives of a number of our members. More or less — or so we thought, innocently — we had become familiar with all the difficulties piled in our path by the Hungarian reaction. Moreover, we had managed to save several individuals from the Polish hell-hole[20] — and all these were about to be wiped out with one blow. How good it would have been to get away from that too-heavy burden and from the responsibility...for each of us to have to deal only with his own problems. But no-one left. Actually, two of the members did retreat into private life, but everyone else remained. And during long nights, I felt the fear of many people right there on the edges of my bed. The many questions that I had no answers to, danced around me in the middle of the night.

The terror dissipated gradually. The discomfort which troubled us, dissolved also. It would seem that we had simply become accustomed to the constant tension.

We paid a group of Poles the full price for the first blank forms. Just as the rats are the first to leave a sinking ship so for many months the Poles were the first to find a way out. They had excellent instincts. They were also extremely stubborn and uninhibited. Several Poles threatened a document forger at gun point one dark night, forcing him to print out several thousand birth certificates. Later on they sold them to us. We could not make use of them, because we discovered a crude printing error on them and anyone who used one may well have had to pay with his life. But they were all right at the beginning, since everyone was in need of documents, and not necessarily to show the officials — sometimes only for a sense of personal security. Once the most urgent work had been taken care of, Meno obtained additional papers, more and more; and Dan worked on the machine with utmost accuracy and quantity. People re-established their self-confidence. The Aryanization was a totally new experience, especially for the Hungarians among us. And there was a dearth of problems. Mercilessly, we pulled out the Hungarians from their natural environment — they were often hesitant and we forced a lifestyle on them, to which they could have accustomed themselves for months beforehand, except that they could never be bothered with the problem.

With the exception of two or three people, who because of their physical appearance were placed in the propaganda department, the entire movement underwent a process of Aryanization. Superficially, we had detached ourselves completely from Judaism. Szilágyi came to us to complain about this. He accused us of betraying our Judaism in the worst way, and that we were refusing to wear the yellow star due to a lack of solidarity. How emotional these people were! How far away the day was when Weltsch[21] called on the Jews in Germany to "Wear it in pride, that Yellow Star!"[22] because since then, the Yellow Star had turned into a death sentence for its wearer.

The first two weeks of the new administration went by almost without our noticing. It was on Saturday night when Dan, Mimish, Pil and I finished the distribution of orders and sat down to eat supper. We felt we had earned a certain respite. There was no specific program for the following day, as if life was moving along as usual. We took a walk along Kaiser Wilhelm Boulevard[23] and found ourselves standing opposite the City Cinema, which was showing the Fernandel comedy "The Unfortunate Pilot."[24] We looked at each other, Mimish and Pil shook their heads and turned to go home. On a spur of the moment decision, Dan and I went into the cinema. We thoroughly enjoyed the French film and laughed our heads off. When we left the cinema, we felt that the sense of fear, on which we had been choking for two weeks, had disappeared. We were free people going about our business, whistling in the wind.

Chapter Four

General Headquarters

In February, the appointment for the Defense Committee arrived from Palestine.¹ Moshe Schweiger was supposed to take command, which was rendered impossible because of his ailing health. A proposal was raised to hand command over to Szilágyi, but we opposed this. We knew the man very well. We were able to assess his ability and talents, and we were wary of his mood-swings. In the end we agreed to appoint Moshe Rosenberg. The committee which comprised representatives of four youth movements, included Moshe Pil, Meno Klein, Leon Blatt and Dov Avramchik.² It was decided that activity would be conducted in utmost secrecy. It was forbidden even to divulge the names of the members of the headquarters. Full military discipline was imposed.

Our ideas as to the working of the Defense Committee were not yet clear enough. This framework too, raised the question of defense versus rescue. Discussions continued for several weeks. Many and varied plans were made up for organizing ourselves. However, on March 19, everything turned out completely differently. Each of the four members was responsible for a specific area of activity. Pil was entrusted with the task of building bunkers, Meno — supply of documents, Leon — organizing the *"tiyul,"* Dov — food supplies, clothing and arms. Money would be overseen by Rosenberg himself. Each field of activity would receive a financial budget according to its needs.

Moshe went to work with great gusto. At that time, the Defense (*Haganah*) had at its disposal some $15,000.³ This sum did not seem very small to us, as until then we had been used to small operations and limited frameworks. Moshe was the first one to realize the enormity of our task. He decided to do "something really great." He wanted to buy an independent printing shop and to establish a Zincography of our own. We smiled a little at his far-fetched plans.

I handled the preliminary negotiations and was joined by Pil at a later stage, since he was destined to become the "commander." He was not reconciled with the task to which he was appointed, did not believe he had the necessary talents for it and did not like it. It was quite clear to him that we were facing a lengthy period of havoc, so very high quality bunkers would be required if we were to hold out for months on end. The quality of an emergency bunker depended on many elements and even the smallest mistake could be fatal and turn it into a trap. The purchase of large quantities of food — enabling a lengthy separation from the rest of the world, was an impossible mission. The munitions problem,[4] also seemed extremely complex, so Pil explained to us. It was no simple matter obtaining an adequate quantity of weapons. On the other hand, in the event that a bunker was discovered, the use of weapons would be symbolic only, since the chances of a small bunker against a serious enemy were extremely feeble. But it was the thought of having to hold out for months on end underground, with no access to daylight, without sufficient food supplies, in filth and sometimes in sickness, which was the most frightening prospect of all.

Our first bunker was on a farm on the outskirts of the city, at Farkasrét,[5] owned by a retired army major, who had smuggled in Moro's mother-in-law from Germany.[6] The man seemed quite willing and eager to participate in any shady deal, as long as he could profit from it.

We despatched three of our Polish members, who would work there as "Ukrainian" laborers. They were given the task of digging out a bunker beneath a deserted hut. For a while, work continued at a reasonable pace, but the three were exhausted from the hard labor and dropped from fatigue, unable to continue any further. One day, his lordship the major appeared with this story: the authorities had been dropping clear hints which could not be misunderstood and conclusions had to be reached. We were therefore obliged to discard this first effort, after much hard work and the loss of a great deal of money. It would appear that the major had found a more lucrative way out for the Jewish relatives of his lady-friend than our bunker; trusting "force majeur," all our deposits were impounded and he no longer had a reason to hold on to us.

Our members, who were incidentally, extremely Jewish-looking, had spent four weeks in the bunker and in the end, we learned something from that affair, too.

On second thoughts, it became apparent that a "bunker" did not necessarily have to be a hole in the ground; a well secured apartment could also serve as a bunker. It was not easy to find such apartments; the housing shortage in Budapest peaked as a result of the flow of Germans into the city.[7]

The many members, newly equipped with documents of Pure Aryans, were now in desperate need of apartments. Those who looked Jewish needed the kind of roof over their heads which would permit them to remain in the apartment for several days at a time. In the end, Pil and his group had to find a suitable workshop for their forging activity and this was the hardest task. Nesher, Uri and Efra L. proved themselves to be the most efficient in this work. A large apartment was soon leased on Izabella Street, and four students went to live there. During the day, these were joined by another friend, Dan, who studied with them. The apartment was used not only by Nesher, Avri, Yohi and other members, it also served as a workshop for us during the daytime.

Several of our Polish members planned to build bunkers in the Carpathian mountains,[8] where they wanted to meet the Red Army. Pil traveled to Satu-Mare[9] to feel out the situation. At first the preparations progressed, but ultimately failed, because the bunker was where the ghetto was to be established.[10] Thus the group preferred to seek shelter in the forests. From their *"tiyul"* period, the group still had connections with local farmers. The program was not without its dangers, but was undeniably imaginative. We warned our friends against any eventualities, but they stuck adamantly to their plans. So we gave them some money and a few weapons.[11] Several weeks later, two members of the group returned and told us vaguely that they had been discovered and dispersed.

The bunkers gradually became superfluous, because the *"tiyul"* went into operation and no-one was willing to sit about aimlessly with nothing to do.

Chapter Five

Jumping Borders

a. On the way back...

Most of the Slovakian members and especially the younger ones, wanted to cross back to Slovakia. The situation there was not good, but relatively better than Budapest.[1] This kind of relativity was sharply typical of our fate. I was inadvertently reminded of Izzy Kaczér's[2] "two shirts" principle. He once told us how he took only two shirts with him to summer camp. He wore the first one until it got dirty and then he wore the other one. He wore this one until it got dirtier than the first. This way, he always had in his possession one shirt which was "cleaner than the other." And after all, this was how we had been living for years: every now and then we would choose the cleaner shirt, hardly noticing how filthy it too had become.

    The way back to Slovakia was not particularly difficult. Up to the last days, movement members had continued to arrive from there, but it was now time to turn the wheel around in the opposite direction. The smugglers were already in the field, our integrating system had become a set-off point, and we were still in the possession of several thousand Crowns.[3] We also had some Slovakian documentation. And thus, we set off during the first few days on a *"tiyul,"*[4] which, in all honesty, was a more of a "second time, return *'tiyul'*."[5] Most of the returning members had some kind of a home base. At that time, the Slovakian members had several bunkers in the mountains, so we need not have worried about the accommodation. Most of the members chose this way, because it was the simplest and most logical. But several of them set off with the clear notion that, once they had crossed the border, their path was a one-way street from which there was no return. They knew they were escaping a situation which had suddenly deteriorated, but actually on balance, they were endangering themselves further. We asked Aaron to go to Romania because the way to freedom led only in that direction. But Aaron wanted to get some revenge and set off for Bratislava, fully intending to join the Slovak partisans as soon as possible.[6] Yoshko Weiser[7] and other members felt the same way.

Three roads led to Slovakia: to the west near Samorin (in Hungarian: Somorja),[8] to the north near Lučenec (in Hungarian: Losonc)[9] and to the east near Košice (in Hungarian: Kassa). At first the simplest route was that near Košice. Duda,[10] who until than had been organizing the integration and continuing transport to Budapest, soon found a band of smugglers, oversaw the *"tiyul"* in an efficient manner, and could be relied upon. The main problem involved accommodation for the people. The train would arrive in the evening so its passengers had to be put up in a hotel for the night. Košice was one of the first towns in which Jews were concentrated in the local brick factory, from which they could be quickly deported.[11] Duda was obliged to leave the town together with his friends. This path, therefore, was blocked to them.

Our route alongside Lučenec, was also beautiful. We had an acquaintance, who owned a house right on the border. Manyi — the name of our assistant there — accompanied our people from Budapest to her home, from where they crossed the border, during a night walk. Manyi was a pretty woman. With her natural charm and wisdom, she managed to ward off curious gendarmes and awkward questions. We had an additional connection in the same village, a Slovakian farmer called Zachar.[12] When the Slovakian *"tiyul"* was over, Zachar blundered and the group he was leading divulged the address of an apartment in Budapest, where members who had not been registered stayed. We received mail at this address too, and it was only by chance that none of us were caught there.

A smuggler who was sent by our people in Bratislava, led our members via the Samorin escape route. His name was Béla.[13] It was him who had brought us the Shapiograph. He had also led several people from Slovakia to Budapest and volunteered to commandeer the return *"tiyul."* We had complete faith in him. Mimish was the only one to suspect him, for reasons which could not be explained. One day we received a telegram from Bratislava warning us about Béla, but it arrived late. The day before we had entrusted him with an additional group, which he handed over to the police a few kilometers from Budapest. Those three youngsters were the only ones to fail during a Slovakian *"tiyul,"* two of whom were deported. We succeeded in over a hundred border-crossings, which we considered a good result. We learned to think in terms of numbers and percentages....

The movement in Slovakia made firm ties with the partisan groups in the east.[14] It integrated completely into the resistance movement. When, several weeks later on August 29, the activity began of the Slovakian partisans, everyone took his pre-determined position. Thus contact ceased with these members. After the outbreak of the uprising, many refugees returned from Slovakia. We treated these people with a certain disdain, believing they would have done better had they also been active in the fighting.

One day a brief note arrived from Banska-Bystrica,[15] the headquarters of the Czechoslovaks. Egon[16] wrote that they were all soldiers. Haviva Martonovitz[17] arrived, as a British officer and part of a military delegation to Bistrica. For a long time afterwards we heard nothing from the members. With baited breath, we followed the development of the military operations and our hearts sank when we heard from the Führer's high command about the final quashing of the partisans' uprising.[18] At the same time, the remaining Jewish population of Slovakia was deported — under the pretext of military considerations.[19]

At the beginning of December we received information from Aaron in Bratislava. His partisan unit had been disbanded. Egon and many others of our members had fallen, many hundreds of enthusiastic young Jews had been killed, Haviva and the other emissaries were imprisoned.

This was the first time we had received concrete news of the death of one of our members. Many of the members we had lost seemed to just disappear in a fog of uncertainty, but Egon had met his death in the explosion of a German hand grenade. For some reason, this death did not hurt so much — at least it did not seem useless. Egon fell when he was armed and in the course of his struggle against fascism.

b. The Way to Tito

Some of the movement's members proposed a *"tiyul"* to Tito's partisans. The Yugoslav partisans had been the first and only one to rise against fascism from the very beginning. It goes without saying that we had only admiration for them. Many Hashomer Hatza'ir members wanted to join them, but we were aware of the problems involved in crossing over. Hungarian counter-intelligence had developed a wide network in south west Hungary, taking into consideration that Tito would send agents to this side of the border, and many Hungarian anti-fascists would join him.[20] After March 20, many people started popping up claiming that they had foolproof routes to Tito. We found out that some of those routes led straight to the Gestapo. Thus, we warned our members against conducting negotiations of this sort. However, we were unable to persuade Avri Lissauer.[21] With the help of a friend — a trades union activist — he met someone and put his trust in him. He went to the designated meeting — and did not return.

The following day, Szilágyi was called to the "Schwab Hill."[22] He was asked if he knew the "Jew Lissauer" and what kind of a person he was. Szilágyi replied that he knew him as a good Zionist. This reply almost certainly cost Avri his life.[23] Had Szilágyi said that this was a foolish young man who is not responsible for his actions, he may have been released. We had lost our first member.

While Avri was spending the time before his deportation in the Sárvár concentration camp[24] we did our best to rescue him. We got hold of the address of a policeman who "could be spoken to," and we sent Metuka[25] to him. The address was false and Metuka was arrested for being a "friend of the Jews" and fell into the hands of the Gestapo. But Metuka was courageous and succeeded somehow in escaping this unfortunate situation.

The fall of Avri Lissauer was also a political epilogue. One day Kastner called our attention to the fact that he would almost certainly manage to implement the emigration plans. He was opposed in principle to the *"tiyul"* and especially to Tito. Here and there the Germans were turning a blind eye, but on this issue they were not joking. After the Avri affair, with Szilágyi facing the barrel of a sub-machine gun, the storm broke out. We were called in front of the "brains trust" (Kastner, Brand, Szilágyi, Rosenberg and Komoly). Joel Brand, a veteran socialist and a man of conviction, expressed his displeasure with us; but this did not sound especially convincing. Kastner spoke rather coarsely and condescendingly. Szilágyi wanted to show an understanding of our youthful hotheadedness, but at the same, wanted to take firm measures with our movement. And this is when something happened which the "brains trust" had not taken into consideration — representatives of the three other movements joined us. They all agreed unanimously with the opinion of the youth movements: "We do not believe the Germans!"

We did not oppose Kastner's negotiations with the Germans, we did not demand the right to do so. Our way was clear: what we wanted were the "little jobs." We wanted to rescue individual human beings, since we knew that the masses were lost to us. We knew that anyone rescued from the Mukačevo (in Hungarian: Munkács) ghetto[26] — was returned to the ranks of the living, whereas those remaining there — notwithstanding the negotiations — continued to be sentenced to death.

We admitted to have operated without discipline by ignoring the specific ban, but we made it clear that no-one had the right, not the movement, or the Zionist Federation — to block the way to the partisans. Not only did all the youths express support, we were also joined by Moro (Moshe Rosenberg). It was the first victory of the youths over the veterans and a rare moment of unity and solidarity for the Zionist youth.

Several weeks later, we were once again making plans for a *"tiyul"* to the Yugoslav partisans. Through the intervention of some trustworthy people, Mimish met a man from Novi-Sad, who came to Budapest on behalf of the partisans to purchase medicines. Someone had to travel with him. He wanted to supply us with a passport from the Croatian consulate. The journey was supposed to be a comfortable one, **in a railway overnight bunk**. It was necessary to go to Zagreb for further instructions. But this time, too, we were reluctant. We had an unaccountable lack of faith in journeys which were "above board." Moreover, there was no-one among us who spoke the language. And what put us off more than anything else was that we had no way of keeping track of the person. It could have transpired, therefore, that despite good intentions, we might have been sending one person after another into a trap.

Later on, Mimish met Toni.[27] Toni was a workman with a careful and level-headed awareness. He was in constant touch with Mimish, received from him and supplied him with many forged documents and helped him in the release of several Yugoslavs from the punishment camp near Székesfehérvár.[28] Toni certainly had contact with Tito, but that particular route was no longer relevant, since our liberation was a matter of only a short time. After the liberation, we met Toni once again at the Yugoslav committee. This time we were introduced to him as Tito's officially appointed representative.

We had dealings with another Yugoslav, who saved the lives of several of our people. Milan[29] was a tough character, a fanatic and an idealist, with the heart of a boy. Although Toni was a Marxist and Milan a royalist, the two were fervent anti-fascists and devoted allies.

c. *The road to liberty*

At the beginning of March, Zoli Hochhauser,[30] member of the Hungarian movement, who was serving in a forced-labor unit,[31] was about to be sent to the front. At the same time the refugees willingly gave up one of their emigration certificates, since a deserter from the army was in as bad a situation, and possibly worse, than that of the rest of the refugees. The departure of the emigrant group was delayed and the date of departure to the battle front was approaching. We advised Zoli to move to Slovakia, which did not seem too difficult to him, since he was originally form Kosice and knew Slovakian. Another idea also arose: Zoli could have just as easily gone to Romania. We had been pondering that idea for a while. It had some daring similarity, since the way to Palestine went through Romania, with a long coastline and port, beyond which was the hope of freedom. We tried several times to make contact with the movement in Romania, but were unsuccessful. We had no information as to the situation there. Not even the contact points at Istanbul[32] or Geneva were able to supply us with any information. In spite of everything, Zoli decided to take a leap into the unknown. On Sunday (March 19, 1944) he was supposed to travel to Cluj, from which Dr. Ernő Marton knew of a safe route to Turda.[33] Zoli set off, in spite of the changed situation. His journey was based on purely personal considerations, because on that same March 19 there was no way we could assess if his army unit was going to be mobilized the following day or not. Zoli arrived in Cluj and disappeared across the border. Only weeks later did we receive news of his transfer to Turda. But after we knew for sure of his arrival in Turda and since the situation in Budapest was deteriorating, we set out — without waiting for Zoli's report — on a *"tiyul"* to Romania. For the Hungarian members this was an easier solution than the possible *"tiyul"* to Slovakia. Both options demanded a daring crossing of the border. They were not familiar with the languages of either of the countries, but Slovakia was completely surrounded by a German zone, whereas Romania was on the fringe. A further consideration set the balance in favor of Romania. The Poles were flowing in their thousands in that direction, and we were very familiar with their instincts…. Leon Blatt, who was supposed to be in charge of organizing the *"tiyul"* on behalf of the leadership, had been opposed to it for a long time and was involved in building bunkers for his friends. The truth is that at that time, we too found several possibilities for bunkers, but were obliged to leave them. Not one of us was willing to sit any length of time in a bunker, at a time when everything was in motion and everyone was desperate to get on the road.

Before March 19, while we were still holding our political discussions, Marton told us of the possibilities of a *"tiyul"* from Cluj. Now that everything had turned out all right for Zoli, we sent out another group. A member of the Zionist Youth movement also set out with them. That same day, an additional group, members of the Ihud and Mizrahi movements set out for Oradea,[34] a place in which the Poles who had lived there for a while, had created several border-crossing possibilities. The crossing from Oradea did not succeed ultimately and the group was obliged to return to Budapest.[35] On the other hand, a group of ours from Cluj made a smooth crossing of the border. Now we were sending a third one and we made the great mistake of sending out a fourth group, before first waiting for news about the third group. Nesher, Yohi, Meir Löwinger,[36] and Ihud member, Eli Sajó, Misho Neumann, his girl-friend[37] and Uri Meir[38] were in the fourth group. The organizers of the operation in Cluj were: a local member of the Ihud, (Hana Ganz)[39] and on our part, Yermi Weiss.[40] The problems were already apparent with the third group. The smugglers betrayed the group, deserted them on the way and they had no choice, but to return to town. As a result, the Nesher group was also obliged to postpone their crossing. To this day, we do not know for sure if this had happened because of the group's diverse character, or whether they had been informed on. Anyway the group was arrested. The only one to get away was Eli Sajó, who returned to Budapest a day earlier, in order to report on the situation. Uri Meir and Meir Löwinger were brought in as army deserters to the military prison on Margit Boulevard.[41] Meirke was sentenced to life imprisonment, Uri Meir was only given ten years, as he successfully pleaded insanity....

Still, this big failure, the first of its kind in such proportions, did not break our spirit. We decided to be more careful, and with gritted teeth set out to find new ways, because the earth in Cluj for a while, was burning. Pil now left the bunkers entirely and took over the organization of the *"tiyul."* The daring and initiative he exhibited during the next few months are hard to describe in words.

The Cluj episode had another small epilogue. As already mentioned, Nesher lived in our workshop on Izabella Street, and according to the rules of conspiracy, it was now necessary to disband this apartment. We did this without hesitation, immediately after receiving news of the Cluj events. This later proved to have been the right thing to do, since Nesher gave away details of the apartment, being sure that we would follow the "rules of the game." Several days later, we moved the workshop to Bethlen Gábor Street.[42] From the outside, this had been made to look like an artist's atelier. Shraga[43] set up his easel, pinned his drawings and some of his completed works on the walls and was back in business.

In Oradea and other border cities, the Poles undertook all responsibility for the *"tiyul."* In these cities, they moved about quite safely, since for several months, they had already been living in these border towns. Their committee[44] was constantly working to remove them from the capital and transfer them to the provinces. On the other hand, we exerted great effort in keeping our Polish comrades in Budapest, so that we were unable to include them in these operations. We were still in a state of helplessness, when suddenly Miko turned up.[45] Miko had been a school friend of Dan's. He had been deported to Poland and succeeded in escaping. In Slovakia, he had been living as an Aryan. When he was caught there, he escaped to Hungary, and here he was living openly as a Pole. He was far from being a coward. When he came to us with the proposal that he would let us have his routes from Oradea (in return for a promise on our part that we would arrange his emigration from Bucharest), we agreed. We sent David[46] with him to Oradea, but warned David to be very careful not to be "taken in" by this Miko. At that time, David was still an inexperienced youth, and what we had anticipated did happen to him. Indeed, Miko made very sure that David saw nothing of what was going on. Oradea was at that time already quite dangerous. The Jews were concentrated in the ghetto, which, incidentally was one of the worst.[47] In this way, we completely lost all our connections, and especially any possibility of finding hiding places. For the sake of security, we replaced David with Hava Auslaender,[48] who had the advantage of being a girl, and therefore less conspicuous and above all, it was impossible to prove that she was not an Aryan.... In Budapest, Pil came across several connections and he too went to Oradea. Hava had still not done much there, and indeed it was very difficult at that time to re-mobilize the wheels of the wagon which had come to a halt.

And now, it would be best if Pil were to personally relate how things started to move, because with all the goodwill in the world, I could never describe the vari-colored and multi-faceted events of those fateful days:

...On my arrival at Oradea, it soon became clear to me that not only were the addresses I had brought with me, together with a great deal of hope, worthless, they had already been "burnt out." Thus, I was traveling with Hava in a carriage, to meet a smuggler who lived a long way out of town. I had all sorts of information on him. The idea of taking a carriage to one of the town's outlying provinces, was not a good one, because it might well have attracted attention, but shortage of time left us no alternative. When we arrived at a small farmhouse, I found an old woman and asked her — very carefully — about the people who had crossed the border during the past few days. The woman burst into tears and told me that the Gestapo had arrested her son that same day. Unfortunately, several more Jews were found hiding in her house, who were supposed to cross the border that day. Needless to say, I was not overjoyed at this news. It was clear that the house was under constant surveillance. I wasn't too moved and we left the old woman to her tears and Hava and I came in the waiting carriage. From out of nowhere, a stranger jumped forward and hopped into the carriage with us. Hava and I gave each other looks saying: well, we seem to have gotten ourselves into trouble! We continued to joke with each other, while I was doing some serious thinking — what do we do now?

Here we were at some river or other, it may have been the Körös,[49] I cannot remember for sure.

When we crossed the bridge, we saw a little boy playing with a wheelbarrow. He was about four years old, washed and dressed and with a round shiny pink face. At the sight of our carriage, the little fellow stepped back in fright and fell straight into the water. Before the carriage had managed to stop, I jumped into the river and pulled out the weeping and bedraggled little boy. I handed him over to his parents, who had come running up to me and then something really strange happened — the stranger, who until then had sat there with us in the carriage in hostile silence, looked me over with a smile, stepped down from the carriage and walked away. Hava and I exchanged looks once again and smiled in relief.

I did not return with any great successes from this trip to Oradea, but I did get an impression of the situation and learned that in Oradea too, it was possible to achieve things. At the same time, Miko turned up a second time, and now his desire to cross the border with us was indeed great. We released Dan from his work. This decision was not an easy one, since Dan was one of the founders and pillars, on whom the fate of the movement depended, but he had already managed to hand his work over to little David,[50] leaving him with a beautifully equipped workshop. It was now clear to us that the *"tiyul"* could not be carried out from one side only, and that we would have to receive help from the other side also — Romania — if we were to work with momentum. This consideration did indeed prove itself, as it turned out later. Dan demanded that I come along, too, and I prepared for the journey. We brought Eli Sajó with us, who was gripped with superstitions because of the many previous failures, but he felt quite secure in our company. Notwithstanding all Miko's promises, things did not work out in Oradea yet again. A few days went by, which we were obliged to spend in a hotel, with no possibility of getting things moving. In the end, we sent Yaffa,[51] Meira[52] and Moshe.[53] I returned to Budapest in order to see how things were there. Strange things were happening here at the same time. At first Michael and Eta[54] were arrested, the next day Avri, Uri, Metuka, Moshe Shapira,[55] Nomi,[56] Hedi[57] and Lea.[58] We were informed that, while under interrogation, the prisoners had informed on Mimish. Mimish was a bundle of nerves in any case, as the underground had been his daily bread since 1942. We changed our plans, therefore: Mimish would set out with Dan and remain with Rafi in Budapest. Thus, Mimish and Yutza[59] packed up their things and traveled to Oradea the following day. The big show was only just beginning. The journey itself involved much suffering. That same day, there was a football game between Ferencváros[60] and NAC[61] and the train was so packed, that we had to travel standing up on the stairs. Traveling under such conditions had an advantage, since any passport control was rendered absolutely impossible. And indeed, the following day we went to see the game, not out of any enthusiasm for sport, but for the sake of security.

Dan, Mimish and I were posing as students, newly arrived, for their vacation, in this provincial town. Mimish had a Ferencváros badge and immediately got into a loud argument with the reception clerk that the NAC team would not win this time (they did, by the way), but the following day, a Monday, was much less comfortable. By early morning, Eli Sajó had been stopped by a street patrol, where he had been holding a too-loud discussion with Glicker.[62] Glicker ran off and Eli was taken into custody. That same day, Hava was arrested at the hotel in which we were all staying. I learned of this by chance in town and immediately phoned Dan at the hotel. Dan understood my hints and reassured me that everything was all right as far as they were concerned. Thus, I went to the hotel, where we hastily packed our belongings. Mimish was furious and cursed us for taking so much luggage when our lives were in danger. Dan reassured Mimish too, with his Olympic calm. I paid our bill and in this way prevented the reception clerk from calling the police, and in the meantime the others left the hotel quietly. This exit from the hotel involved some daring, because we had no idea what information the Gestapo had managed to beat and torture out of Hava. Furthermore, it was only logical that our sudden disappearance would raise even heavier suspicions. We went to Baila-Felix[63] because under no circumstances did we wish to leave Oradea before Dan, Mimish and Yutza had crossed the border; the crossing had been set for the following day.

The following day, Dan went to town to make sure that the crossing would take place the following night. We parted from each other and the carriage took them to their destination, somewhere out of town. This journey was not the most pleasant, especially since it was known that Jews had been falling like flies into the hands of the Gestapo in Oradea; furthermore, they had to return in the same carriage, because the smuggler did not turn up. It was sheer luck that the carriage driver did not publicize his opinion of his strange night-passengers. Mimish decided to take Yutza and board a train to Budapest, which they managed to catch just a few minutes before its departure. But Dan returned, in the middle of the night, to Baila-Felix, woke me up, told me perfectly calmly that they had failed in their objective and then went to sleep. Today, when I recall that football game, the hasty exit from the hotel, and ponder over Mimish's journey and Dan's return in the middle of the night, a smile graces my lips, but at that time, I was living a cruel and bitter reality. We were close to desperation; nothing was going right for us. We renewed our search with Dan the next day. In the meantime, Miko had been captured by the Gestapo and the situation seemed utterly hopeless. It was annoying that the "Zionist Youth" — who had decided in favor of the *"tiyul"* to Romania — were holding on to several good routes, via Oradea and making fun of us. The disintegration of the Rescue Committee was now complete. Each movement carried out its own separate *"tiyul."* To be precise, the Zionist Youth and Mizrahi cooperated with each other on the one hand, and the Ihud and ourselves cooperated on the other. Complete cooperation took place only with regard to documentation. In other words: in the future, too, we were producing everything for everyone.

In Oradea we met an engineer from Vienna and a young Jewish man who spoke perfect Romanian and was living here as an Aryan. Both these meetings advanced us one step forward. The engineer made a habit of traveling to Arad, even to Bucharest, and was happy to place himself at our disposal. Among other things, he gave us a gift of 40,000 Lei,[64] and promised to take Dan's accordion to Arad (Dan was in love with the accordion; while still in Budapest he used to play to us and now there was no way he would part from it. He decided to bring it as a gift to the kibbutz, no matter what). It was agreed that Dan would meet the engineer on a certain day at Arad. He arrived early at Arad and since there was no smuggler available to us the following day, we took a look at the border region. We set out singing and marched along the furrows in the fields and no-one would have guessed that these two jolly students were on a reconnaissance mission. We soon determined that crossing the border would be child's play, and concluded with that Romanian youth that he would cross the border with Dan — without the use of smugglers. Dan took several tools from his workshop, in order to be able to continue with his work in Romania. We obtained a Romanian document, washed it and attached a picture of Dan to it. As a defining feature, we declared that the document's bearer was a deaf mute (I shall never forget that the translation of this into Romanian is: Surdo-mut).

We were meant to meet the youth at ten o'clock in the evening. Until then, we went to one of the local inns for supper. A group of border police were having a great time singing and drinking. In the course of our meal, one of these men came over and asked to see our papers. We pointed out that to the best of our knowledge, off-duty border policemen, especially those involved in drinking wine, did not have the necessary authority to check the validity of anyone's documents. The man informed us that they have a standing order to demand to see documents in the border region at any time of the day or night, of any person who seems suspicious to them. I calmly pulled out my student card. The moron had never seen a document of this kind before and asked to see my identification card. Dan pointed to his coat which was hanging by the door and said: "Our documents are over there. If you want to see them, go over and take them out!" After the check, a man in plain clothes walked over and apologized to us. He introduced himself as commander of counter intelligence and explained that they had to keep their eyes wide open, because there were many Jews and other similar elements running about in the region. He invited us to join him in a glass of wine, but we refused. We were unwilling to forgive him for disturbing us, especially since it was almost ten o'clock.

It was a pleasant night, the moon had not yet risen, and we could barely see two steps in front of us. This made us very glad. Dan took his suitcase, picked up a compass, the forgery tools and a gun and we disappeared into the darkness. The route crossed a forest and I was getting annoyed at not being able to join him. In all truth, I was feeling guilty at leaving him to his own devices in the middle of the night. We arrived more or less at the border.[65] I swallowed several times and held out a hand to Dan. He disappeared into the dark night.

At Baila-Felix I met David Nikurutz. He was a former Romanian policeman and was now living in retirement in his small villa. He was the first Romanian I had ever known in my life. He hated the Hungarians and greatly admired the Jews. I befriended him by telling him that — notwithstanding the fact that I was an Aryan — I felt it my duty as a Hungarian to help the Jews. I wouldn't be surprised if to this day, old David Nikurutz recalls Domnul Szabó[66] since he never got to knew who I really was.... The old man was willing to help me and transfer some of my friends to Romania. He recruited several farmers for this and, in spite his lack of organizational talents, he managed to set up and instruct a small, but serious organization. So that, after a long time, we were once again enjoying some success. On my way on the fast train to Budapest, I started formulating a hundred plans, and felt that the crisis was behind us.

We always received written confirmation of their arrival from the groups we sent out via David Nikurutz. This was important, because many smugglers supplied us with only verbal confirmations, which could not be verified and only weeks later did we sometimes discover that these people had been handed over to the gendarmerie.

It would have been possible to do an intensive psychological research program on the smugglers. Many of them saw the act of smuggling people across the border as a purely financial arrangement and carried it out with the same style and professional expertise as others smuggled coffee or tobacco. They attached great importance to the financial viability of the projects and the number of times they fell into the hands of the authorities. We met a few smugglers with a real "honor among thieves" mentality. Most of them were prepared to desert their wards right there on the border, at the first sign of trouble, and many were even willing to rob the poor souls and leave them to their own devices. There were countless such cases, and we were happy when one or other smuggler "only" robbed his wards and did not inform on them to the authorities....

Old Nikurutz developed a special system for avoiding such cases and each group was given a new secret signal. He had special signals for extortion, betrayal, a difficult route, or an easy one, and when we saw the secret signal — e.g. the torn off left hand corner of a piece of paper, or a sequence of letters — he would deduct mercilessly from the sum promised to his smugglers. Unfortunately, after a while the old man moved into town and was no longer able to work on our behalf. In any case, we could not have made do with only one route. We were constantly in search of new contacts, although each new smuggler presented new dangers, since each of them could have been agents, of which there were plenty in those days. There were also many small-time criminals who made a living out of the suffering of the Jews. On one occasion I reached an agreement with a new smuggler, who aroused my admiration by offering to accommodate people during the day at his brother-in-law's home in Oradea. Finding accommodation for the people waiting to cross the border was one of our greatest problems, and sometimes insoluble. And suddenly, this good man disappeared — he seemed to simply disintegrate several train stops from Oradea. He was probably enjoying himself somewhere, having fooled me out of 1,000 pengős.

Anyway, Mimish's case ended badly. Even after the unsuccessful journey to Oradea, Mimish would not give up his plans for a *"tiyul."* But this time he did not want to go through Oradea. One day, a new and very promising route was discovered via Szeged,[67] which Mimish decided to use. Problems started arising in the train, but who could expect excellent organizational powers from a simple smuggler? And then, as they took their leave of "beautiful Hungary" in the middle of the dark night, there was the sudden familiar hoarse screech of a gerndarme: "Stop!" It all seemed like a perfectly staged comedy. Mimish broke into a run, but it was soon apparent that they were surrounded. The entire group was brought to Szeged, first to counter intelligence and then to the Gestapo. In Budapest, we waited two weeks for news of Mimish. The smuggler who had no compunctions about coming to pick up his payment, told us that on the way back from Timişoara[68] he had been obliged to tear Mimish's letter to pieces, since he fell into the hands of the gendarmes. The story did not seem particularly reliable and we stopped sending out people with this smuggler. It was twenty days after the arrival of the smuggler that we received our first news of Mimish from Szeged. Fortunately, we were able to release him and Yutza, and later, the entire group too. The story of the release is a fantastic one, which I shall tell elsewhere.

There were moments — albeit extremely rare ones — of happiness, small successes which stood out like islands in a deep sea. Much depended on our awareness and caution. I do not believe in chance, but there were many instances, which seemed to us so special and incomprehensible, that they could only be referred to as chance.

Each time I arrived in Oradea, I tried to make contact with the town's remaining Jews. Outside the ghetto, only a handful of Jewish doctors continued to reside, and they were afraid of extending even the simplest kind of assistance. They were gripped by fear and terror of the ghetto, into which they were thrown eventually, anyway. Deportation in Hungary was cruel and accompanied by the merciless and systematic destruction of anything Jewish. And now one such incident brought me to a meeting with a Jewess who might have turned out to be of great assistance to us. From my bunk in the sleeping compartment, I could not help overhearing a conversation from the corridor, from which it transpired that Mrs. Hana is "an exempted person"[69] and as such, was not required to vacate her home. Somehow, I got the feeling that she was from Oradea. I strained my ears in vain, in the hope of hearing something more. The following day, I made my way to the barber. In typical antisemitic style, I struck up a conversation on the Jewish issue and I was especially outspoken against those "exempted people." The barber's apprentice was quick to rise to my bait and told me that in Oradea too, there was one such woman. She was a photographer, who had spied for Hungary, during the Romanian occupation and was now being allowed to remain on her own. Getting her address was now child's play. I was beside myself with joy: after all, not only did I finally find a Jewess, but one that would be well versed in my own profession. I went to her immediately. Trust was established between us right away. She gave me several important hints, opening various new routes.

Had I been writing a tale of "One Thousand and One Nights," I would have devoted whole nights to describing the trees and shrubs at the Oradea gardens, in which we whiled away many an hour. During the long hours of waiting for our groups to set out, we hid under the dense branches. It was here that we sought shelter from the rain. We spent hours watching the monotonous play of straight sun rays filtering through the leaves and prayed to the spirit of this calm fragment of nature to shelter us from the gendarmes and Gestapo men, whose only wish was to harm us. Our most pressing problem — which we never managed to solve — was finding accommodation for people in the town. Thus the public park became the only place in which we could take shelter.

I was unable to travel to the border too frequently, because the town was small and every stranger was very obvious. Again, I searched for a woman, whose job would be easier than that of Hava's, since the project she would be undertaking would be an ongoing one. Our choice was Tamarka.[70] In addition to being highly educated, she was also a young woman with an exceptionally well-developed self-awareness. We had already entrusted her with minor tasks in the past, now she was being given a really difficult one. And indeed, Tamarka soon made all the necessary connections and started working her way into her new job. In fact, she started working with that same Jewish photographer. One evening she arrived unexpectedly in Budapest and related what had happened. Ben-Eretz[71] and his group were spending the day somewhere out of town, where they would wait until it was time to cross (the border). But they were discovered and brought to the police. With them was a young girl from Oradea, whom we had met a short time before, who now, on her very first action, had failed. One of the policemen went to her apartment, where he found Tamarka. Whether out of routine, or stupidity, the policeman did no more than note down her details, which of course, helped Tamarka to be on the next train out of town. Not only had we lost yet another group, but our rhythm was also broken. Tamarka was no longer able to return to Oradea, which left me no choice: once again I put on my green hat[72] and bought an overnight train ticket.

The following morning I made my way straight to Tamarka's apartment, in order to find out all I could about our people. She had not yet been released from custody. A pleasant lady asked me to wait while she called the landlady. This was an old trick and I denied her the pleasure of waiting for the arrival of the police.

The sleeping compartment holds many pleasant memories for me, but also some harsh ones. The train arrived at Oradea in the middle of the night, but it was possible to remain in the carriage until morning, thus solving the problem of overnight accommodation. The detectives who had recently been traveling on all the trains to Oradea, were much more generous toward those who traveled in a sleeping bunk. They estimated that an escaping Jew would not have the daring or audacity to mingle with officers and senior government officials. If you looked reasonably well, the journey passed by uneventfully. I shared the compartment with one or two others — fellow travelers — which made it possible to limit to a minimum any imposing and dangerous conversations. It was a good thing that I was able to shave each morning. We sent several groups to Oradea in sleeping compartments, but we were not always able to obtain tickets to these compartments, nor did everyone have the physical appearance which allowed them to travel this way. On one occasion I got a real scare: at six o'clock in the morning, someone knocked on the door of my compartment. I imagined the worst and even considered jumping out of the window, until it dawned on me that it was Efra, wishing to wake me up to inform me that the smuggler had disappeared.

Once, I was obliged to witness a terrible spectacle. At Szolnok[73] I had already noticed that one of our people who was traveling third class, had been arrested. I hoped it was only incidental. Possibly one of the guards knew the young man. However, at Szajol[74] more men were arrested and soon a gendarme appeared at my compartment, accompanied by a detective, and leading another of our members. I stood at the door to my compartment and was unable to retreat, so as not to attract attention. I barely managed to contain myself at the terrible sight and the sound of the detectives boasting that he had already captured three Jews and only this last one was refusing to admit that he was Jewish. Naturally, I was terrified that he would give me away, with a look or a movement, but we both passed the test. They tied the fellow's hands to the luggage rack and beat him mercilessly, until he admitted that he had indeed been born Jewish. My blood boiled to see the other passengers and their evil pleasure at seeing the young man punished so. To this day I wonder how I was able to contain myself in face of the provocative taunting of the detective, the gendarmes' cruelty and the sound of the terrible jeer: "Zsidó,"[75] with all the other passengers joining in unison. The two hooligans seemed very pleased with their success and waived the chance of checking the papers of passengers in the sleeping compartment. Under those circumstances, the slightest tremble of my hands would probably have given me away.

We did our best to involve as many Aryans as possible in that work. This was how I had made contact with a young and very beautiful dancer in Oradea, whom Dan happened to know from his hometown. Beautiful Harriet was English. Actually, her beauty was marred by one fact only: her mother was Jewish. I was often seen in public with Harriet and the Oradea gossips were surely convinced: that student from Budapest is probably head over heels in love with her. On many occasions, I was obliged to accompany Harriet to the nightclub, and out of this grew an additional advantage: filling those "dead hours," a thing which had always been a great problem in Oradea. And indeed Harriet helped us enormously, and if I am to judge other night-club dancers by her, then I must surely make some fundamental changes to my general opinion of dancers.

My "tiyul" work brought me in contact with many other personalities, who peopled the fringes of bourgeois society. Unfortunately, most of them worked only out of financial greed. Many of them were subject to the effects of alcohol, or simply mood swings. All of these people made money easily and also spent it easily. From operation to operation, they used to raise their demands, until they reached a level of extortion. Many of them were arrested, as was Sanyi, the pimp. It was easier, of course, for them to be released, but we had to lay out large sums of money. In accordance with underworld customs, we were the ones to bear the costs.

Meanwhile, the Poles from Budapest had devised an excellent route, which crossed Szeged. Their situation was still infinitely better than ours. Legally, they were "clean" and as Aryan Poles, were free to travel wherever they wanted throughout the country. Based on the ancient friendship between the Poles and the Hungarians, they had excellent connections in military and governmental circles, and sometimes even with the reactionaries[76] and they knew very well how to take advantage of this. The Polish circles wanted to cooperate with the Zionists, because they needed their money. Furthermore, they wanted us to take their political leaders — whose activity had been exposed, and especially the socialists among them — along with us when we emigrated to Palestine. At first this seemed a very expensive way to act. We also had a kind of lack of trust for the Poles. Anyway, Leon Blatt developed the operation and reached an agreement with the Polish Council. As a result, Blatt was completely independent. He obtained the necessary money by sending out strangers, ordinary Jews — in return for large sums of money. This approach did not seem immoral, since Hungarian Jewry had contributed nothing at all to the refugees. Moreover, they did not even raise any funds to save themselves. But when the time came for the second payment to the Polish Council — a sum of 200,000 Pengő — the issue became complicated and he wanted to involve us in this operation of his. We agreed to his proposal, since the route had proved itself excellently; although we did not know that the route had already lost its secrecy element and the Szeged Gestapo had started "folding it up," which happened at exactly the same time as I went with one of the members of the Council to examine things in the field. Everyone who came with me was arrested and once again, I was the only one to evade death, by a tiny step.

By that time, we had already transferred the point of departure for the *"tiyul"* to the consulate on Vadász Street.[77] Problems with the *"tiyul"* arose in the city of Budapest as well; the most important of these was that of the point of departure. Every day we sent off between five and ten people, and only at the very last moment were we able to divulge to them if, when and how they would be leaving. We behaved in this way, both because of the rules of underground activity and for purely technical reasons — the smugglers made a habit of arriving at the very last moment. The people had to receive accurate instructions, to prepare them mentally and emotionally for their journey, to supply them with all the necessary details and any eventualities which might arise on the way. Alongside this tactical briefing, it was necessary to equip them with money. Sometimes it would take a full half hour to brief just one person. Each one had his individual personality and his way of dealing with problems. After all, their success depended primarily on the people's feelings and their self confidence. At first, our point of departure had been at the Judenrat building on Síp Street, because we could lose ourselves there in the commotion. But it was not long before we became well known and complete strangers came up to us and asked to be taken along too. We were sure that this crowd also included informers, so we quickly did away with this location. But there was another reason for our decision to reject the building on Sip Street.

We had countless confrontations with the "Battlefront Fighters."[78] These were the most reactionary elements in Hungarian Jewry. These assimilated Jews took shelter behind their military rank and thus enjoyed special status. They acted as a "stewards' unit," similar to the Polish "Ordners."[79] This institution produced information and secret reports for the War Office on the mood of the forced labor workers; the "Battlefront Fighters" were the personification of the anti-social spirit. In the Council building too, these toadies ensured their own safety and made a point of upholding the law. They staffed the "Stewards'

Service" and furiously persecuted any illegal activity. We were constantly subject to the tyranny of these characters. One gentleman, a certain Major Kálmán,[80] was not averse to attacking Neshka[81] with a heavy belt. We were forced, therefore, to remove our point of departure to various public gardens. It is hard to describe today, the terrible dangers involved in those meetings. At three o'clock, ten characters would turn up in the St. István gardens. The way the group walked, their physical bearing and their behavior were amazingly alike. Five or six of them — at times all ten — were about to set out across the border and required advance briefing. Afterwards we had to listen to those who remained behind, who had come along for all sorts of weird and wonderful reasons. Some were in need of new documents, others needed money. Unfortunately, our people behaved in a very suspicious manner and I shall always be puzzled by the fact that these meeting places were never discovered. Half an hour like this, which we called "bourse," was more exhausting than eight hours of physical labor. It would drive us mad sometimes when someone, who had already been fully briefed and on his way, would come back to ask if he should wear a cap or a hat. It was a great relief therefore, when we disbanded the "bourse," in part at least, and relocated our *"tiyul"* preparations to "our consulate" building.[82] Under the auspices of this "ex-territorialism"[83] we were now able to talk peacefully with the members. Here too, things were not entirely simple, because the people responsible for the institution rose against us and we had a bitter struggle against them, but at least we felt at home. We had no choice sometimes but to use force in order to obtain what we thought was right. The story of the "status wars" in Vadász Street will be best told by Rafi.

On August 23, 1944, I was once again in Oradea. My Romanian friends, with whom I had spent the night, woke me up in the morning with some happy news: Romania had broken away from the war.[84] My first thought was given over to those three fellows who had set off the previous day for the border, because I assumed that under these circumstances, the border would be more closely guarded. Immediately afterwards, I had another thought: this was my last chance to "hop" over myself into freedom. I knew that the *"tiyul"* was over completely, and my own mission too was now over. But I could not make up my mind to leave my friends. The real work was just about to begin, because we had finally got ourselves into a mouse-trap, from which there would be no way out. I took my leave, therefore, of my Romanian friends, said good-bye to Uncle Peter and my job, this time for good. I also parted from the town which had opened a window to freedom for so many people — and had cost the lives of others....

Uncle Peter was a simple man, a farmer, who was close to Judaism because of his sectarian beliefs.[85] A certain percentage of God-fearing people had placed themselves at the disposal of this holiest task of all — to save the lives of the persecuted Jews. He had a deep understanding of the Jewish issue, more fundamental than that of many intellectuals. We spent long nights discussing the philosophy of religion. I learned to respect his simple and wonderful pantheism and was not at all surprised when my friends wrote that, on arrival at the border crossing point in the middle of a dark night, Uncle Peter would go down on his knees and pray from the depths of his heart. This prayer thoroughly shocked our friends, devout atheists all.

Uncle Peter was a wonderful organizer. He ensconced himself in a small office, which he ruled with a strong arm. It was with him that we carried out the final mission: the transfer of the last Jews of Oradea, who had been hiding and still holding out in various bunkers, across the border. The poor things were so frightened, trembled so hard at any hint of provocation, had been deprived so long of sun-light, that only a few of them dared come out of their hiding places. Uncle Peter was one of the few true righteous people, who dared to challenge the events of that time...

So much for Pil's story.

Chapter Six

Ups and Downs

Topolja[1] could be considered something of a success. Topolja was a shining example of friendship, steadfastness and fanatical determination. Topolja was the second largest experience of solidarity, which extended far and beyond the boundaries of the movement. When Mimish and his group were brought to Szeged, they all decided to escape, no matter what. This decision might easily be taken for granted, but it was not so simple. Very few individuals have the courage to make their escape at a decisive moment. Only someone who had gone through the same bitter experiences as Mimish, only someone, who like him, had known many fates, knew clearly that there was only one way out: escape. Thus, at the first available opportunity, Yutza and Hans[2] made their escape. As free people, they now stood on the streets of Szeged, without a penny in their pockets and not knowing a soul in the town. In one of the town's suburbs, they met a number of Jews from the forced labor units, who willingly put some money at their disposal. Incidentally, this was not beneficial to them, because one of the soldiers who witnessed the exchange, walked over and asked to see their papers. The three ran for their lives but Hans and Yutza were caught. Only Mimish managed to get away, although several shots were fired after him.

Was Mimish's escape fair? He asked himself this question over and over during those sleepless nights. It was quite clear to us that his escape enabled the rescue of the others, since without it, we would never have known what had happened to them and where they were located. Yutza and Hans were brought before the Gestapo and beaten for several days in order to get them to give away Mimish's whereabouts. Since they knew that Yutza was his wife, they used the most terrible forms of torture in order to get her to talk. She was forced to wipe a wet concrete floor dry with her bare body. Yutza revealed nothing, but her body told us — for many weeks later — what she had gone through.

One day a Serb arrived at the Judenrat inquiring about Mimish or Rafi. I spoke to him and discovered that the entire party had been transferred to a German concentration camp at Topolja. Yutza had sent him and he was willing to get her released, but he needed another woman to help him. It was a very difficult decision we had to make. Mimish knew Milan from when he was smuggling cigarettes and shaving tools into Szeged. But we were unable to fully understand him and did not know why he needed another woman. And he refused to give us any further explanations. Mimish was frantic — on the one hand, he did not want to ask anyone to put his life in danger, but on the other hand, his entire soul was torn apart because of Yutza. In the end we decided to send Zippi.[3] When Tamarka was in Oradea, organizing the *"tiyul,"* I had learned what it meant to worry. Now it was Efra's turn to worry about his beloved partner, with whom he had shared the harsh experiences of the last months. But two days later, Zippi, Milan and Yutza were back, according to plan.

Zippi posed as Milan's sister-in-law and told the Gestapo officers that Milan's wife was very sick and in need of help. Milan suggested — by the way — that they might be able to employ the Jewish women from the camp at Topolja, for which they received permission. Yutza understood very well what was going on, having noticed Zippi standing beside Milan and volunteered to act as housemaid in the home of the "cruel Gestapo agent."

Who, in fact, was Milan? There is no doubt that he worked for the Gestapo. He told us that, as a Serb, he had decided to go straight into the lion's den, in order to help his brethren. We believed him. He was loyal to us, willing to deny himself, bravehearted, a real partisan. In the end he was arrested by his employers. When he escaped, we gave him money and documents so he could get away and save his life. How superficially simple this man had seemed to us, yet how important and inexplicable were some of the things he did! Shortly after Yutza's escape, Milan announced that he was going to Vienna, in order to get several Yugoslavs released from one of the camps and that he needed the young woman to go with him — he had once asked us to supply him a young woman for this very purpose. In Szeged, he had registered Zippi on his Gestapo certificate and this time he wanted to take her with him to Vienna; on the one hand he needed an interpreter, and on the other, he was fully aware of the male weakness for the fairer sex, and it was obvious that a pretty girl could attract the attention of certain gentlemen away from their own activity.

This time Tamarka went with him. We ourselves were interested in this visit to Vienna, because an "emigrant group"[4] had set out in the direction of Vienna just a few days earlier and we wanted to know how it had fared. A week later, Tamarka returned, but was unable to tell more about the group than this: the emigrants were somewhere near Hannover.[5] The group had passed through Vienna. However, she had brought some interesting information about the Strasshof[6] transit camp near Vienna. Some 16,000 Hungarian Jews had been brought there before being sent on to various labor camps. Their condition at Strasshof (one of the concessions achieved by Kastner[7]) was more or less reasonable.

After Milan's return from Vienna, we started making plans for rescuing the dozens of people remaining in Topolja. Mimish saw this as his life's work. He imagined the sorry state of the prisoners and was filled with guilt and remorse at having betrayed them by escaping. Milan soon found a solution. He returned to Szeged, bribed people left, right and center and in the end succeeded in getting our people transferred to the Columbus camp. The camp on Columbus Street continued to operate after the transfer's departure, in preparation for a second consignment of people. The camp's management was Jewish. The SS guards at its gates were not dangerous and we reckoned that the best thing would be for the truck with the ten prisoners to arrive at the camp gates and for the ten to be officially registered. Mimish was waiting for the prisoners and happily paid the agreed-upon sum, and like a child whose adventures had succeeded, he asked to hear all the details. The guards became suspicious and telephoned the "Schwab Hill" in order to report the arrival of the mysterious group of ten. And indeed, the Gestapo immediately turned up in two cars and arrested eight men; two of the group had meanwhile disappeared into thin air. We were speechless, thunderstruck. The rescue of the men from Topolja had become a sacred mission for us and for Mimish; we had laid out vast sums of money to achieve it. Had all this been in vain?

We tried to sort things out with the help of Kastner, but the men were taken from the Schwab Hill to Fő Street[8] and then back to Szeged. It appeared that the latter had been the work of Milan, who had not given up the struggle on behalf of the young men. He managed somehow to awaken the honor of the bribed Gestapo people in Szeged. So it happened that the Gestapo gates opened one day and eight of our members walked out, while the guard was busily observing the cloud formation. The battle of Topolja ended in victory and Mimish's peace of mind and mental equilibrium were reinstated.

There was another promise he had to fulfill: it appears that he had made a solemn covenant with Yutza, there in the Gestapo's dungeons of death. Now that they had escaped the talons of death once more, there was nothing left but for him to pave the way to life for little Mimish. Death continued to stalk us, and no-one was more aware than Yutza that her man could fall prey any day. But this baby was hidden in the safest bunker of all. He did not even have the need for forged identification papers! Yutza recovered gradually from the cruel blows and was soon happy with her little Mimish, who had no compunctions about kicking her roundly — from within.

Romania's changed battlefronts did not mean only the end of the "tiyul," it also symbolized the end of an entire period. Weeks of tension and concern were over. Suddenly there was a respite. We were surrounded by a strange, almost audible silence, and inadvertently we began taking stock of the previous weeks. We had sent about 150 members to freedom, many of whom were already in Palestine. Others were in some other free democratic country. This was the positive side. On the other hand we recalled the horrors of the down-side. The cruel border had brought down many of our members, hostile border towns took many others. We had lost Yirmi, Nesher, Yohi, Hava, Chandri[9] and many other good friends. We tried to console ourselves by reckoning our losses in percentages — only fifteen percent — and repeated this to ourselves over and over again, that this sacrifice had been worthwhile, after all, these people had lost nothing, they had merely failed to achieve life. There was only one sacrifice with which we were never able to reconcile ourselves. The futile, insane and inexplicable drowning of the ship "Mefkora."[10] Again and again we could see before the picture of little Renka,[11] who had come from Poland, pregnant. For weeks she wandered the streets of Budapest, always smiling, she was so happy and looking forward to the happy event. And then one day our very first "born musician" arrived, who was issued his very own — legal — birth certificate, bearing his false name. When he was barely two months old, the two crossed the border and arrived successfully in Bucharest, but before they could arrive at their final destination, they found their death among the waves of the Black Sea. The arms of the Nazis were very long indeed. They took Yirmi from us, one of the best of our men from Slovakia, a loyal and honest friend, who helped each of us during those first difficult days in Budapest and was unable to help himself. For the two years he worked in a Budapest factory, he never asked for so much as a penny from anyone. How grateful he was to the movement for granting him a forged Bulgarian passport, with which he was able to cross the border legally and in comfort. The ship of death also bore away my sister, Eva, together with her little Freddy and her husband Imre. They were not refugees. As ordinary citizens, they had lived in Arad, and were among the first to stand by our people who had managed to cross the border from Hungary to Romania. They took care of them, and learned to like our friends; they learned to know and value the movement, too, and once they had decided to emigrate to Palestine, the grateful movement was only too pleased to include them on the ship. How happy was Eva's farewell letter, in which she thanked us and hoped to see us all soon....

It should never have happened. The drowning of Mefkora was a tasteless trick of fate. However, in spite of everything, we found recompense in our sorrow. Those painful months were a kind of raising of the flag to the will-to-live, to the "in-spite-of-it-all," to the bursting out of the boundaries of childhood, of courage and determination. These months had been the realization of our Hashomer Hatza'ir education. We wanted to live because we had tasted life and knew how great a mission it was. We struggled for life, but were ready — if need be — to make a sacrifice for it...of life.

Chapter Seven

Kastner's Grand Plan

Whereas the Jews of Budapest were slow to feel the gradual tightening noose of the Nazi occupation, deportations had already begun in April from the city's suburbs. The first transports set out from Yugoslavia's occupied areas.[1] At the same time there began a round-up of the Jews of Podkarpatska-Rus into ghettos. The Jewish Council had been completely detached from the provinces; no travel permits were issued and no legal aid available. Moshe Rosenberg founded the Department of Provinces, with two objectives:

1) To offer all available assistance;
2) To collect data on the developments in the provinces, in order to supply information and, simultaneously, to collect historical material.

It was a difficult and thankless task. Refugees were flowing in daily from the various concentration camps, supplying an on-going picture of the terrible condition of the provincial Jews. We were already familiar with the various forms of deportation; again and again we encountered the mass terror being waged against the Jewish nation. We were very familiar with the rows of people marching hopelessly to their deaths. One thing we had not experienced previously, was the cruel sadism of the Hungarian gendarmes. Clearly these gendarmes were another example — albeit horrible indeed — of that sector from which were carved the "Hlinka Guards"[3] or the "Ustashi."[4] Probably the most distressing thing of all was the complacency and gloating on the part of the Hungarian people. In every other country, even Germany, there were those who were willing to help the Jews. Here in Hungary, the wall of antisemitism was higher.

We called on all our members from the provinces to come to Budapest, knowing that the capital's turn would come last of all and our first objective was to gain time. Unfortunately some of our members were dissuaded by their parents, who were sure that "maybe after all it won't happen to them…." This was how we lost Koka[5] from Košice, who had only recently given birth to a healthy son. Those of our members who were organizing the internal *"tiyul"* reported to the communities on the situation, but their warnings fell on deaf ears wherever they went. It was not in vain that Samuel Stern[6] had been teaching his brethren to trust, for twenty-five years. The cooperation with Hungarian reactionaries and the gross disillusion regarding assimilation, had now come to an end in a manner more tragic and bloody than we could ever have imagined. It was in these days of chaos, that our Tamarka proved her worth. She traveled the length and breadth of the country, brought money, documents and news about our friends, accompanied the frightened among them to Budapest. She made contact with all the movement's far-flung groups.

Our ties with the aid centers in Geneva and Istanbul were not simple even before the German occupation. Admittedly, we were able to send telegrams, even letters, but everything went very slowly, and, of course, not everything could be entrusted to the official postal services. We took all the advantage we could of courier services, some of whom came from the diplomatic corps, and some from the underworld. Strange as this may sound, we were sometimes assisted by couriers working for German counter-intelligence.[7] At that time they were still with the Wehrmacht. Moreover, they were Viennese! The Jewish question as a political issue, and especially as the political question of the SS, did not interest them at all. It did not bother them to help the Jews and to save the lives of a few hundred of them, if by doing so they could make a little something on the side. As it happened, it was these who maintained the most important ties with the last camps and bunkers in Poland.

All this work was performed by Kastner's people. We barely had a look-in, both out of a sense of caution and perhaps for reasons of party policy as well. After March 19, they were wise enough to form ties with the new rulers — thanks to their previous connections. As far as the Jews were concerned, there were two authorities in Budapest whose importance was decisive. The first was the Operations Commando[8] under the command of the terrible mass murderer,

Adolph Eichmann. Eichmann was under the direct command of Himmler and sent his "work details" from the various countries to Poland. He had a well-honed and efficient system, according to which he operated everywhere he went. He formed a Judenrat (Jewish Council), which at first handed over to him all the Jewish property and then the Jews themselves. In Judenrats throughout Europe there were some miserable creatures willing to sacrifice the lives of thousands of Jews just to save their own skins. But still there were some honest and decent people who were misled by the Germans' lies. These later regretted their tragic mistake and collapsed under their heavy burden of guilt. There is a somewhat piquant aspect to Eichmann's personal history. He had been born in Palestine, son of a Knight Templar, of the Christian cult of Templars, and spoke fluent Hebrew.[9] On more than one occasion in Geneva, Eichmann grabbed a letter from Nathan's[10] hands and gave it to Kastner with a mocking smile, saying that we should tell Mr. Nathan to use more wisdom in composing his letters, if he doesn't want him (Eichmann) to understand what is written in them.

Eichmann brought some of his old friends with him, once again led by "Willy,"[11] as we know, the corrupt supervisor of the expulsion of the Jews of Slovakia. We had no illusions as to what we could expect from this bunch.

The political concept of Becher's[12] office was an enigma. Becher's office — the second most important one in the current administration — arrived ready-equipped with a program. Germany no longer had an interest in annihilating Hungarian Jewry — so they announced. Strategic developments meant that Germany was suffering from certain economic deficits, which required certain measures. Thus a deal was possible. The proposal sounded cynical: blood in return for more blood. Willy, too, participated in the negotiations and it seemed possible for a while that Eichmann's hysterical considerations would be subject to Willy's cold calculations. The negotiations — which referred to the salvation of the whole of Hungarian Jewry — were handled exclusively by Brand and Kastner. Their reports on the progress of the negotiations were minimal and rare. Anyone who was aware of the desperate state of the German[13] battle front and hinterland, would not have seen this deal as lacking in imagination. The big question was, of course, what sort of reply could be expected from the allies?

One day,[14] Joel Brand boarded a plane for Turkey to begin negotiations. It seemed to us that he had been entrusted not only to strive to obtain trucks and chromium, but also to seek out some opening to peace.[15] Brand had only just left, and the deportations began. Possibly the first despatch was only a means of pressure, a well-known political maneuver of extortion. The allies were in no hurry, since victory over the Germans had long been a sure thing. The onset of deportations was seen and understood abroad as proof that the Germans could not be trusted.

I cannot give any more details about these issues, because I knew very little about the whole matter. I am writing this only because it had a round-about effect on us too. Often, we were faced with problems, situations arose, to which the entire Hashomer Hatza'ir movement was required to supply clear answers. We had never had any great faith in the negotiations, and when deportations commenced, we lost it completely. It was clear that we were not for a moment to neglect the "little tasks," but rather were to persevere with them, independently of the negotiations.

When the Jews of the annexed regions[16] had been expelled, negotiations began over the future of the Jews in the "mother country."[17] And when these too had been packed into cattle trucks — the grand plan was reduced to tiny despatches. Thus the big dream of saving a million Jews turned into a plan for sending several hundred Jews to Palestine. This emigration plan too, underwent several transformations. Every day the Germans cut back on their promises. Still, at first this was the only option for the older, less mobile, Zionists.

It was planned at first that the emigrants would set sail from Romania in ships flying the Red Cross flag. Romania was later replaced by Spain, because they wanted it to give the emigrant-train the outward appearance of deportation, setting off in the direction of Germany. The Hungarians were not supposed to knew that the Germans were prepared to participate in deals of this sort.... A ridiculous situation arose later on: German authorities were obliged to "steal" several hundred Hungarian Jews in order to save their lives!

We spent many weeks working on the details of this emigration. Following our first successes, the *"tiyul"* had hit a sandbank and many members were lost. The question then arose whether we would be better off rejecting the *"tiyul"* issue and sending our people via groups of emigrants. Kastner demanded we make a decision. Nevertheless, we remained constant and were never taken in by the "wider concept."[18]

Kastner's efforts first came to fruition, as the most terrible of the deportations were underway. In all the satellite towns, he was able to rescue several well-known Jews from the deportation.[19] Thus some 1,600 people were concentrated in the Columbus Street camp which became the base for emigration.

In Budapest itself, we suffered no losses, with the exception of Avri Lissauer. Every morning the four of us met for breakfast and each one then went on to meet other people. In this way we received a constant flow of information. One day, Michael did not turn up for the breakfast meeting. He did not arrive at eleven o' clock in the morning, nor at three o' clock in the afternoon. Something must have happened to him. We were unable to send anyone to his apartment, of course, but we stationed ourselves nearby. Shortly afterwards, Eta's little brother arrived and told us what had happened. Some time beforehand, a woman had sought refuge in the apartment occupied by Eta and Michael. This woman was a "musician" who had made a recent escape to Budapest from one of the ghettos. Someone had informed on the woman but she managed to escape in time. Michael was aware of all this and thus it was impossible to understand how an experienced "musician" such as he, did not change his address immediately. Thus it happened that the detectives who came at six o'clock in the morning in search of the woman, found a young couple instead, with a miniature forger's workshop hidden in their home. One of his suitcases contained a stock of several hundred registration forms, requiring only a date of issue, which we sorely missed later on. We were totally dumbfounded. Exactly as in the case of Avri, we had no idea as to where to even begin the process of rescuing the couple. We had no connections with lawyers or other people who were professionally involved in rescuing people.[20] Actually, we took seriously the uncompromising style used by all the journalists and politicians.[21] Our only hope was Michael's resourcefulness, which had saved him often before from difficult situations. But instead of rescuing him, we suffered a further blow the following day.

Our friends, Uri, Metuka, Nomi, Avri, Lea and Moshe were caught in one of the apartments which we made the unfortunate habit of frequenting. As if Michael's case was not annoying enough, this case was the fault of the people involved. The Hungarian movement members had not yet developed the necessary self-confidence in their new lifestyle; they had experienced all the "growing pains" of Aryanization. They met each other too often, their sense of helplessness drove them into seeking refuge with each other, hoping to find comfort with their peers. And this was how they did the stupidest thing possible: they spent all their time together. This apartment was visited too often by too many people, and they were probably not as quiet as they could have been. The same kind of forms were found in this apartment as at Michael's and the connection was very soon made. Incriminating information was published in the press. With one eye crying and the other laughing, we read about the resourcefulness of these young people, when, in their interrogation, they unanimously placed the blame squarely on one man, a certain Dan Zimmerman, who at that time had been long gone in Romania.

After several days, the whole group was transferred to the transit camp, to which the victims of the Cluj *"tiyul"* had been brought and several of our members from Oradea. A few days before the emigration group was scheduled to leave, there were thirty-eight of our members in the "Toli." Our last hope was Kastner. For several weeks, he had been promising to rescue our friends before the transfer. Now it was June 28, the day his transport was due to leave at long last. But now, the final hours before take off, Kastner had so many "more important" things to deal with that he had no time to intervene on behalf of our thirty-eight friends. Something had to be done, otherwise what was the point of a transfer which was rescuing people who had been free anyway and not our own thirty-eight dear ones who had been arrested?

At the assembly camp on Bocskai Street[22] we befriended a young SS guard. He was eighteen and his name was Fritz, a native of Cologne. He was a good kid, more interested in his mouth organ than in the entire war. One of the fellows in the camp had a girlfriend who had been imprisoned in the concentration camp at Kistarcsa and he asked Fritz to do him a favor and bring her. Fritz complied happily and within a few hours the young woman was driven over in a car. That was how we got the idea to try the same trick at the "Toli." Fortunately for us, Fritz did not really understand what we were getting at, but was quite willing to cooperate with us. We had in our possession the calling cards for the people on the transfer. They were written in a deliberately obtuse way, so that it was impossible to fathom which authority was inviting whom to join. We filled in these calling cards for our thirty-eight friends. Fritz took his sub-machine gun — of which he was inordinately proud — and I accompanied him as a plain-clothes "Gestapo man." We received a very congenial welcome at the checkpoint by the senior counselor, Mr. Horvát. I explained to him that we were about to transfer a special consignment of workers and were in need of the thirty-eight young experts. The senior advisor ordered that a check be made as to which of them was "at home," and it was already apparent that the scam had succeeded. And then there was a sudden air raid siren announcing an imminent attack.[23] Everything came to a stand-still in the office and everyone ran off to the shelter. Fritz and I went out on a tour of the darkened and threatening lock-up. In one of the cellars, in which hundreds of women were huddled, we found our own movement members. I almost cried at the sight of them among all those whores, but shouted at them instead. I shouted at them that they were to be removed to another place immediately. Judith[24] stood right next to the bars. I pressed her hand surreptitiously. I shall never forget the look in her eyes, as they filled with tears, and at the same time glowed with happiness and hope. She told me that Uri and some of the others had been transferred the day before to Sárvár, but that most of the group was still here.

The air raid lasted three hours. I got into a conversation with the police and gendarmes. They were all senior "blood-hounds." Fritz and I told them tales "from the front"…it was obvious that Fritz was feeling uncomfortable, as he began to gradually sense why and where I had brought him with me. He was terrified at the thought that a German officer might arrive by chance. It was quite clear to me too, that with the all-clear, we would have to make a hasty retreat. So I went up to the counselor and asked him for the signed calling order for handing over the prisoners and he informed me that he would first have to receive the approval of the German liaison officer, to whom he would make a telephone call as soon the all-clear had sounded. I had only one ruse left and I told him that I had to personally go to the German HQ. I returned to the office and asked the clerks to hold that group for a few more days, under all circumstances. Thus I was obliged to leave with Fritz without completing the mission. Hence the last attempt at rescuing the group, had failed.[25]

Chapter Eight

The "Transport"

For several weeks the "Palestine Committee" had been convening non-stop in order to determine the composition of the "transport." It was an awkward situation. Negotiations with the relevant Germans were conducted by Kastner; preparations for the "transport" were handled by the committee presidency, who knew nothing at all about the main issues in the operation. This work method was typical of Kastner. Distinguished members of the presidency, who had just held an election and left Kastner and his party in the minority, were now standing helplessly in front of this man. From time to time, they tried to register a protest, but were silenced with a wave of the hand. Once only, Kastner agreed to avail himself and provide a "detailed" description of the situation. Indeed he told us something, but everyone present felt, both from the tone of his voice and the content of his words, that what he was telling us was what he wanted us to hear. The presidency announced that it was no longer prepared to take responsibility for the entire operation. But immediately afterwards, they lowered their voices, since this operation was a single ray of light in a situation which was gray and indecisive. Although I rejected in principle the way in which Kastner operated, I did get a certain pleasure out of the game this powerful and intelligent man played with these little people. It was a long time since Kastner had been that same dangerous adversary as before. Our cooperation with the Ihud was complete. As far as he did this at all, Kastner was diligent in providing reports to his youth movements and to us. At that meeting of the Palestine Committee presidency, he knew very well why he was holding his silence. Although we were critical of Kastner and did not identify unconditionally with his activities, we were also able to observe the Zionist right floundering in helplessness. Hungarian Zionism had a list of distinguished representatives who were more familiar with words than action. For weeks they had been unable to agree on the final distribution of the places. The compilation of the "transport" list was postponed from week to week.[1] Kastner had a perfect excuse: the entire operation could fail because of their mistakes. We were still so naive as to believe him. Thus, I sat one evening with Eli Sajó and for an entire night we completed the preliminary list. This was followed later by about fifteen additional versions. Incidentally, it was no easy matter to represent the youth movements in these discussions regarding the advance preparations. The discussions were always "complex," "secret," and "special," not suitable for tender ears. But perhaps because this was not a matter of no consequence, we fought over the right to participate in the preparations and decisions. Yet even then, once I had achieved the appointment, it was a major struggle to achieve the right to participate in this meeting or the other.

The youth movements that met once again over the issue of emigration policy, consulted each other from time to time on the large number of problems involved in this kind of emigration. Should we relinquish our members to so uncertain a fate? Almost everyone disagreed; after all, we did not believe the Germans. But this time it was harder to raise objections. The Germans had indeed organized such "emigrations," but only in order to lead them later to the death camps[2] and to laugh with all their hearts that their trick had worked so well. But this had happened in 1942. At that time the Germans had plenty of spare time, which gave them a reason for laughing and their passion for fun and games had not yet been dulled by the murder of millions. Today, the Gestapo does not need to organize this kind of circus in order to capture 1,200 Zionists. It would be much simpler to round them up, and if they want money — as some of us said — all they needed to do was arrest half a dozen prominent Jews and they could extort the necessary sum with no trouble at all. It seemed, therefore, that the plan had some other incentive, something that was proven not only by the efforts extended by the blood hounds who had taken the trouble for weeks to negotiate with Kastner, but mainly in light of Joel's flight to Turkey. After all, the Gestapo were not over eager to take people out of the country, especially not Jews like Joel Brand, whose head was full of not unimportant information. It appears that the Germans were interested in the preparations for the despatch, and thus, it had to succeed, on the assumption that remuneration would indeed be given.

We held discussions on all these issues, within our own leadership as well. In the end we decided that we would have to clarify all the pros and cons to our members, so that they themselves could make a decision about this fateful issue. We struggled over each slot on the emigrant "transport." The principle of equality was still valid among all four Zionist parties; only the Mizrahi were dissatisfied with this. Shortly before the designated departure date, all the arrangements disintegrated; five hundred Jews from the Cluj ghetto "emigrated" to Budapest, and Kastner, devoted son of that city, demanded that they be included. From the Columbus camp too, it was necessary to take more people than had previously been accounted for. And in the end, there were new demands on the part of the ultra-Orthodox and the Neologues.[3] Arguments were endless.[4] In the end Szilágyi took command and in one night dictated his own final "transport." The list was a bad one, hastily compiled and the result of a night fraught with tort nerves. We too, were disappointed because we had not expected Szilagyi to remove so many of our people from the list. The letter he received from us was bitter and scathing and sufficient to cause a rift between us forever.

Nothing went as planned as the time of departure approached. On June 24, the transfer to "Jewish houses" was completed.[5] At the same time it was announced that Jews were allowed to go on the streets only between the hours of two and five o' clock in the afternoon. This presented terrible hardships to the final preparations prior to departure. On June 27, the members of the "transfer" congregated — following yet another stormy argument, let me add — in three camps: in Columbus Street, in Aréna Way[6] and in Bocskai Street. All our friends were taken to the latter. Many dropped out at the last minute and were replaced by others who jumped at the idea. A hundred and thirty movement members went with the "transport," including thirty adults from the Gordon Circle and some thirty children. There was not a single Pole among them, and only ten Slovaks. The refugees were not able to overcome their suspicions. But the Hungarian movement sent most of its members with the "transport," in fact, most of those who had not yet left for Romania. The recently established "Jewish houses," the newly imposed restrictive laws and the loss of Avri, caused the Hungarian members to feel rather confused and to take advantage of the first opportunity to escape. After a long time, they found themselves for the first time with an opportunity not to have to fend for themselves, but to sink and blend into the masses and sense the relief of being able to shed their heavy self-responsibility. (We suddenly understood the full tragedy of fascism, when our own members were also infected with the psychology of the masses!) The only one of the leadership to go was Yehuda[7] who had served on the Jewish Council until now. His physical appearance prevented him from posing as an Aryan, anyway. Someone had to go on behalf of the movement, and this was the best solution.

The transport set out late at night with 1,600 people,[8] instead of 1,200. We heard nothing from them for a couple of days, and then a girl from Mosonmagyaróvár[9] came with the news that the train had been diverted to Auschwitz. A few days later we received a telegram from Bratislava, through which the transport had passed. Only weeks later did we learn that it had "landed" at Bergen Belsen,[10] a small place near Hannover. By the time the first letters arrived, we had been following the story with baited breath and were able to reconstruct the route they had taken. The transport had not been permitted to enter Vienna, because it included two people who were sick with scarlet fever. The train was given moving orders to Auspitz by Brünn,[11] where the transport was supposed to stay, under guard. Someone had misheard the word "Auschwitz" and this caused, rightly, great agitation, until our Fritz checked the matter and discovered it wasn't true. Incidentally, throughout the journey, Fritz had behaved admirably and for the second time, saved the day at Linz.[12] It was here that the passengers were told they could all take a shower. The word "shower" fired their imagination with visions of the monster that was Auschwitz — after all we had managed to hear more than enough stories about the "showers" at that hell-hole of a place.[13] But this time the reference was to real showers. Anyway, it was up to Fritz to prevent the shaving of the women's heads — as was accepted. In Budapest, there were disagreements with regard to the calculations, which was why the train was first sent to Bergen Belsen. In this unique camp the inmates were not required to do any kind of work, and could spend their time as they wished. Their food supplies were meager, but not all that bad. Five children were born at the camp and two old people died.

Following a long sojourn, when many had already determined this transport's fate to be imprisonment, the first 325 people arrived at Montreux.[14]

This, of course was not the end of the affair. But Kastner found himself in a dead-end situation, having too eagerly put his faith in foreign assistance, and he may even have promised the Germans too much. Representatives of the allies had promised, at most, money; merchandise — no way. Some months before, the Germans still had some use for foreign currency, but now that several of the non-aligned countries (e.g. Portugal and Turkey)[15] had deserted them, money no longer had the same value. The Germans stopped asking for money in return for blood. What they wanted now was merchandise in return for blood. The extent to which Kastner's slight of hand succeeded, we would surely learn from the man himself at the end of the war.[16] The fact is that the Germans received no merchandise. I for one, suspected that they received no money either, certainly not the entire sum promised.[17] Nonetheless, the remainder of the people did reach Switzerland at the end of November.

Good for Kastner! All around him and possibly also within him, much was still obscure, but he saved the lives of 1,500 Jews, and these included not only the elite of Hungary's Zionist youth, but a long list of valuable and talented people who contributed to greatly their people and to humanity.

Chapter Nine

"Our Consulate"

The transport had departed and the corridors of the Jewish Council were suddenly empty and silent. Only a few days earlier the place had been full of people, pushing and shoving each other, fearing for their lives, a cacophony of voices filling the air. Now it was almost deserted, only individuals came, slow, heavy of movement, here on some business or other. The struggle for existence had disappeared from 12 Sip Street, and with it the hope for life. The information department was also empty, most of its workers having left. Uncle Federit's pleasant voice was silenced, even Szilágyi's yells had vanished somehow from these rooms. I walked through the building as through a battle field, on which the sounds of war had only just subsided. Were we indeed in the aftermath of a battle — was it one which had ended in victory or one which had ended in defeat? Who was there to supply an answer? Questionnaires, forms, lists, even deserted suitcases, lay scattered all around. It was a strange kind of quiet. In the movement too, only a few remained. Efra was the one to feel this the most, because the seventy movement members to have been included in the transport had been his protégés over recent months. Efra's "bourses" were hair-raising. He had been constantly surrounded by thirty people, most of whom were gripped with fear and asking him thousands of questions. This short respite was most helpful to him.

A further transport was supposed to be leaving a month later. Preparations had begun immediately, but these came to an abrupt halt when it became known that the first group had arrived at Bergen Belsen and not Spain. And suddenly, as if out of nowhere, Moshe Krausz re-appeared. He was involved briefly in preparations for the transport. He soon withdrew; he had been offended to the core by Kastner's methods, possibly because his dignity had been hurt, or perhaps because of his critical approach to the entire operation. Anyway, he presented a completely new line, which appeared both imaginative and promising. He assumed that there was emigration of Jews to Palestine from all of the occupied countries in Europe. Since hiding away in the Swiss consulate, he had managed to study from close-up the mechanism of the principle of "representing foreign interests"[1] and it occurred to him that as the holder of the emigration "certificates,"[2] Switzerland would — somehow — take the issue of emigration to Palestine under its auspices, and implement it. The consul heading the relevant department, Mr. S. Lutz,[3] was familiar with Palestine, having spent several years there in a consular capacity. He was fond of the region and it was possible to enthuse him about a daring plan such as this. These matters developed until the establishment of "Our Consulate" — under the sign "Swiss Consulate, Representing Foreign Interests, Emigration Department," Budapest 5, 29 Vadász Street.

All the emigration affairs therefore, were moved to the elegant glass building owned by Mr. Arthur Weiss.[4] It was not clear at first whether or not this operation was identical to Kastner's, and it was only later that the difference between the two operations became apparent, when the dissent between the two parties deepened.[5] All of a sudden, completely new faces began appearing in the new office. The landlord, Arthur Weiss, also took an active part in the work. We did not pay enough attention to these matters, and this took its toll later on, when all the "new" people — with Arthur Weiss at their head — turned out to be the source of considerable headache and trouble.

An institution of this kind was something quite novel in the middle of July 1944. Most of the Jews in Budapest had no idea as yet how it could serve them, even if it was the first ray of light for them to grab hold of. By the first few days, thousands had already registered for emigration. In fact, this was a mere sleight of hand, but the pride and self-confidence of the entire group reached enormous heights, expressed in a ridiculous game of bureaucracy and management. Only one thing appeared to be definite — that 2,000 people would be able to emigrate via Romania. This time the operation would not be under the auspices of the International Red Cross, but equipped with a genuine collective passport, issued by the Consulate. Again there were numerous consultations and arguments regarding the composition of the list of émigrés. Again the "Mizrahi" requested additional places. The ultra-Orthodox and the Neologues turned up too, and, as a new partner, none other than the Consulate itself. In the end, some sort of an agreement was reached and, in spite of everything, the list of people to be included in the passport was compiled.

The passport was a work of art. Each person with his photograph. The first page consisted of a Laissez Passer, issued by the Swiss Consulate, decorated with a picture engraved on a red background. It was so beautiful. Except for the fact that the emigration did not work out. In vain was the passport, in vain the Romanian permit, in vain the train reservations — the German permit was missing. We finally received it — how ironic — a long time after Romania had withdrawn from the "Axis."[6] This passport was the last job carried out by the consulate in which we took part as a movement. We really did not have the time to "dabble in management" and we left this work to those whose *joie-de-vivre* depended upon it. The consulate had given us the chance of holding semi-legal "office hours." It was here that we were able to receive people, to discuss their problems in quiet, unafraid of being overheard by anyone; which was not so bad, if there were others waiting in the meantime. At long last we had found a place — and perhaps this was the most important part of all — in which we could be located at all times. And this made it possible for our friends to send us from Arad the news that they had arrived. Here, anyone who wanted to could come over and keep us informed that he/she was still alive. Here, anyone who needed to could come and hand in an order for a replacement for a missing registration certificate, or their grandmother's birth certificate — if the need for these should suddenly arise. Friends who had escaped from labor camps could visit us here. Neither Krausz nor Weiss had a favorable opinion of our people. The less than formal attire of our members offended their aesthetic sensibilities. In fact, we were not the usual style of people one expects to see in a consulate.[7] But of course, our people were not about to pay too much attention to the rules of bureaucracy imposed by the older people who considered the place "their consulate," just as they had thought the Palestine Office had belonged to them.

The running of the office was supervised exclusively by Arthur Weiss. This man did a good job of managing his glass business, but had little idea about the workings of the Palestine Office. In accordance with his ideology, his instructions — down to the very tiniest detail — were anti-social. He handled matters in a blatantly reactionary way and we were obliged to conduct a daily struggle for our basic rights. We found ourselves in the sorry situation whereby we had not a single employee in the entire building. This became a bone of contention. Krausz and Weiss repeated often that this was not the Palestine Office, but the Swiss consulate. They were both upset that we had not gone down on bended knees before such a distinguished institution.

One day, the Magyar Szó published a critical article against the institute. On the one hand it attacked the Weiss family, who had succeeded in saving their property behind the consulate door-sign. On the other hand, criticism was hurled at the obscure happenings within the building's glass walls. In fact, everything was going on behind those walls, except emigration. This article was now turned into ammunition against us. We were well aware of the fact — and this new attack did not deter us from this — that the existence of the consulate did not rise or fall because a dozen illegal young men (not wearing a Yellow Star, of course) were coming and going from the building. Undoubtedly, there were good reasons for the existence of an institution of this kind.[8] We knew that we were just as important or unimportant to the authorities as were those distinguished gentlemen who had been given permission to remove their Yellow Stars.[9] Admittedly these people did not, heaven forbid, hand out forged documents to all and sundry, they merely wanted to go on living and working in their small or larger businesses. We too, were interested in the continued existence of the fiction of emigration-activity. But it did not depend on us.

Nevertheless, it was not such a simple matter. More and more frequently, detectives started appearing in front of the glass building. We were being followed, not too conspicuously, but decisively. Just to be on the safe side, I assumed the name Dr. Rafai,[10] instead of Rafi, in the building and when I was being called to the phone. Much more dangerous than the detectives however, was a bunch of Jewish informers, led by a Polish Jew called Steiner,[11] who occasionally blackmailed various people. At first he moved about the glass building; later — when he was no longer allowed entrance — he spent hours walking up and down in front of the building. Surprisingly enough, we members of Hashomer Hatza'ir were the only ones who did not fall victim to this gang, maybe they respected our strength. Anyway, a constant threat of this kind was not particularly pleasant.

In order to clarify the situation slightly, we founded — vastly belated though this was — a department for youth emigration, within the emigration department. Thus we managed at least to obtain a room for Hehalutz. This gave our work some kind of framework, which we ourselves were beginning to find necessary, especially in light of the detectives and informers I have already mentioned. We promised Krausz that we would not deal with forged papers and the distribution of money, a promise which we did not for a moment intend to keep. We had long since stopped bothering with moral obligations to our adversaries and, as far as we were concerned, Krausz had become an adversary. His behavior was decisively hostile towards the youth movements. The blow-up with Krausz came only when Freudiger[12] and thirty more religious Jews, equipped with Romanian passports, crossed the border by train. It was the only emigration organized by Krausz during twenty months of activity and it was typical of the man to have organized it for the ultra-Orthodox. In a dramatic confrontation, in the presence of Kastner and Komoly, he was made to understand the gravity of the matter. His defense was weak and dissolved in no time. The result was that he had to express his reservation at his original claim, that it was a "private matter" and to undertake that — in the shortest possible time — the remaining Romanian passports be distributed among all the streams (as was the norm in the Palestine Committee). But Krausz was wily enough to sabotage the decision and did not fulfill it until Romania withdrew from the war.[13]

Most of the movement members had left via the Slovakian or Romanian "*tiyul*," others on the transport to Bergen Belsen. The group we now had to take care of was not especially large, although many new people had joined it recently. The consulate building made our work so much easier. There was an abatement in the deportations,[14] so that the preliminary conditions were created which allowed us to begin energetic efforts to free our prisoners. In the meantime we discovered several new connections of which we could make good use of. The political climate had undergone a significant change in our favor.[15] There were many clerks and policemen who could be "spoken" to....

Mimish undertook the task of releasing our people, one after the other. One after the other they came from Mosonmagyaróvár, Kistarcsa and other places. The only place we had no access to was the court house on Fő Street.[16] It was the only place from which, in spite of everything, one of our people was deported. This prison housed Ben-Eretz Grossman, Asher Osterwile,[17] Dr. Sigfried Roth[19] and Frenkel.[19] One day a Polish woman arrived, claiming that she could get prisoners released, in return for huge sums of money. Since Frenkel had written several times that he was willing to sacrifice all his property (300,000 Pengős), in order to be taken out of there, we decided to try to rescue him. The woman introduced me to her mediators, and we were told to hand over a certain sum of money. At the same time, Ben-Eretz, Dr. Roth and Frenkel were transferred to Kistarcsa, from whence they could be rescued easily, so that all the original deal fell through. The people, of course, asked for reparations. After some lengthy negotiations, we compromised on 10,000 Pengős, since the three had gone free without our efforts. Frenkel, as I had anticipated, was not prepared to pay that sum. He even went so far as to deny ever having written any such thing about money. This pretense annoyed me enormously. This lie contained in it the meanness, the double standardness and the petty-mindedness of the Jewish petit-bourgeois, which we had learned to despise during our association with the consulate. Among Frenkel's entire circle of friends, not a single one was willing to conduct the negotiations which no doubt contained a certain element of danger. We had nothing at all in common with Frenkel, yet we did not hesitate to confront the danger. But those petit-bourgeois cared for nothing except money. I spelled out all this and a few other matters to Frenkel, and he repaid me with a slap on the face. Unfortunately, I was unable to give him one back because I was immediately restrained and prevented from doing so. But he did get a slap from Mimish, who was quick to settle the debt, as soon as he learned what had happened.

That slap was not actually connected to the problems of that institution, but still it was the apex of a lengthy and stormy "status war," which also reflected in part the generation gap. It was no coincidence that we bore the brunt of this struggle. For a long time the struggle I had been obliged to wage was a Quixotic one, because from the very beginning I had two distinct disadvantages: I did not have a pot-belly and I was not fifty-five years old.

Ben-Eretz, who had just been released from Kistarcsa[20] — arrived at the best possible time. He took over my place in the management, giving me the long awaited opportunity to develop the youth department. At this time a new and unexpected problem arose. Many of the forced labor units had been ordered to the battle front[21] and massive desertion began. This came as no surprise, since we had been telling or writing to our men to leave as soon as they felt that the situation was on the verge of igniting. Thus one day, the "glass building" was flooded with these forced labor people. We were obliged to supply them with accommodation, documents and money. We sent most of them straight to Romania. With their arrival, we resumed our reception hours and the people who came were not necessarily the kind that Arthur Weiss would have chosen. After a long time, Efra's hands were full once again, since he was the only one who knew these men, having organized the supply of information to them as well as their journey back. And again there were confrontations with Arthur Weiss. Following the Frenkel incident, Mimish and Pil were forbidden entry to the "glass building." Now the ban was extended to include Efra. We of course made a moral issue out of it and notwithstanding the fact that Pil and Mimish had more important things to do than wage a status war in the consulate, all four of us went, in protest, to the office. Naturally, we did not recognize the right of the management to take such a decision, since the legitimacy of the management was anyway doubtful as far as we were concerned. For a long time, the "glass building" had not been managed by the Palestine Committee or its presidency. The "management" was in the hands of those people who pandered to Krausz, not daring to say one word of criticism against him. At every opportunity they would defer to Krausz. One of them said once: "Mr. Krauz, we shall erect a gold headstone for you!" We were especially amused by one of these toadies who never mentioned Krausz's name without an added adjective, such as: wonderful, excellent, brilliant, etc.

Apart from two or three "slaves," the office staff were behind us all the way. Even those clerks who worked under Krausz signed the petition protesting the ban on our boys. This "unbelievable" expression of solidarity brought in its wake a storm of fury. We responded by publishing a spiteful and satirical brochure.

One day I was stopped by a policeman as I was about to enter the office. I did not understand what was happening and identified myself as a clerk at the consulate. The gatekeeper whispered to me that Mr. Weiss had instructed him not to let me into the building. Furious and agitated, I ran up the stairs, straight to my room. It was locked. Gradually it dawned on me what had been going on. I returned to Arthur Weiss and demanded the keys to my room. He refused to give them to me and enraged, I picked up a chair and smashed in the glass door. Efra arrived later on and exactly the same scene was repeated with him. He burst into the conference room, where a big consultation was taking place. Efra did not choose the gentlest of words to express his disdain and hatred of the surprised company. The scene was not a pleasant one for Krausz, who asked us to calm down and discuss the matter quietly. A thorough discussion ensued, and Krausz had no choice but to express reservation at the behavior of his management head.

Suddenly the door opened and somebody burst in with the news that Horthy had called for an armistice.[22]

It was October 15, 1944.

Chapter Ten

October 15

The quarrel was forgotten in a moment. I took Tamarka's arm and we walked out into the street. I expected to find the streets echoing with the regent's call. Probably at that very moment Budapest was more than ever true to itself. The street was silent. It was as if the passersby knew nothing of Horty's declaration. People were hurrying by, no-one stopped to talk to anyone else. At the "Bucsinszky" Cafe where we luncheoned we noticed no special joy or sorrow. The customers were excited and whispered among themselves. Suddenly shots rang out from the direction of the "Royal" Hotel.[1] A round of machine gun fire swept the street clean of people. Then a couple of German tanks rode deafening down the deserted street.[2]

At two o'clock we met our friends in front of the International Red Cross building on Mérleg Street.[3] We were unable to compose a clear picture because the radio kept repeating the same message. We split up in order to try to glean some information and arranged to meet again in the evening. On Kaiser Wilhelm (Vilmos Császár) Boulevard we came across a few Jews standing in front of one of the buildings, removing the Yellow Stars from their clothing. We smiled at each other.

We went to visit Kastner, who was lying sick in bed, and extremely agitated. The transport was still stuck in Bergen Belsen and negotiations were in their final stage. Within the next few days he was supposed to go to Switzerland with Becher, to finalize the matter. Now it seemed a lost cause. Unfortunately, even the telephone was out of order. Rezső[4] kept hoping he would be able to find Becher somewhere the next day, and make the journey with him. It was a ludicrous situation. At that moment, Rezső was the only person unable to rejoice at the fact that the Red Army was supposed to be entering Budapest within the next few days (which was, after all, the way we imagined things…).[5] I took my leave of him, it was a friendly enough parting, with a hint of past memories and a kind of look to the future. Suddenly the radio started broadcasting in German and we cocked our ears.[6] We went out with Tamarka but did not return to the house on Buda. We wanted to spend the night in town. It was twilight, the streets were deserted and quiet, and an indefinable unrest could be felt in the air. When we arrived at mother's, we heard at the shelter: "Colonel-General Beregfy will be arriving momentarily in Budapest!"[7] This was followed by a continuous broadcast of German and Hungarian military marches. The Chief of Staff's denial was broadcast over the air just as we were reading Horty's announcement in the evening paper. Afterwards, different calls were heard. We couldn't believe that the entire witch dance was about to begin all over again! That night I slept very little and very badly. In the morning we awoke to the thunder of cannon being fired at the palace.[8] This commotion ended once and for all any hope we may have had that the army was still loyal to Horthy.

There are people who live out historical events in such a city knowing less about them than the news agencies in London and Washington. That was why the first thing I did that morning was make my way to the shelter. This time London was silent. The main item on all the news broadcasts concerned the fall of Petsamo.[9] Horthy's statement was broadcast only in the BBC's evening bulletins. The morning papers printed Szálasi's[10] announcement and the rest of the calls which had been broadcast the previous evening.

The new government seemed to be concerned only with the Jewish issue. Once again Jews were required to wear a Yellow Star and mark their houses with one. All Jewish buildings were closed unilaterally and all exemptions from wearing the Yellow Star were revoked, with no exceptions.[11] Again, Jews were thrown out of many houses. No-one knew where, no-one knew why. It was an ugly and sadistic "game." A terrible torture. The streets cried out: "Yes, they removed their Yellow Stars, they thought it was all over, now let them feel the force of our fury!"

There were long lines of sorrowful, weeping people. For hours on end these poor souls were obliged to bear the curses and spitting of the mob, their arms raised in the air and their eyes filled with terror. Handicapped women in wheelchairs, men on crutches, even stretchers could be seen among these sad processions. These grotesque demonstrations were presented by the government to the people, as a gesture, entertaining, amusing and hilarious. The streets were filled with members of the Arrow Cross. All of a sudden the city expelled into its streets the kind of specimens of humanity seen only in drawings by Doumier.[12] Hundreds of Jews were shot — targets in a shooting range — during those first days in the streets and city squares.

The first people to offer a suitable response were members of the Dror movement. Several of them donned Arrow Cross uniforms and went from house to house rescuing their people. We set out the same day on a similar mission. Efra and Pil put on the uniforms of railway officials,[13] enabling Efra to cross from Buda to Pest, via one of the bridges.[14] Efra, who had come with Yoshko Megyeri[15] to rescue one of our members, was recognized in front of one of the "Jewish" houses by an Arrow Cross member, as a Jewish boy from his hometown. It was a very dangerous situation, because the two were surrounded in no time by an angry mob. Suddenly, out of nowhere, two armed Arrow Cross men appeared and the two captured Jews were handed over into their loyal custody. A few yards away from the incident, the four embraced each other and related what had happened. The two "fascists" were none other than Zalel[16] and Willy,[17] courageous members of the Dror movement.

During the morning hours of October 16, our consulate building was deserted. We were still not sure what would happen to it. Our office too, which had operated under the sign of the International Red Cross, was locked. As soon as all the clerks and volunteers had been successfully taken out of the "Jewish" houses, they congregated in the offices of the two institutions. Furthermore, they did their best to take advantage of the International Red Cross and the Swiss consulate call-up system, to release more of our people. This ruse too, worked nicely! During the first day, a huge crowd had accumulated in the two offices. Those members who could move freely around the city and had secure documentation, were entrusted with the task of supplying these additional people with food.

In actual fact, October 15 did not really affect us. We were an underground movement. We had not been tempted by the various legalization options conducted by the Interior and Foreign Offices. Within a few hours, our well-oiled operation was once again working perfectly. Again, the highly-experienced adults were helpless. They all, even Arthur Weiss, were clamoring for fictitious documents. They had somehow forgotten that it was under their instructions that we had been forbidden to hold false documents in the offices.... Arthur Weiss even asked us for a gun.[18]

Again, we lost no-one. We brought several of the movement's adult members to the consulate. But as far as we were concerned, nothing had changed. Perhaps one thing: the false documents production had now achieved the kind of proportions that Moshe had once prophesied. We had come up in the world. Since the days of the artist's atelier on Bethlen Gábor Street, we had now risen to several workshops. That particular workshop had been discovered for reasons which were unclear; David and Shraga had managed to get rid of the stock at the last moment. Those two were experts at saving our stocks in "hopeless situations." On another occasion we hid two suitcases full of certificates in Kastner's apartment, but the following day he was arrested by the Hungarian counter espionage. Again, David and Pil managed to get out the two suitcases, which were dearer to us than anything else. The prestige of our workshops grew in stature; there was not an official form in Hungary that we did not have several copies of. We had several rubber stamps ready. Thanks to our Shapiograph, we were able to produce any kind of rubber stamp for any purpose. We received Swiss documents from our friends in Switzerland and from our friends in Slovakia, we received Slovak documents. We had blank Slovak passports, Swiss protection passes, various Wehrmacht and SS forms and all the forms issued by the Arrow Cross. In fact, we did not really need such a large selection of papers, which was obtained largely because of the fellows' acquisitive instinct. We even discussed the possibility of setting up an underground museum — after liberation. Up to October 15, the workshop had been called the Company for the Processing and Export of Soy Beans. The owner of the plant, and thus our cover man, was an Italian immigrant.[19] Following Dan's departure, David had been working tirelessly in the workshop. We were forever amazed at this young man's presence of mind — and he was only eighteen years old! Miky Langer[20] had joined in the work only a short while before. Miky was not a movement member. He was a Slovak refugee from Dan's home town. During his stay in Budapest, he had worked as a draughtsman for various engineering companies. His plans for a shelter had won first prize in one of the design competitions. He was brilliant at his job. Many of the most complicated problems involved in the counterfeiting process were solved by Miky's very special genius. And this is one small example:

We were in need of a "Royal Hungarian Ministry of the Interior" rubber stamp. Miky ordered a stamp from one of the relevant manufacturing companies, under the phrasing: "Patent registered under licence no. 5730/1943 on behalf of the Royal Hungarian Ministry of the Interior." He himself chose the lettering and there was nothing suspicious in the stamp he ordered. After cutting away the surplus lettering, the remaining rubber stamp was worded exactly to his specifications. He also designed a most original tool for producing the complex stamp of the Registration of Police Residential Report stations. He always dreamed that after the liberation he would be sent to Germany as a paratrooper, in order to continue with his work. Miky swam like a fish in the sea of false identities.

October 15 was the hardest day of all, but in certain respects, it was easier for us than March 19. Anyone with a little courage, could have taken advantage of the general chaos to rid themselves of the dreaded yellow star, easier than before.[21] Unfortunately, there were many who lacked the courage to take such a decisive step. These miserable souls were later victims of the worst suffering of all. It was terrible to see a procession of three hundred people walking to their deaths, under a guard of only two men, and no-one daring to dart out from between the rows. Was it really worth making so much effort for such cowards? We were forever asking ourselves this question. It invariably arose in the arguments we had in Vadász Street, it turned up in those fruitless hours-long debates and it struck us every time we received one of those letters from our friends abroad,[22] who did not understand our motives. Any expression of condolence had a somewhat false ring to it, it sounded like bitter irony, even though it was uttered with utmost sincerity. We asked for passports, documents from countries outside of Hungary. But it was only in November that we received the birth certificates from Switzerland.[23] Our friends "on the other side" understood nothing of the "new European culture." We were unable to conceive how it never occurred to anyone to come to visit us, with a Turkish or Spanish passport in his hands.[24] We often found it very difficult to continue operating with the same devotion, but once anyone joined that operation, it was impossible to leave it. We loathed the middle class mentality of our people, but this was the reason we did our utmost to save it. We always knew that the day would come and we would take away the young people and lead them into the future. Thus we gradually developed political programs which even outreached our own movement's formal edcucational framework. The Red Army daily brought closer the realization of these plans.

A Trick Known as a "Letter of Protection"

Following a few days of wild and erratic attacks on the Jewish population, an order was issued calling for the conscription of all Jewish males aged between sixteen and sixty.[1] In fact this was the beginning of a new wave of expulsions,[2] except that this time, men were separated from their wives while still in Budapest. What surprised us were the exceptions, which we had not taken into consideration. In addition to citizens of foreign states, people with letters of protection from consulates of non-aligned countries[3] were also omitted from the quota. For a long time the Swiss consulate and the International Red Cross had been issuing such letters. We had been urging our own consulate to issue something similar, although we had still not estimated the importance of the letter. But we were aware of the crucial role played by any piece of paper with an official heading or stamp of any consulate, in the process of getting prisoners released. Through the use of a simple letter from the Swedish consulate, we could obtain the release of anyone we wanted, while our own "Swiss consulate" did nothing on the matter. Nor was Krausz, as usual, in any hurry to prepare these forms. Now that all the men had been drafted and we were finally able to offer something concrete — after so many "bluffs" — the organization failed, because it did not have the necessary form which could have saved the day. And then after a two-day delay, the "letter of protection"[4] appeared at long last from Vadász Street, under the following wording:

"The Foreign Affairs Department of the Consulate of Switzerland, hereby confirms that...had been registered for emigration in the Swiss collective passport. Therefore anyone bearing this letter must be considered the holder of a valid passport."[5]

Now the real work began. That Letter of Protection — it did work! It was honored. Even the forced labor units honored it. Day after day, thousands of poor souls turned up at the "glass building." All of a sudden the consulate was having to face an unanticipated strategic problem. There was also the moral question: the authorities had promised the Swiss a quota of 7,800[6] "Letters of Protection,"[7] a number which, in view of such a calamity, was no more than a mere drop in the ocean. We, the youth movements, demanded the issue of "Letters of Protection" in unlimited numbers. The Soviet army was stationed near Szolnok and we were in a race against time. This position was not accepted and was sabotaged as far as possible. Nonetheless, we began producing forged "Letters of Protection." The consulate had long since used up all the quota, but when it ordered an additional 10,000 forms, we were quick to order the same number. Under a sign bearing the name of the International Red Cross, we opened an office from which we issued the Swiss consulate's "Letters of Protection." Of course, we also had our own rubber stamps. The audacity of marketing "Figaro" chocolate in "Zserbó" wrapping never occurred to us at the time.[8] The whole matter achieved greater piquancy still, because the office on 2 Percel Mór Street[9] was located opposite the real Swiss consulate. The entire ruse was conducted under the nose of the real Swiss consul. Altogether, the whole "Letter of Protection" affair was so chaotic as to be impossible to describe in words. Although Jews were officially permitted to be in the streets only between the hours of two and four o' clock, there was a packed crowd in front of the consulate from dawn to dusk. Counts, generals, advisors-to-ministers, even ministers, intervened, recommended and arrived in person.[10] A ten or twenty strong police unit was stationed regularly in front of the building. But even the mounted police were unable to stand up to the desperate crowd, whose lives were rolled up inside that small piece of paper and the salvation it offered. Pressure inside was as great as that outside. Every day, the number of tenants in the consulate building grew. At first they were only clerks and their relatives. Later on, the building housed Zionists who were running for their lives. But the group grew constantly. More and more people were seeking asylum in this ex-territorial haven. The clerks almost suffocated under the pressure of the crowds.

In addition to filling in blank "Letters of Protection," there was now the problem of ensuring accommodation, food, lavatories, etc. for all the new comers. Ben-Eretz worked tirelessly. During those dark days, he was the one who served as the building's supervisor. Needless to say, he also lived in the building, or more accurately, he worked in the building, because during those weeks, he never got more than a couple of hours' sleep a night.

The committee of the International Red Cross filled a vital role during that period. Even before October 15, we had started planning the establishment of several young-people's homes, which in time, would serve as the basis for the emigration of these young people to Palestine (*Eretz Yisrael*). Now it was our job to establish a large number of improvised young-people's homes, in order to at least save the children from deportation. Within a short time, more than 6,000 children were placed in these homes, which required a vast operating system. Together with Zoltán Weiner, Efra undertook the financial management of this operation.[11] Dr. Kotarba[12] (Dr. Osterweil) was head of medical services. They established a new office at 6 Mérleg Street. The International Red Cross had by now become an important institution and its beginnings were promising. When the management team was removed to 52 Baross Street,[13] I too, moved into the International Red Cross and established the "Political Department." The department was entrusted with forming ties with the underground liberation movements, collecting any information with a political bent which could be passed on to the relevant Jewish organizations. To the outside world, it was all made to seem like a Geneva-based International Red Cross Committee Research Department, publishing lists of missing relatives in Hungary.

In mid November[14] all holders of Letters were ordered to move into the "protected houses" in and around Pozsonyi Streeet.[15] The order was not particularly convenient, because the grand ruse of our issuing all the "Letters of Protection" was now on the verge of being uncovered. And indeed, the chaos was indescribable, because the number of people actually holding the "Letters" was much greater than the number of Letters officially issued. Before people started moving to the "protected houses," we were witnesses to some heart-rending spectacles. This new problem resulted in a renewed surge of people wanting to get into our consulate building, which, housing over 2,000 people, was already at bursting point. We were in desperate need of another apartment building. Several clerks subsequently moved into 17 Wekerle Sándor Street.[16] We fought, of course, and demanded to move some of our own youngsters. The clerks took their own families with them, and the new office soon became home to some 120 people. While Vadász Street remained the place where the "fellers of trees and drawers of water" carried out their work, the "diplomatic" activity went on at the new location, especially liaison with the authorities and the compiling of lists. Ben-Eretz, who had also moved to 17 Wekerle Street, established a supply storeroom. It was from here that food was subsequently supplied to the protected houses. After liberation, this storeroom was the only source of ongoing food supply for a few more weeks. The existence of the storeroom gave us an excuse to introduce a few more people into the building. This was imperative, because the situation in Vadász Street was becoming increasingly dangerous. On the other hand, the situation of the Aryans was also hopeless; every day new recruitment orders were issued and the numbers of exceptions were getting gradually fewer.

For the first time, all the young people vanished from the streets of Budapest; moreover, so did almost all the men. Budapest, which had always been so cosmopolitan in nature, whose streets were always full of thousands of passersby, this Budapest was suddenly silent; the capital was fear-stricken. One day, I took a tram at three o'clock in the afternoon. The carriage was almost empty, and I suddenly noticed that I was the only young man traveling on the tram. Everywhere I turned there were document checks. More and more of our friends had decided to move into Vadász Street. The element of fatigue no doubt had its effect, too; people were exhausted with the constant game of hide and seek. Now that they had the chance to take shelter in some ex-territorial location, many of them had chosen this option, which constituted the easier way out. We were not over-enthused with this solution and did not always recommend it to our friends. Indeed, Vadász Street had proven itself so far, but there were many doubts as to whether the building would hold out to the end. It was like a thorn in the flesh of the Arrow Cross; they were well aware of the fact that Vadász Street was no more than a giant bunker.

Nonetheless, there were great advantages to having our people concentrated in Vadász Street. For the first time in months all our friends were together and able to discuss their problems freely. We made full use of this situation by establishing, as far as possible, a Hashomer Hatza'ir commune. We organized seminars, discussions and even entertainment evenings.

It was during this time that the Betar Revisionist movement began a process of disintegration. Betar had an honest and talented leader in Andy Freiman, with whom we were happy to cooperate in the rescue operation. Andy and other Betar members started having doubts with regard to their movement's ideology. The events of the previous two months had not left them unaffected. The extreme right wing nationalism of the Germans, which had led to fascism and the submissiveness of the petit-bourgeois Jews, on the other hand, were now obviously at their worst, and this brought about changes in the young people's way of thinking. They were obliged to come to some conclusions. With considerable courage, they detached themselves not only from Revisionism, but also completely divorced themselves from their pasts and traditions! The young people who had organized themselves in the Herzl Group met in Vadász Street, with an offer of constructive co-operation. At that time, Andy was lying sick in one of the hospitals. He died of diphtheria at the beginning of December.[17] He was a good friend, one of the few from among the reactionaries who were wise enough to reach conclusions from what he saw.

Chapter Twelve
Our Ties With the Underground Labor Movement

After August 23, 1944[1] we were surrounded once again by the strange quiet we had experienced once before, on the departure of the transport. But this time the quiet seemed ominous and threatening. In fact, we were in a blocked alleyway, with no way out. Whether we liked it or not, we were obliged to remain in Budapest, this time it seemed, for a long time. Our first step was to increase our concern for the prisoners, in other words, to double our efforts at getting them released. This in fact, constituted most of our work, since our day-to-day concern for the others was something that was taken for granted. Everyone was immediately equipped with all the documentation necessary for survival. We had a budget, which we increased from time to time. Life went on, in its familiar, monotonous gray way.

The first period had been that of Aryanization. The second consisted of our efforts in the *"tiyul"* operation. Was the third period going to be one of passive expectation? This lack of activity filled us with a deep unease. It was clear that Budapest would not be able to accelerate the process of liberalization through inactivity. Therefore, we did the one thing that seemed possible: we searched for contact with the underground resistance movement and especially the illegal Hungarian Labor movement within it. It was not easy to find ways to the Hungarian Labor movement. We were not, after all, local people and apart from Ben-Eretz and Efra, we were not even Hungarians. To this day I am amazed that during our preliminary attempts, we did not fall victim to provocation. At first, we managed to make contact with one of the cells in Csepel,[2] which probably had no connection with any central factor. The young people in this cell seemed somewhat confused. Our connections with them were restricted to our supplying them with documents, and later "Letters of Protection" and money. They promised us weapons, which they never supplied.

Many of our friends had become familiar with members of the underground movement in various prisons and concentration camps.[3] We maintained ties with some of them even after the liberation. There were also some members who left the movement in order to join the Communist Party. Later on we kept in touch with most of these. On the one hand there was a bond of friendship between us; they relied on us to keep them supplied with documents. One of these young men introduced us to someone from the 'line.' It was a simple laborer, who demanded that we participate in the distribution of flyers, supply of weapons and production of documents. Although Haim[4] had given him certain information about us, he was unable to relate to our specific problems. Anyway, we rejected the first two demands. We explained to him that our people are probably not suited to the task of distributing flyers, since they are compelled to lead a double underground life, both as Jews and as Socialists. Not only would they be jeopardizing their own lives, they would be endangering the movement as well. We rejected the demand for weapons simply because we had no way of knowing whether our counterpart was the right man to receive any weapons we had to give. Anyway, our own means were limited and we were unwilling to hand out weapons to all sorts of cells. We were however, most willing to supply him with documents, and surprised to see that a "representative" of the Labor movement was unable to give us the addresses of some workers, who could house some of our own Aryan members.

A certain Kovács was the third member of the Labor movement we met with. We described our activity and political outlook and wanted to hear some things from him, too. But he was reticent at first. It appeared that he preferred, on that occasion, to hear us out first and he himself said as little as possible. He circumvented all our practical questions. His own demands of us were pinpointed thus:

1. To supply material from various foreign sources and edit it for the underground press;

2. Translations into Slovakian and where necessary into Serb, for their Slovak and Serb members;
3. Documents.

He, for his part, offered us the following assistance:
1. Ongoing information on the legal, political and underground life in Hungary;
2. Accommodation for our members;
3. Larger bunkers, for emergencies.

The man was much more open and communicative at our second meeting. He told us outright that he had been collecting information about us, which was positive. He was not representing the entire working class. There were two communist factions in Hungary: one was known as KMP and the other, KP,[5] the one he was representing. For a long time we maintained close ties with Kovács. We supplied him with documents and met occasionally for discussions and clarification, on the Jewish question. These talks encouraged us to begin considering the possibility of taking an active part in the formation of Jewish policy in the Diaspora, after liberation. We knew little at the time about life in the liberated territories and about Soviet policy. We believed that, after liberation, the working classes would take over the Government of Hungary and we were prepared to undertake the political education of the Jews and of turning them into a productive part of society. Obviously, we had no desire to relinquish our dreams of emigrating to Israel, but were convinced that it was still possible to work hand in hand with the Jewish communists. After all, we would be together only until the time came for us to emigrate, and this for practical rather than ideological purposes. It was in our mutual interest to transform the masses of Jewish petit-bourgeois to productivity and to change their social status in order to prevent these poverty stricken people from drifting into the clutches of the black market profiteers.

We prepared a plan for Jewish-socialist cooperation which we presented for discussion and review to the Labor movement, both via Kovács and via the 'line.' We had come to a decision that it was up to us to participate in the formation of future Jewish policy in the Diaspora and not to restrict our activity to the work of the educational movement. While still underground, we had to solidify the principles of this political activity. We tried to concentrate all the progressive forces in the forced labor camps, for political propaganda and study and, in a limited way, to supply them with weapons as well. We established contact with several communist cells in the camps, introducing them to our people and in many places, ties were formed between them and the local labor movement cells.

Later on, Kovács came to our aid when hundreds of forced-laborers were coming to us asking for documentation, money, accommodation and clothing. He supplied us with the addresses of workers, who accommodated many of our young men. Without this assistance, we would barely have managed to cope.

Our "document producers" uncovered some interesting connections. Yoshka B.[6] was also a member of the 'line' and was soon liaising between them and us. Every day, he received many and diverse documents from our workshop — forged of course — and he also helped us greatly. With his help, we arrived after a long time at a certain printing shop, which supplied us with birth certificates and ID cards. It was just in time, since our supplies were seriously dwindling. We spent many hours with Yoshka B., discussing the political situation and the future.

Iván[7] was one of the active organizers of the partisan movement. As an army captain, he had his own cells. Later on, he housed our forgery workshop in one of his units. The brief period spent there by our boys was one of our most fruitful ones.[8] We had been obliged to disband this workshop when the great officers' conspiracy was uncovered and the senior officers were arrested.[9] Ivan too, was involved in the affair and forced to go underground.

Gradually we got to know more and more members of the underground. We also learned about the Hungarian workers' movement. We had the opportunity to examine the reliability of the information we were receiving and were somewhat disappointed by the situation. It was not possible to sense the existence of a united leadership; nowhere was a common line apparent. We were able to evaluate the meaning of a situation in which we were capable of offering more than we could expect to receive. We did not delude ourselves that this proved the power of our movement; it would only be right to indicate the weakness of the Hungarian Labor movement.

On all sides, we were inundated with rather negative information about Kovács. His real name was Demény.[10] Many accused him of being an informer. Some real allegations were also lodged. Mimish warned us at every opportunity, against cooperating with the man. Mimish received most of his information from one of our members who had worked at the Ganz[11] factory. This man had once worked alongside Demény. Yoshka B. also accused him, and we decided to invite Demény and ask him to clarify a few issues.

We had no fear for ourselves, in talking to an informer — he had always been very fair with us. Moreover, we believed he was quite intelligent; someone like him would not start informing the Germans five minutes before midnight. As far as we were concerned, the clarification was more a matter of socialist conscience, because we did not want to cooperate with a working class traitor, even if it was in his power to offer us anything. Indeed, our main reason for cooperating with the Labor movement had nothing to do with any kind of assistance we could or could not expect during the war, but rather the desire for a relationship with them during peacetime when it came.

We called on Demény for an open confrontation.[12] We have no written recording of that meeting and I am obliged to recall from memory what Demény said to us; I believe that I have remembered everything that was said, because it was a special occasion, on which we made a verbal attack on the Hungarian Labor movement, completely disillusioned, since any illusions had long since been erased.

"You must not blame the Hungarian Labor movement absolutely," said Demény. "The way I see it, it is one of the best," he went on, "anyway, it is better than the Czech or German Labor movements. I would put it on a par with the Bulgarian movement. Don't forget that the Hungarian Labor movement has never been legal.[13] For twenty five years [the party] was underground, during which time it struggled and founded, under the harshest conditions, an outlawed organization, an underground press and a team of responsible political activists. The movement is not uniform, because it never had the chance to conduct open discussion, nor the opportunity to convene congresses.[14] There has never been democratic, wide scale discourse...."

"It is absurd to accuse me of being an informer. The reactionaries murdered my brother. I myself have spent the best years of my life in prison. There is no truth in the accusations that I always managed to save my own skin. I can give you plenty of examples where I was sentenced, when many others got off free. You must be asking yourselves why I never tried to dispute the accusations against me. Well, you are not naive, and are quite capable of understanding how such rumors can be used politically against the reactionaries. On one occasion I asked Schweinitzer[15] with a wink, why he chose to arrest me of all people, after all, everyone knows that I am an informer...that "distinction" gave me a certain freedom of movement, which was only useful to the Labor Party. By the way, there is nothing concrete to accuse me of. You'll laugh if I tell you that the fable of Demény the informer is spread around loud and clear and very often by my very own people. The time has not yet come for clarification. We are cooperating closely with all resistance factors. After the victory, I shall be only too pleased to face a party tribunal. I myself am not at all important. Throughout the years of my illegal activity, I have often risked my life; I had no reservation on this score. In time, all communists learn to play down their own self importance. Now, we have joined up with the 'line.'[16] We did it for the benefit of the revolutionary Labor movement. The 'line' is well aware of the value and power of our organization. Their accusations are only against me personally. I would be more than willing to cease my activity at any time, if this would be in the interest of the Labor movement. Maybe I'll write books; by the way, it is this program that has been occupying my mind for quite some time. As I said, my prestige is a completely marginal issue. Just as you have hurt me lately with your lack of faith in me, so your honesty today has been good for me."

Even after this confrontation, we were unable to reach a final decision on the matter of Demény, since we knew little of the many and diverse problems facing the Hungarian Labor movement. We reduced our personal contacts with him, but continued to meet other members of his group. The KP and the KMP eventually united. We read about the merger in the journal of the united Communist Party — Szabad Nép,[17] — in an underground publication.

At the same time, our friendship deepened with other members of the 'line.' These were rather firm on the Jewish issue. It became absolutely obvious that liberation would bring about a democratic Hungary, not a dictatorship of the proletariat.[18] For this reason, the line of the united front was stressed, but the members were not updated on many matters. Everyone praised us for being a

Marxist movement within Judaism, but they neither wanted, nor were they able to promise us recognition as future political partners.[19]

As we look back today, we must be honest and admit that our expectations were too high and we were disappointed. From our closest confederates in the underground we had hoped for a deeper understanding of our plight....

In the labyrinth of underground movements, we encountered many members who were affiliated to various streams and nationalities. For quite a long time, we had connections with a certain civilian protest movement.[20] What we expected mainly, were addresses of bunkers, but we were soon to learn that this bunch were dabbling more in government and politics than in the kind of activity they could and were actually capable of performing. We left those good bourgeois souls to their little games.

A small group of British and Dutch officers[21] who had escaped from German POW camps, were most sympathetic. It was interesting how much those fellows could do and how much they were capable of giving us, despite the fact that they did not speak a word of Hungarian, which severely restricted their freedom of movement. These fellows, so self-involved as they were and despite their unemotional way of thinking, were excellent people with whom we could easily find a common language. When Joel[22] the paratrooper chanced upon them during his escape from the deportation train, they asked to be introduced to us. I shall never forget the surprise on the face of the brave Captain Tim[23] when he brought Joel to us and discovered that we were actually old friends.

Garany, Detention Camp.1943, Members of Hashomer Hatzair movement
Upper row: Simha Hunwald, Aryeh Funk, Nesher Adler.
Bottom row: Levy Weiss, Moshe Eisenberg, David Lavi (Liszer),
Avraham Fueredi, Uri Hermann.

Hashomer Hatzair Winter Camp in Kospallag, December 1943.

Jitzhak Herbst (Mimish).

Rafi Benshalom (Friedl)

Miklos (Miki) Langer

Moshe Alpan (Pil)

Efra Agmon (Teichman)

Dan Zimmerman

David Gur (Grosz)

Nonika and Peretz Revesz

Simha Hunwald

Tzipi Agmon (Schechter)

Tamar and Rafi Benshalom (Friedl)

Zwi Goldfarb

Neshka Goldfarb (Sender)

Alexander Grossmann (Sanyi)

Jews waiting in line in front of the Swiss Consulate, 29 Vadasz Street, to receive the "Schutzpass" (Protection Certificate).

Humiliation of Jews by the "Arrow Cross".

Jews being transferred to the Budapest Ghetto.

Deportation of Jewish Women from Budapest on the main road to Austria.

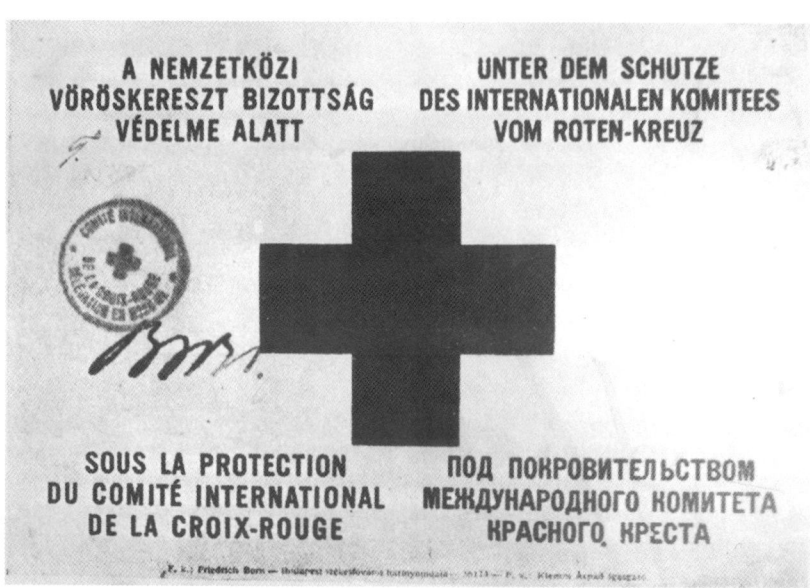

Embleme of the International Red Cross On a Childrens Home.

Charles Lutz, Swiss Consul, at the Embassy.

Temporary Swedish Passport (Schutzpass).

Josef Meir (Megyeri Joska) in "Arrow Cross" uniform.

Ing. Natan (Otto) Komoly, President of Zionist Movement in Hungary and Chairman of the "Rescue Committee".

Friedrich Born, Representative of the International Red Cross in Budapest.

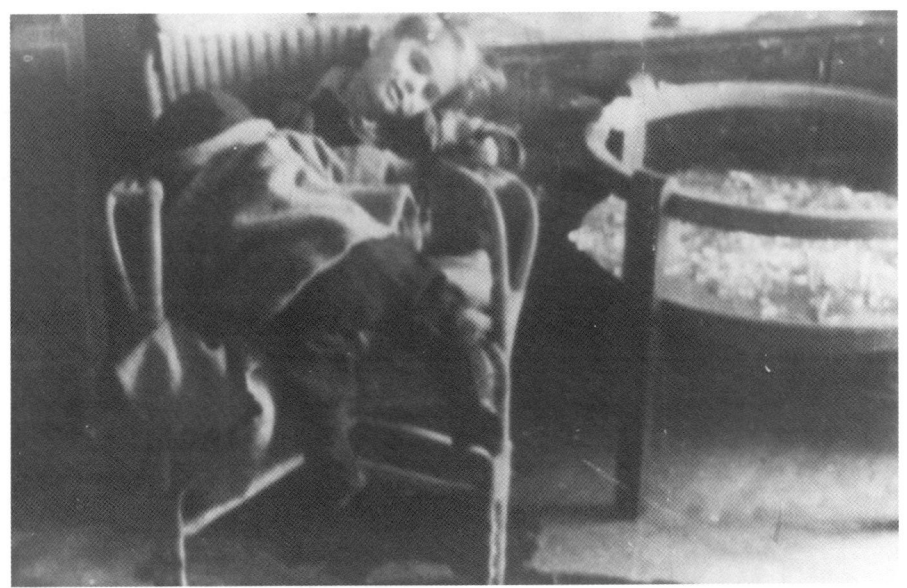

Jewish child in Budapest 1944

The "Workshop" for Forgery of Document
at the Bethlen Gabor str. Budapest Sketch of Shraga Weil.

Forged "papers" (documents) produced by the "Workshop" of the Underground Movement.

Chapter Thirteen

The Parachutists

In the middle of April, I received a phone call from Erzsi Kurtz, Kastner's secretary, who asked me to come over immediately because she had an important message for me from Palestine. When I arrived at her apartment I met Zvi Goldfarb and two fellows I was unfamiliar with, all deep in conversation. The two introduced themselves as emissaries from Palestine.

My first thought was: be careful — because at that time we were used to provocation and were prepared for them. I decided therefore, to ask them a few questions first. It appeared that they were indeed emissaries who had come equipped not only with Kastner's address, but with mine and Zvi Goldfarb's. We were naturally very pleased and immediately started asking a myriad of questions, because it had been a long time since we had had a chance to talk to people from Palestine. But they were surprisingly closed-lipped — something which would turn out to be to their disadvantage later on — and first demanded a detailed report on the situation. We told them all about the way things were going in Hungary, about our own activity, the process of Aryanization, the *"tiyul"* operation, the bunkers, everything — and we had a lot to tell. The two, Joel Palgi (Nussbecher) and Peretz Goldstein, were emissaries on behalf of the Histadrut (the General Labor Federation, who had parachuted into Yugoslavia and their job was to organize the defense and rescue operation). They were fully aware of the fact that they were very much overdue; but their delay, as they explained to us, was due to various technical dificulties.

First off, it was necessary to make some kind of arrangements for them, and indeed, we compiled some ducuments and handed them over that same day. They had already spent two days in Budapest, staying at a small hotel, but they felt they were being followed, so that Joel was keen to move out as soon as possible.

They arrived at a very inconvenient period; it was during the days when Jews were being tranferred into "Jewish houses," which were marked by Yellow Stars. There was great commotion and agitation, and we were having to find accommodation for many new members, who until now had been living as Aryan sub-tenants in Jewish homes or in houses which had now been turned into "Jewish houses." A serious housing shortage had ensued and arrangements for the two emissaries involved considerable problems. Peretz spent that night at Yehuda Weiss's home, although Yehuda did not let him get much sleep and he was obliged to stay awake talking.

As I said, Peretz and Joel had come via Yugoslavia. They brought with them a large-scale "*tiyul*" plan to Yugoslavia, with the aim of transferring Jewish youths to the partisans. The problem was making arrangements for the old people and their families, because the partisans were not over eager to take on people in need of protection, without their being able to contribute their part to the war effort. But the emissaries were convinced that this problem could be solved by forming brigades of Jewish partisans who would undertake this task. We told them about our own experiences in this field, about Avri Lissauer and of our efforts in this direction, which had all turned out to be useless and expressed our doubts as to the possibility of efficiently organizing such an operation and its chances of success. Nevertheless, we wanted to get down to business and we thought they would be able to help us a lot.

It was a big mistake on their part that they did not supply us with all the details, because had they done so, things might have turned out quite differently. As I have already pointed out, they had Kastner's address and they contacted him immediately. It later became clear to us that Kastner had known for a long time of their expected arrival and the plan at first had been that they would parachute into Hungary itself, in the Lake Balaton region, where a villa had been rented to supply them with a starting point. That villa was Jewish property, so that the program was canceled because of the early and unexpected crossover and because of the delay in the two men's arrival. They came via Yugoslavia and this fact was the cause not only of a further delay, but of the failure of the entire program.

Their fear that they were being followed was verified. The man who had brought them from Yugoslavia to Hungary was an agent for the Hungarian counter espionage, and they had indeed been followed from the very first moment. Kastner, too, had been under surveillance from the moment of their arrival. The Hungarian counter espionage were convinced that they had uncovered the center of a large espionage operation, after having seen that the route of the English parachutists had led them straight to Kastner.

Minor events and instances proved to the two parachutists that their assumption had been correct. On the tram on their way to meeting Zvi Goldfarb and myself, they noticed two men whose behavior was suspicious. They decided immediately to jump off the moving tram and hop onto another tram going in the opposite direction, and they arrived at their destination via a circumvent route. Thus they managed to shake off their "tail." They asked Kastner how they should behave and actually followed his advice.

But in order to understand the course of events, we must go back and repeat a few details:

At that time, Kastner was working on the 'German line.' He had placed all his hopes on this card and based all his plans on it. The head of the economics department at the SS, Obersturmbahnführer Becher, with whom Kastner maintained constant contact, had suggested bringing a JDC[1] emissary from Palestine to Hungary — since Joel Brandt had not returned — in order to seal the business with him. Menahem Bader was selected for the task of emissary, but for various reasons, this did not materialize. And now, wanting to keep the Hungarian authorities away from the game, Kastner thought it was right to simply inform the Germans that the emissaries they had mentioned before, had arrived in Budapest. In this way, he hoped to ensure their immunity against the Hungarian authorities.

It was a daring idea and also extremely dangerous. If we had been asked at the time, we would have advised them firmly to join our 'little line' and to maintain only indirect contact with Kastner. But since we knew nothing of this bundle of problems, we were not in a position to help them with this kind of advice.

The two did indeed accompany Kastner to the Gestapo and SS special HQ, in order to introduce themselves. They were sure that by doing this, the matter was closed, and they moved into Hansi Brandt's apartment, which they believed, as did many others, to be ex-territorial. The following day Joel Palgi was arrested in that apartment by the Hungarian authorities. Peretz moved immediately to the protected camp on Columbus Street, and joined his parents, who had come to Budapest from Cluj. Since the Hungarian authorities continued to follow Kastner, it was quite logical that they would then look for Peretz at the same place; but the SS guards prevented the Hungarian detectives from entering the camp.

Kastner and Hansi Brandt were called to the Hungarian counter espionage and interrogated. It appeared that they knew a lot more about the two parachutists than Kastner had estimated. They also threatened Kastner with arrest for espionage. Naturally, Kastner's German partners were not prepared to intervene with the Hungarians on behalf of the parachutists, because they were interested in hiding their long-term plans regarding the Jews from the Hungarians and thus they were unable, or did not want, to promise Kastner their protection.

And this was how the tragic situation was formed, whereby this incident could jeopardize the big transport, whose exit date was due at exactly that time. Apart from that, Kastner was informed by the counter espionage that Joel would be executed immediately, if Peretz did not hand himself in. Kastner asked for permission to leave just for a few hours, and went straight to Columbus Street to inform Peretz of the true situation. Peretz decided to go to the Hungarians. All this took place over a few days. It looked like the mission of these two men, of whom we had such high hopes and whose mere arrival had brought us such joy, was coming to an abrupt end.

After a lengthy interrogation, the two were brought to the military prison at Margit Körút, where they joined some very distinguished and highly respected fellow prisoners, including members of the political and military elite, who had been arrested one by one. As Joel told us later, even in prison, these continued to play at "governments" and handed out portfolios freely to each other. Hanna Szenes, who had parachuted in before Peretz and Joel, had spent time in that same prison, but we never met her, because she was captured as soon as she crossed the border. From time to time we received brief snippets of information from Joel and Peretz and we sent them parcels, which it turned out later, never reached their destination.

Kastner undertook efforts to get the two released. He had still not given up hope of getting them out with the help of the Germans. When we saw that nothing was moving, we decided to act on our own initiative. With the help of "our consulate," which had been visited by several influential Hungarian politicians, during our "protection letters" period, we managed to make some important contacts. The matter took on some concrete form: one day we received the good news that the hour had arrived.

But October 15 spoiled all our plans. Hanna Szenes was shot. Joel and Peretz were deported. Joel succeeded in escaping from the train, together with several French officers. We never heard of Peretz again. At first, Joel went to the French consulate in Budapest, where he was given clothes, money and identification papers and here, too, he met the group of French and Dutch refugees, acquaintances of ours, to whom we had supplied documents. At that time, Joel had no idea which of us was still alive or where we were. But the officers were able to give him our address. They did not know that we had already had contact with Joel before. Van der Vaas, a Dutch officer, the leader and cleverest person in that group, came to us one day and asked if we would be willing to take care of an escaped parachutist from Palestine. We agreed, of course, and were most curious to know who the man was. When it turned out to be Joel, we fell into each others' arms with tears of joy.

And again, we were faced with the problem of where to hide him. After some brief consultations, we decided to transfer him to the "consulate building" on Wekerle Street, for a short while only, because it was already overcrowded, and Joel's presence might jeopardize this hiding place. We then appropriated a Slovak passport for him, so that he would have some freedom of movement and, of course, the appropriate licence from the Foreigners Department of the Hungarian Police, allowing him to stay in Budapest. (The Slovak consul in Budapest, Spisiak, had taken Yoshkó Laufer as his secretary, whose job it was to prepare the Czechoslovak consulate in Budapest. Through Yoshkó, a loyal and courageous friend, we received these passports at that time, and we supplied them to a large number of Czechoslovak refugees in Budapest. Spisiak signed these passports and it was clear to us that he did this in order to supply himself with an alibi once the war was over.)

Joel spent quite a long time in Wekerle Street and had no reservations about taking part in our activity. He then moved into the apartment of Mr. Railroad Officer, János Szabó, who was none other than Moshe Pil.

After liberation we immediately began to restore Hehalutz and the other Zionist organizations. And from the beginning, we were aided by an emissary from Palestine.

The mission of the two parachutists from *Eretz Yisrael* (Palestine) had in fact, failed, and lives had been lost. Nonetheless, in those tragic days, when we were standing orphaned, alone, we found this mission to be of enormous symbolic significance and it will never be forgotten in the history of the Jewish defense and rescue operation.

Chapter Fourteen

52 Baross Street

With the foundation of the political department on 52 Baross Street[1] I brought in Neshka from Dror, because I planned to concentrate all Zionist-related political activity together with all other Jewish activity, within the framework of "The Working Palestine." Thus it was imperative that close cooperation be maintained between us and Dror. The relationship between us was very good, as we had been working together constantly since March 19. Dror had a small leadership, headed by Zvi Goldfarb[2] and his wife Neshka, both of whom were enthusiastic and extremely courageous people.

Founding the political department turned out to be a very difficult job, much harder than I could have imagined. Any political activity in those days had to be much more conspirative than could be contained in one office. I had to move around, so it was impossible to involve Neshka in many of the activities. In the meantime, she had set up the Dror secretariat in one of the rooms, which meant a continuous stream of people dressed in various strange and highly impressive uniforms, because Dror members loved uniforms and made a point of dressing only in those of the Arrow Cross, masquerading as soldiers or members of the Levente.[3] It was from here that people were sent to the bunkers; food was supplied to the bunkers and hundreds of people were supplied with documents. We often had to ask Zvi or Neshka to restrict the commotion, since this could prove harmful to the operation. The number of "clients" increased from day-to-day as it became widely known that this was the place to obtain documents.... Neshka was enjoying herself; she wanted to help everybody and was unable to turn anyone away. Her kind heart may well have been her downfall. Later, when she was arrested, she identified one of the detectives as a man who had received documents from her only a few days before.

Actually, we too, were not overly cautious, because for a while we were also handing out documents in the office which was very convenient, but also extremely dangerous. We therefore decided, to stop the distribution after four or five days and Marek[4] went down to the street once again, to the tried and trusted meeting places. Except that lately these meeting places had also become extremely dangerous, since the young people had vanished from the streets. Number 52 Baross Street had an additional disadvantage: Yoshkó Meir (Megyeri)[5] had been taking part in illegal political activity for months and had surrounded himself with a group of brave and ever-ready people. He too, had moved his base of activity to this place and his partisans would appear every day between two and four o' clock. Number 52 Baross was also somehow incriminated when certain members of the Megyeri group were captured. Anyway, we were warned in time. Shortly before that, Yoshkó folded the operation, because it seemed too complicated. At that time, he lived with György Nonn[6] who had just escaped from the military prison on Margit Street. Gyurka was one of the young communist leaders, whom he had known from Transylvania. For days on end the two engaged in stormy arguments on the Jewish issue. Nonn was a stubborn young man, the son of a farmer, and was unable to understand why we wanted to be Jews and not Hungarians.

Despite all the dangers, Yoshkó maintained contact with us, visiting us every Monday or Tuesday. We were always happy to see this young man in the shiny uniform of the "Hungarian Legion."[7] Later he made a habit of appearing with a sub-machine gun and grenades. One day he told us, laughing loudly, that only the day before, he had "purchased" a small tank, and was now worried about where to store it. It was a period of relative chaos. Budapest was full of various uniform-clad militias, including illegal ones, of course. Everywhere you looked you saw these fantastic uniform-clad people, whom nobody could identify or relate to. In "KISKA"[8] there were hundreds of young Jewish men dressed in uniform; even one of the most senior officers — as it became apparent later — was a Jew. Had the underground been able to unite under a single leadership, there could have been an armed uprising in Budapest against the Nazis, at the last moment. In the absence of such a leadership, there were random courageous uprisings which were quashed because of their being scattered and alone.⁹ In 17 Wekerle Sándor Street, we also had one of these fake units, masquerading as a guard unit. Those serving in it were almost without exception, members of the "Historic Class." The young Kállay[10] was among them, as were several others including sons of ministers in the new Hungarian Government.[11] In the heart of hearts of these young men, churned a revolution which was absolutely unique. They were prepared to adapt themselves to a new social order, except that they did not know exactly how to set about doing so. They were young people, utterly ignorant politically, and they started to sense the suffocating hold on their necks of the grave period they were living in.

One day, we decided to relinquish the house on 52 Baross Street. Three days after that, two Dror members were arrested in front of the building. This signaled a series of tragedies. Zvi and Neshka, together with some other friends, were arrested the following day at their meeting place on "Városliget."[12] Three days later, the authorities uncovered their three bunkers. The bunker on Hungarian Boulevard[13] put up a brief but ineffective struggle. The others surrendered without a struggle.

It was already difficult to determine during those stormy December days, exactly where our people were being held prisoners. It took us a few days to discover that the entire group was "sitting" in Margit Boulevard. We had been misled by Patyu's[14] testimony, after he had succeeded in escaping from a moving car which was supposed to be taking him, Zvi and the others to Sopronkőhida.[15]

We were desparate to find a way to rescue our friends, unable to reconcile ourselves to the possibility that so short a time before the imminent downfall of the evil regime, our whole movement could simply topple.

And then all of a sudden, like a bolt of lightening, we were hit by another blow. Our work-shop had to change place once again. David, Feigi and Miky did not return to their home after the move. For reasons of security, no-one knew where they were moving to, so we had nothing to grasp. We had ties with an Arrow Cross member, who had a Jewish fiancé and who had helped us with several minor incidents in the past. Some time before, he had secured the release of three of our friends from the prison on Markó Street.[16] We made our way straight to this Tony, who received us with a smile. He was sure we would be arriving today — he said — because they had some fantastic arrests in the

Seventh Quarter! He was especially interested in the affair, which from the start was obviously connected with us in one way or another. He reported that his "brothers"[17] had arrested three young Slovak males, who had a print-shop, equipped with a fantastic array of forms, stamps, passports, party membership cards, etc.; in short, everything imaginable. One of the young men committed suicide, the other two were in Margit Boulevard.

Full of contained fury, we considered the possibility of getting our friends released. We knew for sure that any hour wasted could cost them their lives. And now that same Pole, who had on several occasions claimed that he could get prisoners released, appeared at Wekerle Sándor Street. On the one hand, he demanded hair-raising prices for his services (one hundred Napoleons[18] for each prisoner), on the other hand, he did not seem especially reliable. But this time, we had no choice and he was given the job. The price was determined at three hundred Napoleon coins and in return for every additional person he managed to get released — according to a list we had made up — we promised him a further twenty "Napoleons." Of course we had no idea where we would get the money from, but still….

The whole thing took four days. On the fourth day,[19] a beaten and battered group of prisoners turned up in front of 17 Wekerle Sándor Street, a larger number than we had dared hope for. We were happy to hand over five hundred Napoleons. It took us a while to collect the money, and only then could we embrace our friends. Miky was not among them. He had not committed suicide, the Arrow Cross had beaten him to death. Marek, too, was missing. He was not among them, that brave young man who had attended all the meetings with his "explosive material." Marek had disappeared without trace, forever. A coward's bullet had hit him in the back and brought him down, together with so many other nameless people, into the flowing River Danube.[20]

All the fellows were in a terrible state. Feigi could neither sit nor lie down, he had concussion and vomited up anything he ate. Pil took Feigi back to his apartment. David went to Mimish's apartment.

The following day, that same man had over a hundred people released from Fő utca, including sixty-five Dror members; the others were mostly communists,[21] many of whom were acquaintances of ours. It was only now that we gradually came to know what in fact had happened. The arrest of the Dror group was the work of a Jewish informer,[22] with whom we were very familiar even in Vadász Street. The print shop was the victim of a miserable circumstance. Miky lost his life in the party offices of the Arrow Cross, in the arms of his two close friends. His slight physical build and gentle facial features ignited a special kind of fury among the hooligans.

The incriminating suitcases actually saved the lives of the young men. Had the contents of the suitcases not been "so interesting," they would have eliminated our men on the banks of the Danube. Thousands were being exterminated at that very same time. But as "special cases," they were brought to Margit Boulevard.

We were appalled by the horrible cruelty of the Arrow Cross. We were already fully familiar with the methods used by the Hungarian counter espionage, the gendarmerie and the Hungarian Gestapo, but this new branch of the Arrow Cross, known as "Nemzeti Számonkérö Szék" (Chair of National Prosecution), far outstripped anything we had been accustomed to, in it's sheer inventive cruelty. Zvi, who had been taken for interrogation by the Gestapo at Sopron, told us that there, too, the treatment was not exactly "gentle." He was required to write out his life history, and they knew that he should be treated as leader of the accused group — also, incidentally, of the attack on the public meeting of the Arrow Cross at the Culture Center.[23] They tried to encourage him to talk, by tying him head down and pouring several liters of water into his nose, while his mouth was blocked.[24] We wondered how accurate the information was that these institutes had on us and were completely unable to understand why, given the circumstances, they did not come to arrest us all.[25]

Chapter Fifteen

Budapest Under Siege

On December 24, 1944, the siege tightened around Budapest.[1] We felt a certain relief; this was the day on which the danger of deportation was over. Indeed, we had to take into consideration that there would be further rioting, worse even than before, but the greatest danger always concerned the fear of deportation. In the middle of the city — in sight of its civilian population — the fascists did not dare commit large scale acts of murder. Thus we were also quite unaware of the dangers involved in demolishing the ghetto.[2]

One day[3] an agitated policeman arrived at Wekerle Sándor Street and told us that an armed group of Arrow Cross had surrounded the consulate on Vadász Street. Several grenades were thrown into the building and the inhabitants were expelled into the street. We all held our breaths for a second; here it was, the moment we had all dreaded. But within a minute, we had picked up the telephone and informed all the relevant authorities of the incident: the Foreign Office, Police, the capital's military HQ and all the other elements. Fortunately, all these interventions were successful and almost immediately police and municipal officers arrived at Vadász Street. To this day, I am not sure who should be thanked for preventing the mass deportation[4] of some 1,500 people who were already filling the street, but one thing was certain at that moment: the great ruse of the consulate was working wonderfully. The authorities respected the building's ex-territorial status and our people were saved. Vadász Street could claim a great victory, and…five dead.

Good for Krausz! During all those months we had not really learned to like him, but his creativity was brilliant; no-one can deny that! During the first few days following liberation, he received a letter of appreciation from us, for his achievements. He deserved it! We had had serious reservations about him, but now we were thanking him with all our hearts.

Those same Arrow Cross people came to the consulate another three or four times, but on those occasions they made do with a few minor objects. After one of these visits, they asked Arthur Weiss to accompany them, "in order to discuss a few economic issues." The invitation was most courteous and Arthur Weiss believed them. He joined them in their car and never returned.[5] Thus the man became, ultimately, a martyr to the cause. That same man, who symbolized for us the epitome of all that was Jewish bourgeois reactionary, the man against whose blatant anti-social stance we fought for months on end....

Our military guard force acted adequately throughout the attack on Vadász Street; they went straight out to the attackers and were responsible for the success of the defense. But they did not function as well as they could have and were somewhat irresponsible. Their uniform was a source of ridicule (after all nothing serious could happen to them). They acted more out of fear of the Red Army than anything else. Even then, during the worst period of all, when a car ride could have saved lives, they made constant use of the available cars in order to obtain spirits and other frivolities. So when they went off one day to collect some things, they asked for a couple of workers to go along to help them. It was no longer a pleasure to travel along the streets; but the Arrow Cross were especially on the lookout for cars; they reckoned they could burst through the blockade to the west and then — a car meant salvation for them. But bombs also started falling from all around. No wonder, therefore, that two brave young men went out with the soldiers, ready for any task. They were stopped in the street, together with the car and taken to the Arrow Cross building on Molnár Street.[6] Sergeant-Major Horvát[7] came out immediately to investigate the arrest. That same day, he released his two demi-soldiers and the car, but not our two members. A few days later, one of our underworld contacts — who had a Gestapo certificate — informed us that he was prepared to search for the two prisoners. He was told nonchalantly that the two young men had been "eliminated" some time before. In those days, human life was cheap....

The final days of fascism inadvertently caused us two more great losses. The day[8] Arthur Weiss was arrested, the engineer Ottó Komoly — president of the Zionist Federation, and now manager of Department A of the International Red

Cross — was also kidnapped from the lobby of the Ritz hotel.[9] He too, disappeared without trace. Thus we lost a man who was honest, straightforward and pure, the kind of man that was a rarity here. He may not have been an outstanding personality, but his honesty and decency earned him the respect of people on all sides. With the loss of Komoly, Hungarian Zionism suffered a great deal, not only its president — the loss of Komoly also meant the loss of Hungarian Zionism's equilibrium.

Two days later, one of the runners was shot dead in front of the consulate building on Vadász Street. At the same time, Simha Hunwald and Tibor Szemere drove past the spot in a diplomatic car. Their tragedy was that they stopped for a moment when they saw the body. This was enough time for the Arrow Cross to arrest the two, throw them into their own car and drive off quickly.

Arthur Weiss, Ottó Komoly, Simha Hunwald…. Once again we tried all the impossible ways to find and rescue them, but the telephone was no longer working. The "Rata" planes[10] flew ceaselessly overhead, and the worst part was that all the leads we had led to nowhere. The three had disappeared and it was impossible to trace them. After the liberation of Pest, we hoped that they were being held hostage in the palace[11] and as such, would be freed. A few days later, Tibor Szemere was found. He knew nothing about Arthur Weiss or Ottó Komoly. He had been separated from Simha some time before, but was told by one of the prison guards that Simha had been shot dead on January 20.[12]

The death of Simha was the worst, most shocking trick that insane fate could have played on us. Simha had returned from the Carpathian mountains only in November,[13] having spent many months in the Ukraine.[14] He recovered from a severe case of typhoid fever and in the end, dressed in the uniform of a "Honvéd,"[15] walked many hundreds of miles back to his friends. Only a few days after his arrival did he resume his activity, adapting himself to the circumstances in the most admirable way. Simha was the last victim we sacrificed to fascism. He will remain a kind of exclamation mark in our lives, and will never permit us to forget a thing….

Budapest, April-May 1945

Epilogue

Two years have passed since January 18, 1945 — the day the Red Army battled for the liberation of Budapest. These memoirs were written a short while after liberation, in the form of brief notes, but even now, as I hand them over to the public, I feel no need to correct or add much. In the meantime, we have only had some matters clarified, which were not very clear at the time and we now know the fate of many of our friends who we considered at the time as "missing." But I have no desire to change my impressions from then, since it is my intention to pass on our experiences in a direct manner rather than to write an historical essay, based on some thorough research, nor is this meant to be a literary masterpiece.

In Budapest, we were among the last of our active guards to be rescued from that apocalyptic dance of death, and liberated from the terrible nightmare that was the Nazi rule. We were almost the last people to witness firsthand the birth of the people's democracies in central and eastern Europe. We were exhausted when we met the first heralds of a new life. The first were soldiers of the Red Army, including some Jewish soldiers, who offered us help in overcoming our great suffering. Later, people started gradually returning from Bucharest, Belgrade and Moscow — Jews who had been in forced labor camps.

But we were unable to rejoice in the joy of liberation; there was no time to even contemplate all this. We were faced with enormous tasks. Some 120,000 Jews remained in Budapest, most of whom did not have a roof over their heads. Even more serious was the problem of feeding and clothing them. From all sides, people started emerging from bunkers, from the rubble of bombed out houses. They came out of the most imaginative hiding places, the children's houses were in the most desperate situation, the ghetto was about to be disbanded and there was nothing edible to be found. For the time being, there was no possibility of bringing in foodstuffs from the provinces. Throughout Hungary there was not a single train, car or gas. In short: there was nothing. And thus began for us a new and difficult task. Again we encountered the kind of problems that were beyond our experience and power and were not even within the framework of our authority. But over the years, we had been weaned from questions of authority. We had only to see the need, and will and willingness soon followed.

Months passed and life gradually went back on track. But there was something wrong. At some point, our account had not been properly settled. The last years had seen a war of open and cruel annihilation against the Jewish nation and we had waged our own "wars of the Jews." All the historical and geographical borders had been blurred, because as far as we were concerned the SS was the same enemy as the Ustashi, the Hlinka guards or the Hungarian gendarmerie. They too, never asked about nationality, but looked only for Jews.

And now suddenly, everywhere we looked, people began to talk in new terms.

The Jewish question no longer officially existed. Only the matters of the Hungarian war for democracy and the Hungarian victims of the war were discussed. It seemed to me that this was the only point on which we did not accurately assess the development of things and where reality found us politically unprepared. At first, it was even difficult to understand. It was a strange feeling of pain and stinging insult, because even unconsciously, we had been hoping for some reparation and compensation, for some grand ceremonial act, in which Europe would mourn the martyrdom of the many millions of our people, from which our remaining members could draw hope and security for a different future.

Through this we found ourselves facing a situation which could barely be understood, in which we were denied even the right to our own martyrs; because statistics referred to such and such a number of Hungarian victims, Slovak victims, Poles, who died in the gas chambers. Even the numbers remained silent and did not reveal the torturous path followed so recently by the Jewish nation.

We even anticipated the attitude to the fascists to be something rather different. As far as we were concerned, fascists were not only party members or gendarmes, but also the thousands of concierge, tram drivers, ordinary citizens and even children playing in the streets. And now the term "fascist" was restricted to a handful of war criminals. That vast and omnipotent conductor, which encompassed all our lives, suddenly vanished. Once again there was the "nation" which had even become "democratic," because it was now no longer possible to arrest and execute millions, so that amnesty has to be given the "small fry." No-one asked us, we were even expected to understand. As time passed, we began to understand, but it was not easy. We fought this war on the most diverse of fronts, as partisans for the honor of our nation and to save its substance and sometimes only to save its honor. It was a desperate struggle and the forces were not equal and the balance was sad. We managed to save but a few thousand from the claws of fascism and with these few thousand we hoped to create a new life and to bring a solution to the Jewish problem. And we discovered that, for us, the war was still not over.

How easy it was for all those nations with their embryo democracies! They rehabilitated themselves, slowly and through hard work, from this war and have built themselves a better future. First they put their own homes in order, then their cities and finally, they put order in their country. People have learned once more to laugh, they have learned to handle their own affairs and enjoyed the rights and the liberty which were returned to them.

But we have emerged from this war dispersed and with our roots cut, more than ever before. We saw how antisemitism had been hidden in an ambush, just waiting for the right moment to pounce once again. In this war, no-one heard our cries of desperation and it seems that no-one can hear them even now that the war is over. Likewise, there is no-one interested in hearing them.

Our people are still on the road, in camps, by the wayside. They are still asking for a new life.

We did not imagine that starting a new life would be an easy matter, but we were convinced that, through our struggle, we would achieve some kind of foundation for a new life. Now it is apparent that we are going to have to take a pragmatic look at the future, without any illusions. We must continue with that same 'small line' that served as our motto during the war. Continuous and systematic action, with the full awareness of our objective, action which does not denigrate those same small components which in the end, together, will form the large goal.

This truth was learned by our movement during those years of supreme effort and it knows it today, too. From within a flood of speeches, lectures and illusions, it also knew to educate the young person and to point him in the direction of pioneering which is hard and lacking in pathos. This generation which grew up within the battle shall take care to make education the focal point of its activity. All our members now undergoing training, in all the various countries, on their way to the Land of Israel, in the camps and on ships, it is they who are the fighters — against the British blockade which forbids their entry into Palestine — it is they who are offering the most appropriate answer to the question of why we Jews retaliated.

Prague, June 1947

Josef (Joshka) Meir's Testimony

Germany's occupation of Hungary on March 19, 1944 found me in one of the Hungarian army's forced labor units, as a political prisoner. I was arrested and interrogated about my connections with the communist underground.[1] There were some thirty members of the Halutz (Zionist Pioneer) movement with me in the forced labor unit. I maintained contact with the members of the movement in Budapest. Efra and Cipi visited us, bringing forged documents, enabling our escape.[2]

I arrived in Budapest a few days before Szálasi's coup on October 15, 1944. We held a meeting and decided that I should exploit my former contacts with the workers' movements[3] and examine possibilities for mutual assistance in various fields.

The events of October 15 forced us to organize ourselves according to the new situation, as quickly as possible. In the evening of the same day I renewed my contact with a political body that had left the Arrow Cross Party and now operated as The Hungarian Socialist Party.[4] It was headed by Colonel (ret.) Kálmán Rátz,[5] a past member of the Hungarian parliament. Ratz courageously demanded the return of Hungarian forces from the front. He also wrote and spoke much against the persecution of Jews and more than once made efforts to assist individual Jews.

György Juhász, an energetic activist, and his sister Gyöngyvér — at whose estate in Pestszentlőrinc we later established an arms cache — were central members of our inner circle. My acquaintance with them went back to the underground days of the Arrow Cross people.[6]

I received some party service-unit armbands,[7] a few badges and hats. In those days, even veteran party members did not possess such accessories. The following day, members of the Halutz underground went about their rescue work equipped with these accessories and documents, while making the most of the chaos; within a few days following October 15, Budapest was bombed repeatedly.

The first thing we had to do was concentrate all the candidates for the rescue operation from the "Jews' houses," whose gates had closed on them. We compiled lists and split into teams of two to carry out the mission.

As an example, I will describe one incident typical of the many we experienced in those days. It was the day after the Szálasi coup, on October 16. Efra and I were a team. We decided to go to one of the houses on Népszinház[8] Street to rescue one of our comrades who, to the best of our knowledge, was stuck there. Just then, Tiger[9] type German tanks were shelling the "Jews' houses."[10] Corpses were sprawled in the streets. Arrow Cross thugs equipped with sub-machine guns gathered from everywhere. They led Jews by the hundreds, with raised arms, to an unknown destination.[11] Ten and eleven year old children tied stones into their sweaters and beat the unfortunate Jews who crossed their paths.

Efra was in the uniform of a railway-officer, with an Arrow Cross armband and I wore a mixed military and Arrow Cross uniform. The two of us entered the house with drawn revolvers. The occupants of the house were scared of being taken out and executed. They thought that the Germans would wipe out all the Jews of the street. It hurt us to see the fear that our appearance aroused, but we had no choice. The concierge claimed that he did not know where our comrade was, so we checked the shelter into which all the tenants of the house had squeezed. We discovered that our comrade had escaped the night before.

We left the house and were calmly proceeding along Erzsébet[12] Boulevard to our next objective, when two ruffians aged between fourteen and fifteen stopped us. One of them asked Efra if he "...wasn't, by any chance, from Kisvárda,[13] and wasn't his name Teichmann...like our neighbor?..." Efra denied everything and I tried to change the subject:

"Why are you wandering around the streets? Come to 60 Andrássy Street[14] and I'll give you some work!"

The two boys did not give up; they continued to follow us. We tried to leave the main boulevard, veering towards Ferenc Liszt Circle.[15] The two ruffians discovered and rapidly approached an armed "Levente" man and pointed at us. We increased our pace, only to hear the sound of a rifle being loaded at our backs. The "Levente" fellow was chasing us, rifle in hand. Suddenly we heard him say:

"The boys have informed against you!"

Apparently, one of them had really recognized Efra. We turned around and to our great surprise, saw that the armed "Levente" man was none other than Tzalel, a member of Dror. Meanwhile, we continued to walk ahead — all three of us. On the other side of the square we found a soldier. The boys had made sure by reporting us to him as well. But the soldier was Patyu — also a member of Dror. By chance, they were preparing for an operation in the area. The four of us now walked on in some confusion: two members of the Arrow Cross were facing us, behind us were another two with rifles and ten meters behind them, the two ruffians who wanted to witness what was going to happen. In this way, we reached the western train station.[16] Here we decided to act. A railway worker was coming towards us on a motorcycle. Efra, who was his senior in rank, stopped him. When he found out where the motorcyclist was headed, he said that he was going in the same direction and mounted the bike. They disappeared at full speed. I ran the other way and the two members of Dror also took off in opposite directions. Our problem was solved.

After the Szálasi coup, we concentrated our members from the forced labor units and the districts in Budapest. We divided our people into two groups. The first, which was composed of suitable members, was to carry out missions.[17] We were worried about the safety of the second group. Only as a last resort, when all hope was lost, did we hide our comrades in bunkers. The Dror tactic — to hide all the members of their movement in bunkers far from the city — did not appeal to us. Sadly, the Dror movement paid a heavy price for this strategy.

We preferred to house our members temporarily in various industrial plants.[18] Here, thanks to our contacts with groups from the workers' movement, we could house them for various periods. Nobody was ever caught in these places.

We were helped in this activity by the communist Demény group.[19] We also sent people to the districts; we rarely agreed to the idea of bunkers. In these cases, too, we took into consideration our comrades' ability to participate in our activities, should the need arise. We considered a joint resistance movement with the Hungarians. However, through no fault of ours, the comprehensive armed operations and open resistance never had their turn. Through one of my liaison people (a Communist by the name of Futó),[20] I managed to reach a few industrial plants in Kőbánya.[21] Here we constructed some interlocking bunkers in cellars and storerooms. Our members spent the day here as workers and at night they stayed in the bunkers. We had designated a role for these plants in one of our operations. This was not put into effect, although through no fault of our members; they were prepared.

In Almássy Square,[22] we were helped by an officer in the Civil Defense,[23] a veteran communist. There was an emergency hospital here, which we used for comrades (among Polish refugees) who could not move around freely in the streets and who posed as patients. Generally, we tried to obtain Civil Defense badges and papers, since it was a recognized military service. More possibilities of rescue were open to us through this service, since the Jews feared the uniforms of the army and Arrow Cross, but not of the Civil Defense, whose help they agreed to accept.

We even had a hiding place equipped with electric light and a supply of food in a spacious paper warehouse in Erzsébet Boulevard, in the center of the city.[24] We also had a few bunkers in the suburbs. These were on the premises of certain industrial plants, where our comrades were together with communists and participated in their seminars, distributed their leaflets and other underground work.

In fact, we had a special group of technicians and bunker-builders. The group spent the night in the "glass house" on Vadász Street, rising early for work and returning late at night. There were a number of comrades on Vadasz Street who wanted action at any cost.[25] We put them in touch with one of the Hungarian underground cells, which they joined. To all outward appearances, this group was a genuine military unit which received provisions with the aid of their army papers. A supervisory authority discovered the unit's true identity by chance and our comrades were forced to go into hiding. They were attacked by some men of the Arrow Cross, but were proficient in the use of weapons and the attackers were shot in a brief exchange of fire. Luckily, none of our men were injured.

Hungarian underground groups slowly crystallized in Budapest. As the front came closer to the heart of the country and its capital, more and more of the fighters began to consider disregarding the orders to withdraw to Transdanubia[26] together with the Hungarian troops and instead, to try to remain in Budapest. I had good relations with the soldiers serving in the military airfield at Mátyásföld.[27] On one occasion I learned directly from them that all the men in their unit were ready to desert, if only we could provide them with civilian documents. I managed to organize everything quite soon and the whole guard unit, some twenty to twenty-five men, deserted.

Through them, I established contact with the major in command of a company. I met him in a private apartment in Kohári[28] Street. He and his men were wary and disbelieving. I was also apprehensive. In the end, I braced myself and went to the appointed place. Each side was afraid that the other had set a trap.... The company consisted of infantry, a mortar squad and a machine gun squad. They were supposed to go westward, to an unknown destination. Anyway, I established contact between the above company commander and military center of the Hungarian underground, operating in Apponyi Square,[29] headed by Vilmos Tarcsay.[30]. The order to move westward was received twenty-four hours in advance from the underground military center. To be on the safe side, I organized receipt of the company's "superfluous equipment." When the company entrained at the station,[31] we also left, equipped with an "open" pass ("direct orders"), ostensibly from the Arrow Cross. I received the items — a few boxes of hand grenades and sixty rifles with ammunition — from the commander's adjutant. These went to the stores at Pestszentlőrinc.

Several days earlier, they had handed over a more interesting "item": a tank that had been "lost" on the way back from the workshop. By arrangement with me, the crew had parked it in a closed yard at the workshop. To my regret, we were unable to make use of it and later sabotaged it.

At the end of November, some of the men of the Mátyásföld guard unit were arrested and almost turned me in. The office at 52 Baross Street, shared by Rafi Friedl (Benshalom) and myself, was under surveillance. Had they succeeded, quite a few "sensitive matters" would have been exposed. However, at the last moment, just before the house was searched, we managed to disappear.

The Hungarian underground was disorganized, lacking leadership and operational efficiency.[32] There was no alternative: we had to adapt ourselves or be forced to take initiative to change the situation.

I organized a few groups of youngsters from among past members of the trade unions and the workers' party — eighty percent of whom were non-Jewish Hungarians. Our center was in the church on Lehel Square.[33] The church organ player was the head of a cell. The youngsters carried out underground activities — distributing leaflets and information, infiltrated "direct orders," releases and military industry papers to the factories, for workers who wanted to desert.

Directives for sabotage operations were also passed on in this way. Later, when I was totally occupied with what was known as the 'military line,' I transferred the cells to a man whose underground name was "B...,"[34] on the orders of György Nonn.

Nonn was a young man of Schwabian origin, born in Transylvania, who was sentenced to eight years in prison in 1942 for being a member of the central committee of the underground Communist Party. He managed to escape from prison and immediately contacted us. We supplied him with forged documents and a hiding place for the first few days.

It was from him that we first heard about Hanna Szenes' final days in the Margit Circle prison. György Nonn, as a prisoner, was put to work as a clerk and it was he who compiled the formal notes on Hanna's execution and an inventory of her personal effects. He escaped a few days later. He soon became one of the leaders of the Hungarian underground.

He put me in touch with the commander of the Kőbánya partisan unit.[35] I was asked to organize a supply line[36] parallel to the 'military line.' In addition, I placed the arms and ammunition from our stores in Almássy Square at the disposal of the partisan commander. I also connected him with several unrelated cells.

The organization in Kőbánya was superb. Underground units were established in barracks and schools — outwardly as regular military units. These units often attacked Arrow Cross patrols or fighting units.

Budapest then fell under siege. I organized armed patrols from among the young groups. These patrols, which appeared to be Arrow Cross party patrols, had two aims: a) rescuing Jews from the mobs and 'party services' under the pretext that their execution was part of our duties; b) when conditions were right, we shot a considerable number of Arrow Cross men. I infiltrated some of our members to the Civil Defense forces camped at Almássy Square. Our people were on the alert day and night and conducted armed patrols in the ghetto area. They disrupted Arrow Cross plans for murder and robbery and chased them away from the area. Two members of this group struck up a friendship in a bar with the man from the National Prosecution Seat[37] and he enrolled them in his unit![38] Through them we reached a direct source of information. They were also helped by the editor of an illustrated weekly published by the Arrow Cross Party; he supplied the most exact — even the most guarded — information.

During the siege, I again concentrated the youngsters who operated from the Lehel Circle Church. German vehicles, tanks and troop carriers were crowded in Eskü Circle[39] or in Apponyi Circle, unable to move through shortage of fuel. My fellows placed explosives with a time fuse under these vehicles.

At the beginning of January 1945, movement in the streets became very difficult. The city was bombarded day and night by Russian artillery. My transport consisted of a motorbike I received from 'Pil' (Moshe Alpan) which served me faithfully. I had to maneuver among the gaping shell holes, human corpses and horse carcasses. I preferred as far as possible to move at night, even though I did not always have the correct password required for moving around.

On January 4, I arranged with László Zircz[40] and Károly Pulacs[41] to meet at the Juhász family villa in Pestszentlőrinc, where we had an explosives and weapons cache in the cellar. On our arrival, we found the family sitting in the salon with guests, including one of the leaders of the Arrow Cross (our next 'meeting' with him was to be in one of the main Budapest squares, some months later, when he was publicly hanged for his crimes). We joined the conversation about politics, Jews, etc., impatiently waiting for them to leave so that we could go down to the cellar. The mission that night was to assemble explosive bricks with fuses and take them to the city for use by the groups.

In the cellar, we could hear the thunder of cannons and the echo of shots, but we were used to this. When we had finished our work, we decided that Pulacs would stay at the villa until morning and Zircz and I would leave. We were wearing hats decorated with the cock feathers[42] and in the uniforms of the Hungarian military gendarmerie. We had just left the house when we heard the shout: "Stoy!"[43] In front of us stood soldiers in fur hats with the red star badge. It emerged that a soviet vanguard unit had penetrated a few score meters beyond where we stood.

In the first few seconds of the encounter, we were not sure what our situation was. We burst into roars of joy and ran towards them with open arms. We saw our liberators before us. They recoiled and aimed their weapons at us. Only then did we realize that, in their eyes, we were enemies. It seems to me that throughout the Holocaust I was never closer to death than in those few seconds. To this day I do not know how we managed to convince them not to kill us on the spot, but to take us to their command post, where a discussion ensued between a Mongolian officer with slanted eyes and a young Jewish officer who also spoke Yiddish. The former insisted on killing us (I think he was drunk) while the Jew demanded proof that we were indeed members of the underground, and Jews. We showed him the underground newspapers we had with us. I also passed the 'anatomical' test that proved me to be one of our Father Abraham's offspring — a test I feared so much during my time in the underground. However, my friend Zircz, being a Gentile, failed this test. The young officer found an alternative: an examination in Marxism. We also informed him about the arms cache in the cellar of the villa Juhasz and about the third comrade, Jaacov Markovics, who was waiting there. When he had verified all this, he let us go.

We were rescued and freed. On my own initiative, I looked for a front command post in order to convey everything I knew about the German deployment and the Arrow Cross in the capital.

June 1946

Efra Teichmann-Agmon's Testimony

Until 1943, I lived in Kisvárda.[1] When my annual call-up notice arrived, I decided not to go. I returned it to the postman saying that I was not the addressee. Since we were eight brothers and sisters, the postman could not tell us apart.... I decided to leave Kisvárda immediately and go to Budapest. My father, who was not enthusiastic about my Zionist activities anyway, would not hear of it. I left against his wishes. Later, when the Germans conquered Hungary, I wrote to my father and asked him to join me in Munkács, where I was living at the time. Then and only then, did he give me his blessing to follow my own path. My parents and four of my brothers perished in Auschwitz.

In Kisvárda, I belonged to a not particularly active Hashomer Hatza'ir cell. My contact with the movement in Budapest was through my friend Shmuel Frenkel,[2] also from Kisvárda. He introduced me to the members of the Slovakian movement, who crossed the border and had wide experience in underground activities.

I knew the order from the forced labor unit would be forwarded to me. I also knew that I had to sign a police form giving my last address when I moved in and my next address when I vacated an apartment, if I wanted to avoid being declared an army deserter. For this reason, I changed my address fortnightly, all according to regulations. To the best of my knowledge, the "accepted channels" took two weeks to run their course, so after three months there was still no sign of my mobilization papers.... But I saw that I would not be able to continue like this for much longer and therefore, I disappeared. I gave up my identity and, as we used to say, went underground.

This was also useful in terms of movement activity. The Hungarian movement was hard hit; many of its adult members were mobilized. Members over the age of twenty-one served in the forced labor units at the beginning of 1944. Most of the experienced operatives were in concentration camps for helping and hiding refugees from Slovakia. The top echelons couldn't operate. Josko Baumer carried the affair of the Slovakian refugees on his shoulders. New operatives were needed and as soon as I arrived in Budapest, I was given missions.

On March 9 and 10 there was a meeting of the executive. The movement cells in the outlying towns were hit hardest, owing to the mobilization of the most experienced members. For this reason, the executive decided to send agents to those towns. I was sent to Munkács where I stayed for a full month, from March 15 to April 15. The Germans entered on March 19, while I was still there. When they came to Munkács the Germans immediately demonstrated what their arrival meant for the Jews…. From the very first day, Jews were beaten in the streets, brought from the villages and concentrated in the town. There were some 20,000 Jews in the town and surrounding areas at the time.

Munkács was a Jewish 'metropolis' with an active Zionist center. The youth movements, which had hundreds of members, represented all the Zionist parties. It was clear that something had to be done. I was there as a representative of the movement; my task was to try and help my comrades. However, it was impossible to do so for a long time. Munkács was close to the border and thus cut off from the rest of the country, so much so that even the Christian population had to request travel permits; travel was restricted.[3]

Those born in 1923 were being mobilized for forced labor and we seized the opportunity to make a change in the prevailing situation. The youngsters were summoned to Jászberény.[4] We told the recipients of these call-ups: "Return the order! Go to the town Command and tell the authorities that you want a travel permit to Jászberény. Say that you have been ordered to report there, but that you have lost the paper, or someone took it and tore it up by mistake!…." In this way someone else could travel with the original or the copy. We explained: "In Hatvan,[5] don't take the train to Jaszbereny. Instead, you must carry on to Budapest. If anyone questions you on the way, tell them that you're going to the capital to buy equipment. After all, the mobilization order states that you have to come with a rucksack, blankets and so on…."

This was how I returned to Budapest on April 15, 1944. The leaders of the movement convened to assess the situation and its possibilities, to crystallize our aims and determine what we should do. When Haika Klinger came and spoke to us, the reality of the German occupation of Hungary became very clear. Her lecture was a turning point; in its wake we established the "Senior Group"[6] — together with two Mapai youth movements, Dror and Maccabi Hatza'ir. Our Senior Group engaged in weapons training in the Auslender family's apartment on Pusztaszeri Street.[7]

But the situation in Hungary was different from that of Poland and Czechoslovakia. Here there were no forests, there was no Hungarian partisan movement with whom to cooperate and justify the establishment of a parallel Jewish movement. Hungarian Jewry did not feel spiritually or physically connected to its brethren. The Jews believed that "Here, it couldn't happen!" They tried to convince themselves that "There are deportations from Munkács because it is a border city!" There were also those who put their trust in the Regent, "Horthy won't allow it!" The absolute majority believed that, "the Law is the Law and Jews are law-abiding![8]" We felt that Hungarian Jewry felt no solidarity with the refugees coming from Slovakia and Poland. The Jewish leadership claimed that they were anxious for their own flock. We, the young Zionists, claimed that they were fearful for their own skins.

This was the official point of view of the central Jewish organizations in Budapest,[9] directed by Shmuel Stern.[10] Budapest's Jews tried to live with the unquestioning self-conviction that Hitler's exterminatory intentions did not apply to them...! They applied to rural Jews, or to those with sidelocks[11][r1] and later raked in the occupants of Budapest's Jewish Quarter in Dob Street and its surroundings....[12] They believed that the assimilated Jew — always a loyal son of the Hungarian nation, who fought as an outstanding soldier in World War I[13] — would never be treated in this way!

The rural and district Jews had no understanding of the situation; they were hurt by the decrees imposed on them day after day. Furthermore, all the men under forty-five[14] served in the forced labor units, as a great Jewish journalist was to observe: "They were in Hungarian captivity!"[15]

Our comrade Pil stated that 1944 was not 1942! In those days the Germans were at the peak of their victories. Now they were approaching their end. The

Nazi collapse was no more than a question of time. Their end was in sight, it was just impossible to know the exact hour. One who gains time, gains life. Thus we established a guideline: the movement, our comrades, had to be saved. This was an objective in itself. Furthermore, from among these, an active rescue unit for the future had to be formed. Our direction was thus fixed from the start in terms of practical possibilities geared for rescue.

We did not understand our Polish comrades, why they insisted on concentrating the people in bunkers[16]; people would be immobilized and shut in. Our method was different: it was better for our people to move about freely. Freedom of movement was the basis of our activity. This did not mean that we didn't establish bunkers. We did, and even equipped them with food and weapons, but we did so more to create another option in case of need. Our main work and activity was in a different direction.

Some of our members were in country towns, where they lived or to which they had come on movement missions in the short period of the movement's legal existence between the end of 1943 and the beginning of 1944. With the restrictions on Jews, it was absolutely forbidden to travel between the country towns and the capital. The journey involved inspections and was life-threatening. One after another the district Jews were expelled — at first to the ghettos — including the pioneer youth. Our movement had 500 members, according to which I estimate the total membership in the pioneer youth movement at 2,000.

Following our decision to concentrate our members in Budapest, we employed the method of sending them forced labor unit leave permits, which enabled them to go to and from Budapest. Failing this, we sent mobilization orders or soldiers from the guard units of the forced labor units who, for a sum of money and with the help of our members serving there, agreed to carry a "small package" containing documents and money to our comrades in the countryside. From the outset, we were assisted by female comrades who looked Aryan and carried forged papers.

The "Department of Districts" in the Budapest Jewish Council was run by our comrade, Moshe Rosenberg, of the Gordon Group. He called on us for gathering on-site information, forwarding money and general assistance. The Hehalutz (Pioneer) Youth were asked to send emissaries for the Council to the districts. There were twelve such emissaries; I do not recall all their names. Ester Schechter[17] was sent to Kisvárda, but was caught at the railway station. After being cruelly tortured, she was sent to prison and from there to Auschwitz; I did not succeed in rescuing her. One of the Fettman[18] brothers was sent to Debrecen.[19] Hava Barmat and Tamar Benshalom went to the Transdanube Districts. Miky Gotteszman[20] was sent to Munkács. Moshe Rosenberg briefed us and gave each of us 15,000 pengo for operational expenses. The district Jews had already been transferred to the ghettos and it was very difficult to make contact with them. Other comrades were caught on the road, or in railway stations, under suspicion of trying to contact the segregated Jews. Two of the women who were arrested were "encouraged" by a Gestapo officer, or one of the gendarmes, to give themselves up to the troops to earn their freedom...both refused. One of them who rejected the "polite suggestion" with disgust was taken to the Sárvár concentration camp and deported. The other, who said "maybe in Budapest..." was taken to the capital, where she managed to escape in the tumult of the railway station.

I was sent to Mátészalka.[21] I tried to discover whether there was anyone who could leave and enter the ghetto, apart from those who were authorized to do so. I found out that one of the dentists could leave and that he attended patients in his house opposite the ghetto. As it happened, they needed dentists in Mátészalka. I went to him and when we were alone, told him who I was. He didn't believe me, told me to pray and subjected me to a physical examination. He was a member of the local Jewish Council; an elderly, intelligent and poised man. He was moved to hear that in Budapest they were concerned about the Jews of Mátészalka and had even sent an emissary. Nevertheless, my mission ended in failure. The dentist said frankly that there was no moral strength or will to live among the Jews sealed in the ghetto. Nobody dared to try anything, not even for themselves. Furthermore, nobody would dare to participate in joint schemes. That is, even if we established contact — as in Mátészalka — we achieved nothing, since the first condition for rescue was that the candidate should dare to escape. Even though we endangered the lives of twelve of our youngsters on mass rescue missions, it emerged that the mass rescue of Jews from Hungary's country towns and districts was an impossible mission.

The result was different when we tried to bring organized Halutzim. Here at least, we managed to save individuals. It did happen, that a few of our comrades, on hearing that the movement was rallying to their aid, stayed out of the ghettos, or fled from them. However, it was extremely difficult to survive with no documents, food, or cover. Some of them, sick of the protracted anticipation, set out on their own. Taking advantage of favorable conditions, they actually reached Budapest.

Josef Rosenwasser[22] and Ester Schoen[23] of the Kisvárda cell were rescued after two weeks of starving in a hay-loft until we brought them to Budapest. Josef Jung of Munkács was still a young boy. He hid in a forest, God knows what he lived on. One day he met his school friend, a Gentile, in the forest. Josef persuaded him to go to Budapest and contact the movement to get him money and papers.

With rather mixed feelings, we trusted this simple boy not to inform on our organization and turn us in, even if beaten or tortured.... In the end, after all, he had no contact with us, our aims or our work. Josef Jung arrived. He slept, showered, put on clean clothes, ate his fill — and went into action. He was an energetic lad. We sent him to the Gestapo center with food parcels for the prisoners. During inspection, they cut a loaf of bread in two and found many interesting items: money and documents. Josef was arrested on the spot. But today he is here, a member of Moshav Alonei-Abba.

Miky Gotteszman — today Moshe Golan of Tel Aviv — was sent to Munkács accompanied by a corporal. We did movement work under military cover.

I have mentioned that we also sent soldiers equipped with leave permits to the districts. Later we obtained leave permits and became "soldiers" ourselves. In this way, we got Josef Meir, Jehoshua Weisz and Josef Scheffer[24] out of Pecs.

When Dr. László Somogyi[25] was with the "Kastner group" he gave me two railway documents. We pasted our photographs on the documents, sewed uniforms and I traveled under the name of Imre Benko, an officer of the Hungarian Railways.[26] By chance, I once visited a forced labor camp in one of the districts. I was talking to one of the men when we were approached by a lance-corporal of the guards detachment who made a great fuss and dragged me off to the all-powerful sergeant. He tried to interrogate me. I told him I was not the one who had approached the man I had been talking to, but that he had approached me and asked if his parents' house on Király Street in Budapest had been damaged in the bombardment. While he was checking my papers, the sergeant realized that I was an officer in the department where he worked as a civilian, and that I was his direct superior in rank…. What does a Hungarian junior officer do when he sees his superior? He clicks his heels and comes to attention, saluting and apologizing to the officer for having troubled him…. After which, the sergeant rebukes the lance-corporal for daring to think that a railway officer would approach some Jew. Our comrade was punished with two hours in bonds for having the cheek to address a Hungarian railway officer. The sergeant escorted me to the railway station; he was delighted that I deigned to speak to him at all….

October 15, 1944. This day will forever be remembered for two critical events that took place within two or three hours of each other. That morning Regent Horty broadcast an announcement on the radio declaring that Hungary was ready to lay down its arms and enter into negotiations with the Allies. The announcement was also stunning because it included the declaration that the Germans had imposed their anti-Jewish policy on Hungary. It is easy to imagine the joy that erupted in our ranks, even though we felt that the event was too beautiful…. Indeed, that same day German army divisions appeared on the outskirts of the city and under their auspices the leader of the Arrow Cross Fascist Party, Szálasi, was called on to form a new government. This time, the situation became worse and more dangerous than anything that had happened before in Budapest. The next day, gangs of fascists established a reign of terror in the streets. All exemptions given to Jews were canceled, it was absolutely forbidden to leave the house, and exhilarated, armed gangs rounded up Jews with raised arms. It was a time of wild, spontaneous, terrible bloodshed. Hundreds were led to the banks of the "Beautiful River Danube," where they were stripped naked and shot with automatic weapons; few managed to escape this hell.

In those days of horror, our most urgent task was to muster anew and get our comrades out of the closed houses in which they were trapped and return them to the rescue and defense activities. It was also very important to disrupt the activities of the street gangs, mostly boys of sixteen to seventeen.

Josef Meir and I organized commando patrols for ourselves, as did several other groups from our movement and from Dror. We obtained Arrow Cross uniforms, armbands and arms; we also equipped ourselves with forged command documents used by the Arrow Cross. With the help of these documents, which also included "execution orders," we managed more than once to rescue Jews who were really being led to execution by rioters. Joshka (Josef Meir) wore the uniform and leather coat of a Hungarian-Fascist army officer, and I wore the uniform of a railway officer. We proceeded according to a prepared list and by instinct to places where people were congregating and rioting. Thus one day, we found ourselves going in the direction of Népszinház Street, where there was terrible rioting. Gangs were breaking into houses, indiscriminately dragging people out, mercilessly beating them and shooting them on the spot. The street was running wild and filling with dead and wounded. We joined those units that were leading Jews. We were now an "Execution Squad" and people were handed over to us without difficulty. We went into one house by ourselves because we had been informed that one of our comrades — Jehuda Alpár — was supposed to be there, in his parents' house. It was not easy to maintain the tough facial expression when we heard the weeping and shouting rising from the shelter, when we appeared with our loaded weapons. Jehuda was not among them; apparently he had managed to escape earlier. But his mother fell at our feet, bitterly weeping and pleading for her son's life. She didn't recognize us in those clothes and we could not reveal our identity. We could not obey our natural urge to console her, to speak a few words of comfort and encouragement. This was a lifelong lesson for me.

When we left the house, there was a tragi-comic incident which fortunately ended well. As I was walking with Joshka, a boy of about fourteen popped up. "Look," he yelled, "that's a Jew! That one in uniform's a Jew!" He was the son of Gentile neighbors of ours in my hometown and he recognized me in spite of my costume. Curious onlookers rapidly clustered around us. I could feel the blood thudding in my veins. There was no possibility of withdrawal. I fell on him with threats and shouts, but he persisted. The crowd began its own action, insisting that the matter be cleared up at the police station and closing us in; the situation was getting hot. At that moment, two fellows in Arrow Cross uniform appeared and on hearing what was going on, drew their revolvers, held them to our backs and ordered us to move on. Walking at a brisk pace, they dispersed the crowd and shoved us along until we reached a quiet street. There we fell on their necks.

They were two brave members of Dror, on patrol like us, who had come to our rescue at the last moment.

The idea of the Schutzpass (Protection Pass) came up in November 1944. This project clearly demonstrated the essence of Zionist-Halutz activity. The original concept — which nobody questioned, daring as it was — included several hundred and a little later, several thousand people. For these, proper protection was assured through documentation. The youth movements refused to agree that such protection should be limited to the official framework. Therefore, when all other factors (including official Zionist circles) were trying to keep to the numbers previously fixed in the agreement with the Hungarian authorities, the youth movements saw to it that the Protection Passes were distributed in numbers that made it impossible to keep track of them. The aim was that anyone who asked for a pass would get one; and that's how it was in reality. We forged Protection Passes and supplied them to everyone. We received orders and supplied the "goods." We printed forms and set up a special office with a staff, typewriters, lists, announcers and ushers.[27] In the end, even those involved in the matter did not know what was going on. The Russians were already on the other side of the Tisza River[28]; they preferred to rescue more of our people, with less safety, rather than rescue less under relatively safer conditions.[29] We squeezed the people into "safe houses." The crowded conditions were beyond imagining. We also established "safe camps" in Kolumbusz Street and in Abonyi Street.[30] Here too, there was room for thousands of people.

The establishment of the International Red Cross' Department A was the result of a meeting during which Nathan Komoly said he had managed to convince Friedrich Born,[31] (the International Red Cross special emissary to Hungary), to help in rescuing the children. We held a discussion on the mode of operation and the various tasks. In addition to Komoly, those at the meeting included Dr. Kastner, Offenbach, Hansi Brand, Pil, Rafi and myself, among others.

Department A of the International Red cross included the following branches: the children's branch — under Perec Révész and Zoltán Weiner; the staff branch — under one of the leaders of the Zionist Youth; the economics branch — under Efra Teichmann and Hansi Brand; the political branch — under Nathan Komoly and Rafi Benshalom.

Mothers sat in long rows with their children, and there were also children on their own, in the Central Office in Mérleg Street. At first they came only at the specific times when Jews were allowed free movement, then they came all day long,[32] in order to reach one of the houses, some kind of refuge.

Only the Pioneer Youth knew how to organize all this. Moshe Krausz, director of the (Mandatory) Palestine Office, was able to conceive the idea of Protection Passes, whereas only the Pioneer Youth could turn it into a tool for the rescue of tens of thousands. International Red Cross protection was obtained as a result of the diplomatic activity of Nathan Komoly. However, this protection eventually became an instrument for rescuing the lives of thousands of children when the Youth Movements turned the concept into a reality.[33]

The determination of masses of Jews to live, stimulated us to improvise children's homes every day. We had to supply them with food, equipment, working staff, local and central management — everything. One by one, the homes were established. The first was in Orso Street and the rest were in Budakeszi, Garay, Nürenberg, Percel Mór, Dob, Király, Akácfa, Nagyfuvaros, Lajos, Teleki Pál, Szondy, Munkácsi Mihály, Kövér Lajos, Magdolna and other places. Only one or two were struck[34]; 5,000 children were rescued!

We had to support these little human beings. The economics section, which had its branch office in 6, Merleg Street, was in charge of this. The central storeroom was in Kolumbusz Street. The office staff consisted of some twenty to twenty-five people. Vera Görög[35] was my secretary. About twenty buyers worked with me, most of them veteran food merchants and wholesalers. I had many quarrels with one of them, whose name I do not recall, because by force of habit, he wanted to make a profit on the food!... The unforgettable Uncle Somló[36] was a great help to me. We needed each and every one of our comrades; Josef Schőnberg (Ben Porat)[37] was director of the home on Dob Street. Yamoy[38] was a counselor at one of the homes.

The economics section had to supply the needs of all the children's houses, shelters, and safe houses and we had to provide everything, from the first slice of bread. The ghetto did get an official provisions allowance, but this was not sufficient, of course. It needed to be constantly supplemented. Actually, our task now was to feed all the Jews of Budapest! But Arrow Cross and other army units also turned up frequently, because they too were short of provisions.[39] Uncle Rudi Weisz,[40] a veteran in transportation, was in charge of transport and kept our books in strict order.

The following is a list of provisions taken from the stores of the economics section, between November 28 and the December 23, 1944:

28.11.44: 40 crates of preserved tomatoes — to the central ghetto storeroom
30.11.44: 14,550 Kg flour — to the central ghetto storeroom
30.11.44: 500 Kg coffee substitute — to the central ghetto storeroom
3.12.44: 4,000 Kg beans — to the central ghetto storeroom
3.12.44: 2,000 Kg beans — to the central ghetto storeroom
3.12.44: Various foodstuffs
7.12.44: 10,000 Kg dried noodles
8.12.44: 20,000 Kg Pumpkin for baking
11.12.44: 9,000 Kg barley flakes — to the central ghetto storeroom
13.12.44: 500 Kg hard yellow cheese — to the central ghetto storeroom
15.12.44: miscellaneous — to the central ghetto storeroom
15.12.44: 200 straw mattresses — to the central ghetto storeroom
15.12.44: 5,000 Kg preserved tomatoes — to the central ghetto storeroom
15.12.44: 5,000 Kg flour — to the central ghetto storeroom
15.12.44: 10,000 Kg flour — to the bakery on Holló Street[41]
15.12.44: 2,000 Kg fine coal — to the old people's home on Hungaria Blvd.
16.12.44: 10,000 Kg flour — to the central ghetto storeroom
16.12.44: 14,415 Kg dried peas — to the central ghetto storeroom
16.12.44: 20,000 Kg beans — to the central ghetto storeroom
18.12.44: load of tomatoes — to the central ghetto storeroom
19.12.44: 10,200 Kg flour (204 sacks) — to the ghetto bakery
19.12.44: 10,200 Kg corn flour (120 sacks) — to the ghetto bakery
20.12.44: 1,100 units of eggs — to the central ghetto storeroom
20.12.44: 465 Kg hard yellow cheese — to the central ghetto storeroom
20.12.44: 10,000 Kg white beans — to the central ghetto storeroom
21.12.44: 4,500 fine coal — to the central ghetto storeroom
22.12.44: 100,000 Kg squash — to the central ghetto storeroom
22.12.44: load of dehydrated vegetables — to the central ghetto storeroom
22.12.44: 20,000 Kg shelled dried peas — to the central ghetto storeroom
23.12.44: load of green peas — to the central ghetto storeroom

23.12.44: load of cleaning utensils — to the central ghetto storeroom
23.12.44: 200 straw mattresses — to the central ghetto storeroom
23.12.44: 10,000 Kg salt — to the central ghetto storeroom

(At this time, loads were delivered to the section storeroom from the supply sources; many loads were also sent to the children's home storerooms and other places).

This was the most "prosaic" part of the pioneer activities: the epic of the beans, potatoes and dried noodles. But while hunger, chaos and murder reigned in Budapest, the Jews in and out of the ghettos did not suffer from continuous hunger. We were able to supply amounts sufficient to sustain life. When the Russians entered the city, we still had stocks.

The money — untold amounts — for all these operations was made available to us by JOINT, with the Rescue and Aid Committee as a go-between. About twenty wholesalers did the buying for us; they were the ruling "big sharks" of the food market in Budapest. Transport and storage were carried out by our people, since this was life-endangering. Later, it became necessary to hire Arrow Cross men and Germans for these jobs — at a time when it was impossible to defend our storerooms against the Arrow Cross.

We had a big sugar storeroom near the Western railway station. We received information by telephone that the Arrow Cross had confiscated it. We quickly turned to an old helper of ours — a German sergeant who stood two meters tall. The sergeant enlisted the help of a German soldier and together they deterred the robbers. With the help of our friends, Uncle Somló and I loaded the sacks of sugar onto a truck. We started the engine, everyone jumped onto the truck and then, with a deafening roar, a shell made a direct hit on the storeroom.

This happened three days before the ghetto was liberated.

David Gur's Testimony

I was born in Okany, a village in Hungary. My father was a wood and grain merchant. Remote from Jewish tradition, our family was among the village's ten assimilated Jewish families. I completed my high school education in a Protestant school in a nearby town. Jews made up a small percentage of the student body. While most of the teachers were not noted for their sympathy for Jews, there was no overt antisemitic activity.

In 1943, when I was seventeen — with a matriculation certificate — the gates to the institutes of higher learning were closed to all young Jews. I went to Budapest and began work as an apprentice to a Jewish building contractor. The building workers — both trained and untrained — were antisemitic to a marked degree. An "educated" young Jew like myself was an unusual phenomenon for them. During the day I worked and at night I studied construction draughting.

In September 1943 I looked for and found my way to the underground Hashomer Hatza'ir movement. We held our meetings in private apartments. However, this only lasted from December 1943 until the Germans entered Hungary on March 19, 1944, when the movement went underground again. The movement's main activists came from among the Hungarian-speaking Slovakian refugees who lived in Budapest, some as Jews and some as Aryans. At the end of March, I was equipped with forged Aryan papers, like all the other members of the movement.

Shortly afterwards, thanks to my draughting skills, I was made a member of the team in the forged documents workshop. Later, I became supervisor of the shop until we were caught on Christmas Eve 1944.

The production of forged documents was just a means to an end in the

European underground movements, whereas in Hungary and Budapest it was one of the most important and independent branches of underground work. This fact was due to the special circumstances of the Hungarian underground and the possibilities for Jewish rescue activity. In other countries, the main goals were: armed struggle, sabotage, and active resistance. In Hungary, Jewish underground activity centered — for lack of choice — on rescuing the living. A similar situation prevailed in the non-Jewish Hungarian underground movements. The question arises: Why was there no armed resistance in Hungary? Was this merely by chance?

Some people — unfamiliar with the situation in Hungary at the time — have attempted to compare Hungarian underground activities with those in other countries. In doing so, they overlook some of the objective circumstances that pre-determine the nature of a movement, as well as the fact that the only possible way, under prevailing conditions, was active rescue.

The following factors determined in favor of rescue:

1. **Lack of personnel capable of bearing arms.** Most Jewish men between twenty-one and forty-five had been in service since 1942 in the framework of the special forced labor units, mainly in occupied Russia. Those who had not been mobilized prior to this were called up after the Germans have entered Hungary. It was impossible to organize armed resistance with only women, children and the elderly.

2. **Unfavorable topographical conditions.** Most of Hungary consists of wide, poorly forested plains. The only area with suitable geographic conditions for partisan warfare is the Carpathian Mountains. However, the Jewish population of this area was among the first to be rounded up in ghettos and deported within days after the entry of the Germans.

3. **Lack of time.** With the German occupation, events followed one another with dazzling swiftness. By the time people became aware of what was happening, they found themselves in Auschwitz. The concentration of Jews in local ghettos and their deportation from Hungary was carried out in various parts of the country with maximum efficiency, within a few days. The entire process of the deportation of

Hungarian Jewry (apart from Budapest) was completed within the amazingly short period of six weeks! There was no time to get organized.

With the German occupation of Hungary, the forged-document project acquired major importance.

The regime imposed by the German occupation was based on the exercise of force and violence against the Jews. These actions were camouflaged as the bureaucratic procedure of a seemingly law-abiding state. Government orders were published in the press, on the radio and by bulletins on notice boards. These orders multiplied daily, their content became more and more severe, their range extended further and further and they isolated certain groups of Jews from the Jewish population as a whole. From the day they entered Hungary, the Germans pulled all the strings, sometimes openly and sometimes behind the scenes and their shadows hovered over everything that took place at the time.

To stay alive meant to quickly and carefully evade carrying out the new orders every morning. This had to be accomplished alone by each individual. The only way was with forged Aryan documents. This was made necessary by the constant, strict inspection by the gendarmerie and special police in the streets and public places. Concierges also served this purpose, as the loyal servants of the regime in blocks of apartments. Only those with suitable papers could hope to avoid being deported — that is, to stay alive.

Constant changes of names and addresses required a massive quantity of documentation. In resourceful hands, such documents provided the opportunity and basic conditions for survival. For members of the Halutz movement, the forged papers served mainly as a means of freedom of action in rescuing others.

The remaining ways of rescue — such as, the 'safe houses'[1] under the auspices of neutral embassies (Switzerland, Sweden, the Vatican), or documents that placed individuals beyond the scope of anti-Jewish laws[2] — attested to their Jewish identity and exposed them to German and Arrow Cross terror. On the other hand, the forged papers allowed their owners to remove themselves completely from actions directed against the Jews.

The German Occupation on March 19, 1944 found the Halutz movements more or less prepared, compared to the rest of the Jewish population.

Hungarian Jewry refused to believe for a moment that they would share the fate of European Jewry. Their attempts to demonstrate loyalty, to the point of fawning on the authorities, their lack of resistance, their lack of interest in the problems of the refugees[3] and the Zionist movements (particularly the Halutz movements), was the official line of the leadership.[4] As individuals, the Jews intuitively reacted fearfully, enclosing themselves in the narrow confines of personal destiny and passive anticipation of what lay in store.

The first refugees arrived with the beginning of the expulsion from Slovakia in 1942. In addition to finding accomodation and work for them, it was necessary to provide them with papers. At first, most of the refugees tried to settle down in everyday life as Jews. They acquired copies of forced labor identity cards, or of deceased people; only seldom did they change themselves into Aryans. The main problem was the Police Residential Reports,[5] which had to be forged because nobody wanted to be legally registered with the police. In the beginning, these needs were supplied by professional forgers, naturally at a high price: a resident's permit or identity card cost sixty pengő! The average weekly wage was only forty pengő! Most of the refugees had no fixed employment and fought hard for subsistence; they could not afford the sums demanded. Among the Halutz movements, Hashomer Hatza'ir was the first to decide to solve this important problem, to shake off their dependency on the criminal underworld. They began with the forgery of signatures on the Police Residential Reports. From a technical point of view, this was an exhausting process, because each document had to be made up by hand. Obviously, it was impossible to meet the great demand in this manner.

At the beginning of 1944, Hashomer Hatza'ir decided to turn all its members into Aryans. The first step was to provide the Slovakian refugees with forged Aryan documents. Dan Zimmermann was put in charge of the operation. He worked mainly with original Aryan documents, birth certificates, identity cards, and "Levente" I.D. cards.[6] We copied the required data from the voters' roll, which was open to the public. The information thus obtained could be used in applying to the Population Registry in various areas to get birth certificates, with which it was possible to obtain baptismal certificates, certificates of citizenship, documents testifying to parental origins and many other papers. This was not an unusual activity, since many non-Jews applied for documents, in view of the "Jewish Laws," to prove that neither they nor their ancestors were Jews.

In 1944, the *Haganah* (Israeli Defense Forces) headquarters was founded under Moshe Rosenberg's command. One of their most important tasks was the organization of large scale forged documents. Meno Klein, Dan Zimmermann and Viki Fischer were responsible for carrying out technical operations. The Defense Headquarters, established in 1944, went out of operation after a short period of indecision and attempts to organize. Its only achievement was the establishment of the document forgery workshop. This was the result of the cooperation between Hashomer Hatza'ir and Maccabi Hatza'ir.

In the beginning, Dan worked under temporary conditions, mainly in his own apartment. Later, he moved to the Jewish working boys hostel in Zöldmáli Street, where the staff were members of Hashomer Hatza'ir. Afterwards, when the scope of work expanded he rented an apartment under the assumed name of a university student. As a student, he was able to host a number of friends under the pretext of studying together for examinations. His guests included Mimish, Avri and Michael.

When Dan's flatmate, Nesher Adler, was caught crossing the Romanian border it became necessary, according to underground rules, to leave the apartment at once. Thus the forged document workshop moved to an attic in Bethlen Street,[7] where an 'artist's studio' was established. The studio idea appealed to us and Shraga Weil and I moved in immediately. We hung Shraga'a drawings and paintings on the walls. In addition, there was always a "work in progress" in case of an unexpected visit. Here the stamps were drawn in chemical ink and duplicated by the shapirograph method. The place was used solely for the production of the stamps. The forms were filled in and distributed in various places, by others, in order to guard the secrecy of the central aspect of the operation. The work of filling in and distributing the forms was organized by Efra Teichmann-Agmon. During this time, another branch of the workshop was operating in 5, Nagyatádi Szabó Street,[8] where police residential reports were prepared by the conveyor belt method, under the supervision of Viki Fischer.

The entire workshop staff consisted of amateurs, by any professional standard. There was not one printer, blockmaker or rubber-caster among us. We lacked basic knowledge in every field of technology regarding document and stamp production. Actually, we had talents in other fields. Shraga was a graphic artist, Miky a draughtsman, and I had also passed a course in draughting. Nobody foresaw, or could have foreseen, the professional requirements or the increased strength and scope of the demand for forged documents. In consolidating the workshop team, we were influenced more by considerations of loyalty to the movement, volunteering, and sometimes chance, than by reasons of profession. The team had to invent and improvise, quickly and independently, complex work systems that would normally take years to master. However, in meeting the standards and professional requirements of our work, we learned what we had to know through practice. We discovered how we had to work, how to overcome and bypass difficulties we encountered.

Against this background, the workshop operation stood out as a unique phenomenon in the whole of occupied Europe and the anti-Nazi underground, from the point of view of production methods, quantity, diversity and the massive demand that it supplied.

The main methods of operation were:

a. **Drawing.** Some stamps were hand drawn directly onto the documents with black ink or stamp pad ink. This was done mainly at the beginning, when the scope of operations had not yet expanded.

b. **Copying the stamp.** This was done by using chemical ink on transparent drawing paper. The sample was placed on a gelatinous sheet — a Shapirograph — which allowed us to produce twenty to twenty-five stamps in twenty-four hours. We received our first Shapirograph from Slovakia. After a while, the surface was damaged and the stamps developed a halo. Hence, we began experimenting with a material for the shapirograph produced from gelatin and glycerin. With this method we produced all the stamps we needed in only limited quantities.

c. **Ordering stamps.** Using the above method, we stamped an order form and a regular stamp factory supplied us with ready-made stamps.

d. **Montage.** When we did not manage to get a suitable order form, or when it was particularly dangerous to produce one — for example, in cases where we needed government or military stamps[9] (which included the crown and Hungarian state emblem) which private individuals could not order — we had to use a complicated method. We ordered generalized versions of stamps, from which we assembled the required version by cutting the text into separate letters and re-pasting them. This work demanded dexterity as well as cleverness, design and montage skills. Miky Langer was great at this work. With methods c and d we obtained 150-170 different stamps, which we re-used in any required amount.

e. **Steel framed lead letters.** This method was rather clumsy and did not stand the test of precise comparison with the original. However, when we were producing the police residential reports we had no choice but to use it, mainly in April-May 1944 when we had to print great quantities of these documents. In October-November, we again faced this problem, because Budapest was flooded with Hungarian refugees from the east of the country, fleeing from the Russians and Jews escaping from the Death Marches from Budapest to Vienna. We could be inventive in the production of country district documents, because it was no longer possible to check the validity of the data.

f. **Authentic original documents and forms.** A certain type of document was available on the open market, because the non-Jewish population also needed forms. We bought vast quantities of these from various sales counters. Another type, not on open sale, was partly supplied to us by "sympathizers" (such as a Protestant priest of Jewish origin, a population registry clerk whose first husband was Jewish, etc.) and resistance groups.

g. **Altering original documents.** In certain cases, we washed original documents in chemicals, partly or wholly erasing what was written, replacing it with different data or style.

h. **Self-duplicating.** The basis of the document was a form duplicated by us in the workshop: Polish birth certificates, various Aliens Control[10] documents, Refugee Certificates and so on.

The forged documentation in itself did not provide sufficient protection during street inspections and did not overcome the danger of prolonged stay in shelters during alerts. The forged paper had psychological value; it gave its holder the basis for a confident facade — since anyone who did not appear natural and confident would not be saved even if he had a document in his pocket. One needed to know which document to present and when to present it. During a street inspection, if someone took out a sheaf of papers, he was immediately suspect. The rank and file Christian citizen had nothing more than a residence permit and identity card. Minors now and then might have a Levente document and, later, one from the military industries.

Others fell into a different kind of extremism: they went about with no papers at all. They asserted that a Christian did not have to prove that he was Hungarian and not Jewish. But these were extreme cases, not in any way typical. Forged documents and suitable appearance of their holders were helpful in most cases.

Shortly after the German occupation of Hungary, the order of the Yellow Star was imposed.[11] Those Halutz movements whose people had been Aryanized, as mentioned above, assumed underground discipline. Some Jewish leaders did not approve of this.[12] Voices were raised accusing us of separating ourselves from Jewish destiny. "The Yellow Star should be worn with pride! It is sanctification of God's Name!" they claimed. As time passed, these voices fell silent. Our daily lives were organized on a conspiratorial basis: division into cells, communication, prohibition of group meetings.

However, the inexperience of the underground way of life, sense of isolation that created attractions between people, unavoidable contact with the criminal world — smugglers, forgers — whose services we needed, all these brought disaster and mass arrests in the early stages of organizing the underground. Our comrade Avri Lissauer wanted to open the way to Tito's partisans, but instead of reaching Yugoslavia, he fell into the hands of the Gestapo and from there was sent to the Mauthausen Death Camp. Misho Neumann was arrested, some weapons and the first and only printing equipment, which had not even managed to go into production, went down with him.

The only place where we could meet, under cover of course, was the congregation hall and Jewish Council at 12, Síp Street. Here, deserters from the forced labor units were gathered and escape groups set out for Romania. Those who had been Aryanized received their documents here. The Department of the

Districts, in which Moshe Rosenberg played a central role, became the departure base for Halutzim dispatched to the country ghettos. This was the only contact with those ghettos. The Halutzim transferred various permits, forged documents and information to almost all country communities. They endangered their lives in doing this, because since the German occupation, railway travel was forbidden to Jews. The comrades whose Jewish appearance made it dangerous to travel with Aryan documents were given forged papers from the Information Department of the Jewish Council, where our comrades Jenő Kolb and Yehuda Weiss worked. These documents were recognized in some districts. As stated on the document, "The Jewish Council confirms that the holder may travel to Budapest".... At the time, during the deportation of the country ghettos, a document allowing departure for Budapest was a great concession; to gain time was to stay alive.

The artist's studio was a good idea in itself, but the neighbors' curiosity and imagination were boundless: they spread the gossip that the studio was a secret radio station and it reached the ears of the police. Luckily, the police came at a time when there was nobody in the studio. When we heard what had happened from the confused report of a well-meaning neighbor, we immediately left with Shraga, taking the best of the equipment with us.

Since we didn't have a new place for the workshop, we took the suitcases with their highly incriminating contents to my apartment at 7, Veres Pálné Street, as a temporary measure.[13] Yet this was inadequate, even as a temporary solution. A few days later, Hansi Brand offered her apartment. This was after her husband Yoel had flown to Turkey, as an emissary of the Germans, on approximately May 22-24.[14] The day I moved the suitcase to the Brand apartment at 15, Semsey Andor Street,[15] Hungarian counter espionage arrested all the members of the Aid and Rescue Committee, including Hansi Brand. Her home was searched. We knew nothing about the search, except that all our equipment was lost: forms, stamps, chemicals, work tools, everything. Its practical worth was beyond estimation. It was the product of hours of backbreaking labor that during many months. Could we replace what had been taken? To reproduce it in a turbulent world, under pressure of the riots, when the country ghettos were being deported at dizzying speed? Each hour, each minute that the workshop was out of operation, determined life and death. We had to find out at all costs what had really happened in the Brand apartment, in spite of the fear that the place was under surveillance. I undertook this task.

Pil followed me at a distance of twenty to thirty meters with a loaded revolver, to come to my assistance if necessary or to report on my fate, in case of a disaster.

Pil stayed at the entrance to the house and I went into the apartment. I found old Mrs. Brand, Yoel's mother, alone. She gave me the suitcase at once. She had hidden it under the bed in her little room. Happy and moved, I went out, knowing that Pil was covering me. I took the suitcase back to Veres Palne Street and, in time, we re-established the workshop in the apartment of "Uncle" Federit. The house at 1, Darázs Street[16] was a residential building in Buda and seemed suitable.

The daily visits by Shraga and myself did not attract attention. Through "Uncle" Federit we made the acquaintance of a Protestant priest who gave us a considerable number of forms and birth, marriage and baptismal certificates — most of which had original stamps. In this period, we also received original forms, although in smaller quantities, from a number of other sources. For example, from a Christian woman who was the widow of a Jew and worked at the Population Registry. She endangered herself by coming without fail to underground meetings, bringing original forms for birth and marriage certificates.

I must mention my meetings with the two parachutists from Mandatory Palestine. I met Yoel Palgi at Yehuda Weiss' apartment, three days after he arrived in Budapest, and gave him a set of documents for two people. I spent almost a whole day with Perec Goldstein. I changed his documents and guided him around the hostile, foreign city. This was after Yoel Palgi's arrest and one day before Perec turned himself over to the Gestapo.[17]

Until June 24, all the Jews of Budapest, who were made to wear the Yellow Star, were concentrated in special, marked houses. We had to change places because of this and also because "Uncle" Federit had gone to the temporary camp in Kolumbusz Street on June 27, prior to joining the Aid and Rescue Committee's Train, which was to leave three days later. We rented an apartment at 52 Kerepesi Street,[18] declaring that it was to be used as an art studio. Shraga and I moved into the new place to start working, but Shraga soon had to leave for Slovakia and I was on my own.

The day after Shraga left, a bomb that was apparently aimed at the nearby industrial plants, hit the house on Kerepesi Street. What we called the "studio set" was damaged, but the main equipment was fortunately spared when a table was thrown onto it by the blast, saving it from damage. The bombardment halted the tram connection for a few days and I had to carry the precious, heavy suitcase for many kilometers until I reached my apartment in the city center.

At this time, my flatmate took the escape routes to Romania, on the way to Palestine. I moved into Efra and Cipi Teichmann-Agmon's apartment at 19 Retek Street.[19] Here, I continued the work of forging documents, mainly on my own and with occasional help from Efra.

In the period between the concentration of Budapest Jewry and Szálasi's rise to power, relative calm prevailed regarding the demand for forged documents. The activity continued to a lesser degree: doccuments for escapees from the labor camps, for changes of address, etc. There was no room for more comprehensive activity, since after Romania dropped out of the war in August 1944, the border was hermetically sealed and the Hungarian authorities eased up on persecution, for a while. Horthy also hoped to break off his pact with the Germans. His attempt failed, however, and government passed to Szalasi and his cohorts. For the Jews of Budapest, this meant terror in the streets, cold-blooded killings, wild mob incitement against the remaining Jews. The terror was fed by deep hatred, but it also helped to distract attention from military activity on the front.

The "Jewish Houses" no longer provided any relative quiet or safety. The occupants were deported in the direction of the Danube. In November, the Death March to the Austrian border began. Past experience, the lessons learned from earlier events, were of no use now.

Special stratagems were required in order to "extricate" even one person from the closed houses. Movement people dressed in Arrow Cross uniforms, as "Levente," as auxiliary security men.[20] In these uniforms, carrying weapons and Direct Orders,[21] or with execution orders, they rescued people from the "Jewish Houses." The members of Dror displayed special courage and resourcefulness in these operations.

The terror operations finally prompted the neutral legations to act. "Protected Houses" were established under the auspices of neutral countries. The legations issued protection certificates in limited amounts to those who were entitled to live in the "Protected Houses." We helped them, while issuing wholesale, self-produced Swiss, Swedish and Vatican protection papers. Demand for the Swiss papers grew so great that our workshop became too small. Therefore, we established our own "legation" opposite the Swiss one, in Szabadság[22] Square. From early morning till late at night people — among them many Christians — gathered here to get protection papers for themselves or their Jewish acquaintances. Nobody was refused. According to estimates, every second Budapest Jew was in possession of some sort of protection document.

These documents produced miracles, mainly in the beginning: entire forced labor units were brought back from the German-Hungarian border. It was even possible to save people from the Death Marches to Hegyeshalom,[23] or from execution on the banks of the Danube, if we could get these protection papers to them in time.

After October 15, there were inspection barriers at the bridges over the Danube. Most of the movement people were concentrated on the left bank of the river, in Pest, where the ghetto and "Protected Houses" were. Air raids were frequent. We feared that we would be cut off from the arena of operations and our comrades. Therefore Efra and I moved from his apartment in Buda to Pest. I went to live with the Pil sisters in 52 Damjanich Street.[24]

From mid-July, the workshop was in 93 Rózsa Street,[25] under cover of a soyabean factory. This cover was provided by an anti-fascist Italian by the name of Rossi,[26] a connection made through Perec Révész of Maccabi Hatza'ir. His Italian citizenship gave him special status in Hungary. Miso Wetzler, Endrei Feigenbaum and, later, Miky Langer worked with me in the workshop. Efra Teichmann-Agmon and Feri Eisenberg took care of distribution of the papers.

Mob terror by the Arrow Cross was not aimed solely at Jews. The rope was tightening around liberal circles and the workers movement and it finally shook them out of their lack of action. First and foremost, they also needed forged documents for any operation. They began to look for us and did succeed in finding us. We, the Jewish rescue movement, were the one and only active organization. They needed us, because only we could supply them with first-class forged documentation.

Some of the main underground groups that established permanent contact with us were:

Van der Vaas[27] and his group, which contained British and Dutch officers who were escapees from German POW camps. Among others, I supplied them with Swiss birth certificates.

Van der Vaas acquired weapons, since he had excellent contacts with liberal Hungarian and anti-German military circles. Following his escape, Yoel Palgi re-established contact with us through Van der Vaas.

We had extensive contact with the Pál Demény group of the workers' underground movement. We supplied them with documents and they made hiding places available to us in factories in the fourteenth district; mainly for those of our comrades who simply could not be housed in the "Glass House" on Vadász Street for lack of space. Efra Teichmann-Agmon kept in touch with them and managed to house the constant flow of comrades from the forced labor units and the "Jewish Houses."

Futó Galambos represented the official Communist Party line in the underground. Through him, our documents reached the leaders of the illegal Communist party, including Károly Kiss.[28]

Our comrade, Josef Meir (Joshka Megyeri in the underground) developed contacts with a number of military groups and members of the workers' movement, as well as with some Arrow Cross units which were working against the official Arrow Cross, mainly those who patrolled and guarded the ghetto.

Lieutenant Iván Kádár,[29] represented university student circles, the officers who had a hand in the uprising, Vilmos Tartsay[30] and László Sólyom.[31] Iván Kádár was one of the few who were able to make a valuable contribution.

György Nonn[32] escaped from the notorious military prison on Margit Avenue.[33] He found his way to us through Josef Meir.

Pál Fábry,[34] a clerk in the foreign office, represented Hungary's minor aristocracy and "gentry."[35] He was among those able and willing to help, although his contribution was doubtful.

To complete the picture, we wish to mention the names of some among the many for whom we provided forged documents, and who have held important positions in Hungarian public life:

Tibor Déry[36] and Iván Boldizsár,[37] among the pillars of literature, József Köböl,[38] Lajos Drahos[39] and György Markos[40] — who held key positions in the Hungarian trade unions, government and the party.

There were many others who received our false papers indirectly. László Rajk[41] and Péter Gábor,[42] who later held central positions in the Hungarian Communist Party, received documents from our workshop. Other communist activists were equipped with documents from our workshop, such as: Mátyás Timár,[43] Béla Szilágyi,[44] Gyula Mikala[45] and Károly Klement.[46]

The soyabean factory was only a cover, but this cover could not be maintained for very long without actual activity. The concierge had been coming to sniff around more and more often — it was time for us to disappear again. One of our newest contacts, Pál Fábry, had found us a suitable place in the bookstore of Virág Móric,[47] in Baross[48] Street. Her father was Zsigmond Móric,[49] the renowned author, who was among the thirty-eight leaders of Hungary's cultural life who signed the petition against the violation of civil rights, at the time when the first anti-Jewish law was being conceived, in 1938. We were not the only ones to be kindly received; Virág Móric also hosted a long line of deserting army officers. For this reason, we thought it better to get out of there after a day. One hour after we left, the Gestapo arrived.

Our next stop was at 14 Nádor Street.[50] We left the same evening owing to an encounter with a policeman, as we did not observe the blackout precautions.

After this, we were helped by Iván Kádár, the communist. He arranged a "safe" place for us in a building owned by the fascist students' organization, Csaba,[51] on the premises of the Academy of Science, in Baross Street. Here we posed as an auxiliary security unit, dressed accordingly. We had a few calls from students volunteering to join us. During this period, the workshop did not operate exclusively for the Jewish underground; it grew into a serious asset to serve the whole Resistance Movement. The equipment consisted of six suitcases. We were capable of producing any document used in Europe. All of us — Feigi, Miki, Misho and I — spent the entire day working diligently in the workshop, without rest, without pausing even to eat. We would leave the place only when absolutely necessary.

In mid-December, the Russian steamroller reached the gates of Budapest. Various mobilization orders were published one after another; first, the exemption for military industries plants, grade C, was annulled. The workers had to leave for Germany. The exemption for grade A and B plants was also annulled after a while. The government offices moved to West Hungary. The Levente leaders were transported to central Germany by S.S. trucks. Everyone was urged, of their own free will, to move to the West. One could walk in the streets only on special errands, with "Direct orders" or with special disability certificates. It was dangerous to be in the streets after dark; people were shot without reason, personal accounts were settled by informing. The fate of anyone suspected of communism was sealed. There were many Jews with "Protection documents," but these documents gave no protection and Jews were hiding in cellars, in bomb-damaged buildings, often with no papers at all. A slip of paper meant life to them.... Only a slip of paper. Something.... A paper from the Foreign Ministry certifying some function, an exemption from the War Ministry — these had the power to ensure that they could remain in Hungary with the hope of rescue. Those who were ordered to go to Germany, could stay. Those who chose active resistance, needed documents from László Vajnay's Arrow Cross unit,[52] the Skull-Legion,[53] and the Prónay Unit,[54] in order to carry out their night missions: eliminating Arrow Cross groups, attacks, raids to obtain arms, ammunition and vehicles, exploding arms dumps. We worked feverishly, without pause; we knew this was the end. Every moment, every slip of paper meant human life, successful missions, sabotage, contribution to the struggle for liberation.

All movement members were engaged in saving people. Jews, communists and the bourgeois all placed their hope in us, in our piece of paper. We were the support of all those waiting for the liberators, we were the ones who cleared the way for their coming. Our work was the basis and pre-condition for all other activities.

Feri was arrested at the beginning of December. In accordance with the basic underground law, we acted quickly. We immediately left the workshop, taking all our equipment. The work, on which so many lives depended, had to continue. We trusted Feri, but this was not enough. Until we knew clearly what would happen to him, we had to leave the place at once. Temporary interruption of our work would cause less damage to the whole underground than the loss of equipment and means of production. We had not a moment to waste; we packed and left. But where would we find, in this crumbling world, in the general chaos, another more or less suitable place where we could go with all our equipment? A place where four or five young people, who should long since have gone to Germany, could stay? We were helpless. We hid the suitcases in Erzsi, Hava and Bruhi's[55] apartment. We mobilized everybody: Workshop! Workshop!

We began to search. A day passed, another, a week…nothing. Who was letting apartments or shops in Budapest, in the middle of December, 1944? Even if we found something, we couldn't feel secure. Ten days had gone by already. Requests were coming from all sides, they pressed us and finally, demanded. Accusations flew: You are saboteurs! And threats: You'll pay for this after the war!

Day and night we scoured the city for a place for our workshop. We got most of our assistance from Futó Galambos; however, his suggestion that we pretend to make short films in an abandoned studio, at the end of December, so close to the frontline, seemed out of the question. Pál Demény offered a safe place for us in Zugló,[56] where there were a number of chemical plants that were completely under his control. He would also place armed sentries around the place. This experienced labor leader, who had twenty-five years of underground activity behind him, did not understand that what we needed, was not armed protection, but an unsuspected place, a roof over our heads, and a suitable alibi. Another day or two passed. We were afraid of a forced solution.

Miky was a designer-draughtsman, almost an architect, and since his escape from Slovakia had worked in Budapest's Municipal Building Department, in the seventh district. He had formed close relationships with his fellow employees. Now, in December, inspectors that Miky knew well were the only ones left in the department. Having no choice, we decided to reveal our secret to them and ask them to let us work in a back room at the office. It was the only place that provided both an alibi and the required camouflage.

On the December 21,[57] we moved into the first floor of 13 Erzsébet Circle. We were arrested shortly afterwards. On that day, the production of forged documents in our workshop came to an end.

In nine months of operation, we managed to produce a considerable quantity of papers. To give some idea of the scope of our work, I present the following list of the types and quantities our workshop produced:

LIST OF FORGED DOCUMENTS

Type	Units	Originals
Birth Certificate	10,000	500
Marriage Certificate	8,000	300
Personal I.D. Card	10,000	150
Catholic Baptismal Certificate	3,000	300
Catholic Marriage Certificate	1,500	100
Protestant Baptismal Certificate	1,200	
Protestant Marriage Certificate	750	
Unitarian Baptismal Certificate	50	
Unitarian Marriage Certificate	300	
Polish Birth Certificate, printed	300	
Polish Birth Cert., duplicated	300	
Polish Birth Certificate, typed	150	
Slovak Birth Certificate	80	
Slovak Baptismal Certificate	80	
Slovak Residential Identification	200	
Croatian Baptismal Certificate	5	
Swiss Birth Certificate	5	
Death Certificate	80	
Book of school-grades (by subject, index)	25	
Matriculation Certificate	7	(washed)
Junior High Certificate	2	
Student Identity Card (polytechnic)	10	
University Students, "St. Imre" Institute (Catholic)	20	

Military exemption cards (with photograph) stating that the bearer worked in military industry and did not have to join the army or go to Germany:

Type	Units	Originals
Hungarian Wolfram Factory, Kremenetzky	2,500	
Hungarian Steel Co. Ltd.	1,500	
Haverland	600	
Weisz Manfred, Atheneum, Terla, Mikron, Kárpát Furniture, Weltzl, etc.	800	
I.D Card of VI-XII District Police H.Q	2,000	

Identity cards without photograph:

Type	Units	Originals
Mabi (health insurance)	30	
Fortuna Commercial Co. Ltd.	60	
Sevics Luggage Shop	30	
Terla Pharmaceutical Co.	40	
Ministry of Foreign Affairs	25	
Embassy of San Salvador	50	
Embassy of Paraguay	50	
Embassy of Switzerland	120	
Refugee Certificate	2,000	
Swiss Schutzpass (protection pass)	120,000	
Swedish Shutzpass	30	
Vatican Shutzpass	450	
American Citizenship Certificate (valid also after USA joined Allies)	15	
American Citizenship Certificate — from KEOKH Szeged (as above)	25	

Slovakian citizenship certification for Slovakian refugees who did not speak

Hungarian. (Fascist Slovakia was Germany and Hungary's ally. The certificates were very useful to bearers):

Type	Units	Originals
Slovakian Citizenship Certificate	30	
As above, permission from KEOKH to stay in the capital	80	
Slovakian passport	12	
Slovakian, Bulgarian visas	20	
KEOKH Yugoslavian Citizenship	45	
KEOKH Polish Citizenship	45	
KEOKH pass of Szentendre	300	
KEOKH pass, Tab, residence permit	200	
KEOKH travel permit of Szatmárnémeti	50	
Citizenship Certificate	200	
Residency Certificate/"Police Residential Report" (character, residence, occupation, taxes)	4,000	
Gestapo Certificate	20	
Arrow Cross Certificate	170	
Arrow Cross open orders	250	
Levente I.D. card	450	
Military I.D. card	70	
Military Paybook	120	
Discharge Certificate (Military)	180	
Immediate call-up order (Military)	50	
Travel pass (Military)	25	
Temporary leave pass (Military)	700	
Direct order (Military)	400	
Disability certificate (Military)	3,500	100
Food Authority (sugar) ration card validation	7,000	
Police Residential Report	60,000-80,000	

The Arrow Cross detectives came in search of Jews and found us. This arrest was the result of our own negligence and stupidity. We had left our revolvers in our jackets, in the hall. Feigi and I began to unpack one of the suitcases, feverishly looking for the other revolvers. However, the detectives entered before we found the weapons. One of them pushed the door of the small, dark room. "There's someone here!" he shouted, poking his revolver into the doorway. He shouted again and cocked his revolver.

We had no choice but to come out. They tied us up and confiscated our watches, money, valuables, fountain pens — and the interrogation began.

They opened the suitcases only later, when they were looking for something to steal. Actually, it was only then that they realized who we were. Hoping that we had a large sum of money on us they began to beat us and ask questions. They tried to break open the Municipality's steel safe, certain that they had uncovered a far-reaching underground base.

One of the interrogators went through every apartment in the building, checking the occupants' documents. One of the tenants phoned the police and informed them that drunk Arrow Cross men were causing a disturbance in the building. The policeman they sent did not dare enter the building alone and asked for an emergency squad from the Arrow Cross Party offices in the seventh district. Meanwhile, we tried to reach a compromise agreement with the Arrow Cross. We offered them 10,000 pengő to let us go.

But, unfortunately for us, the emergency squad arrived. They also beat us, robbed the apartment and, at nine o' clock, took us to the party headquarters in Erzsebet Blvd. The six suitcases contained documents for the whole of Europe, starting with a "Tito Note," going on to a certificate of the Arrow Cross armed unit, a Swiss passport, Hungarian army booklets and permits from military industries. They regarded us as a "big catch," which was lucky for us.

An hour before we came, they took a group of fourteen to fifteen people to the Danube. On their return, the murderers reported the details: "One was still moving...still shouting...we shot again..." and so on. They looked at us indicating that the same fate awaited us the following day.... Close to midnight, they let us be. We used the time to destroy the documents we still had in our pockets; we chewed and swallowed them. As a result, they didn't discover where we were living. At midnight, they lined us up, removed our overcoats, sweaters and shoes. They demanded our personal data. Naturally, they found excuses to beat every one of us.

They broke a rubber truncheon on Miky Langer, because the Jews of Slovakia had, as it were, given Benes[58] a thousand planes. Feigi was thrown into the corridor for mentioning his father, who was one of the founders of the Hungarian Party in Nové Zámky.[59] I was beaten because they did not believe that, at my age, I had passed the matriculation examination. They then ordered us to organize the rich material, with which they were unfamiliar. We began by removing things from the suitcases. We threw whatever we could into the wastepaper baskets under the table. With the rest, we disposed of the order envelopes, which bore the code and the name of the person making the order. In this way we destroyed the incriminating material, leaving no trace and ensuring that nobody was turned in. The Arrow Cross amused themselves with trying out the stamps, of which there were over 150. For some reason, they liked the colorful forms. They pulled out an Italian school certificate at random and asked which of us had made it. Feigi said it was not made by us. For which they fell on him and beat him senseless. They used clubs and chairs on him, kicking wherever they could reach.

They moved Miky Langer to the other room, and until Feigi regained consciousness, "dealt with him." From midnight until five o' clock, we were beaten without a break. They stripped us to our underpants, the better to see their blows on sensitive parts of our bodies. The fourteen to fifteen year old boys were the cruelest. Ambitious to prove themselves to their elders, they intensified their blows. The victim's groans and cries were fuel for the flames. But, in spite of the cruel "treatment," not one of us broke or handed over any kind of information — neither names nor addresses.

My turn for "personal attention" came later. Since I was the youngest, I suffered relatively less than the others. They wanted to know the location of the communists' printing press and our relations with them. This was because they found some issues of "Szabad Nép" and a copy of a "Tito Promisory Note."[60] The troops slowly grew tired and allowed us to sit down. They presented us as a special phenomenon to the dignitaries who began to arrive after seven o' clock. By this time, Miky was in the worst shape; there were blue circles around his eyes, his face and body were covered in bleeding wounds. They sat us at a distance from one another in the corridor.

At about eleven o' clock, we saw Miky, who had till then been sitting withdrawn in a corner, and collapsed. We were powerless to give him any real assistance. We tried desperately to help him: we seated him on a chair, gave him water, rubbed his body, tried giving him artificial respiration. But his condition was worsening by the minute, his pulse weakened, his breathing became irregular and his heart stopped. Our dearly loved comrade died in our arms. Despite our agitation, we were unable to stop the brutal, vicious Arrow Cross men from giving him a few more kicks and stripping him of his clothes before removing his body. We were left without Miky....

In the afternoon, detectives experienced in criminal interrogation arrived from police headquarters and tried to influence us by psychological means. They then drove us under armed escort to the military prison in Margit Blvd.

By then the material, which had filled six suitcases, had shrunk to fill four: the "Brothers"[61] kept a few fine souvenirs for themselves, such as eight revolvers, a duplicating machine, food-ration cards, etc.

In Margit Blvd., we were taken to Lieutenant Balassa.[62] The following day we learned that Zvi Goldfarb, of Dror, was also imprisoned there, together with a group of people who had been discovered in two bunkers. On the afternoon of December 23, Feigi was summoned for interrogation. He had suffered severe concussion from the earlier blows and was unable to eat or stand on his feet, so I went instead of him, limping and doubled over.

After a few electric shock softening-up exercises, they took some items at random from the suitcases: for example, one Protection Pass (Schutzpass) and one stamp. Even when I was telling the truth, they didn't believe me. They mentioned all the Zionist leaders and asked if I knew them, who had done what, and where? They were pleased that they had finally been given someone from Hashomer Hatza'ir as well as members of Dror.

They promised another interrogation on the following day, with protocols. With this, the beating phase came to an end and it was time for the verdict....

I discovered later, that since I had not come home from the workshop to sleep, Pil understood that I had been caught. They began to look for me at once. They learned that we were being held at the Arrow Cross Party building in the seventh district. As they were working for our release, we were moved to Margit Blvd.

On December 24, Christmas Eve, the Russian assault on Budapest began. That same evening the officials of the National Seat of Prosecution left the prison on Margit Blvd. Only the professional jailers remained. However, the officials of the National Seat of Prosecution were too late: they could not get through the surrounded city in time, so they returned to the prison, dressed for a journey and armed to the teeth.

The Margit Blvd. prisoners were separated into two groups: Jews in one and Christians in the other. The Christians were taken away and we Jews also expected to be taken to our deaths, or to be machine gunned on the spot. But nothing happened that day or the next. Actually, on December 25, we had already begun to negotiate with our jailers. We offered them money — millions. But they wanted guarantees, documents of protection from the Allies' delegates, ensuring that nothing would happen to them when the war was over. We promised everything.

We considered all possibilities of escape. We planned a ladder of sheets and hangers, but this never went beyond the planning stage.

We were called on parade in the afternoon[63] and made to stand in rows. An officer of the City Command appeared and read lists of names. The jailers' faces indicated that our fate was sealed. But the list sounded strange. Among the names being called, some were not even in the prison. The names of those present did not match those on the list. Apparently, whoever had compiled the list did not know for sure who was actually in the prison. We took advantage of the confusion and did not respond. Suddenly I noticed a name that was read: Tibor Rapos Farkas.

Rapos was the name I had assumed when I was living in the apartment with Pil. He was the only one who knew this name. In the street, I used the original papers of Tibor Farkas.[64] My first act on being arrested, was to eat the paper under the name of Tibor Rapos, to protect Pil.

I understood at once that Pil had a hand in this. I identified myself as Tibor Rapos and stepped forward. The others, seeing what I did, followed suit. The guards did not understand this peculiar behavior, but were happy to get rid of us, so that they would have as few prisoners as possible when the Russians arrived. Therefore they did not check the issue of names very carefully; they took out the whole group of those who had willingly come forward, being sure that we were going to our deaths.

We marched through the empty streets of Buda escorted by soldiers armed with sub-machine guns. The officer of the City Command played his part very well. When we crossed the Lánc Bridge over the Danube, I turned, at the head of seventeen of our people and, without a word, headed for the central party headquarters in 17, Wekerle Sandor Street (one of the houses under the protection of the Swiss legation).

"How did you know?" the officer asked in amazement.

When I saw my friends waiting for us at the entrance to the building, I understood the true meaning of brothers in arms. I was happy to have been rescued by my friends.

The ruse was repeated the next morning, with a new list that we helped to compile. Those who were still in Fő Street., mainly communists and members of Dror[65] were also taken from the prison, ostensibly to their execution.

Budapest was surrounded. A Ukranian unit captured the city, house by house. Anyone in the streets was in danger of his life. Katyusha shells were exploding all the time. I was living with Mimish near the City Park, in the Sixth Quarter,[66] when I was liberated by the Red Army on January 17, 1945.

THE WANDERINGS OF THE FORGED DOCUMENTS WORKSHOP IN 1944

1. The Apprentice's Home, Zöldmáli St. (Operator: Dan Zimmerman).
2. 86, Izabella St. (Operators: Dan, Avri Fischer, Mimish, David Gur).
3. 12, Bethlen Gábor St. (Operators: Dan, Shraga Weil, David Gur).
4. 7, Veres Pálné St. (Operator, tenant: David Gur).
5. 25, Szigetvári St. (Operators: Viki Fischer, Misho Wechsler).
6. Semsey Andor St. (Operator: David Gur).
7. 1-3, Darázs St. (Operators: Shraga, David).
8. 52, Kerepesi St. (Operators: Shraga, David).
9. 19, Retek St. (Operator, tenants: David Gur).

10. 93, Rózsa St. (Operators: David, Misho, Miky, Feigi).
11. 52, Damjanich St. (Operator, tenant: David)
12. Bookshop in Baross St. (Operators: David, Misho, Miky, Feigi).
13. 24, Nádor St. (Operators: David, Misho, Miky, Feigi).
14. Baross St., Csaba students organization (Operators: David, Misho, Miky, Feigi).
15. 9th District, Erzsi, Hava and Bruhi's apartment, (storage only)
16. 13, Erzsébet Circle (Operators: David, Miky, Feigi).

Arrest and destruction of the workshop: December 21, 1944.

Cwi Erez
Hungarian Jewry in World War II

At the outbreak of World War II, there were some 530,000 Hungarian citizens who declared their religion as Jewish and some 80,000 Christians of Jewish origin. In the twelve months preceding the outbreak of the war, Hungary doubled its area. In October 1938 and March 1939, vast areas, taken from Hungary under the Trianon Peace Treaty in 1920, were returned to the Crown together with a considerable Jewish population.

Thanks to the extensive diplomatic backing of Nazi Germany, Hungary re-annexed part of what had been, so to speak, stolen from it. Owing to the annexation of Austria in March 1938, the Third Reich became Hungary's western neighbor. It was not only due to this fact and direct Nazi influence, but mainly owing to pressure from internal Hungarian elements, that calamity struck the hundreds of thousands of Jewish citizens on September 1, 1939 in the form of discriminatory legislation. The process had been going on since 1920, when Law 25, the "Numerus Clausus Law," was passed in the Hungarian parliament. This law made Hungary the first country in twentieth century Europe to renew discrimination against citizens for being Jewish. The law, which was intended to prevent certain professions from being flooded with Jews, led to Hungarian Jews being sent to the death camps two decades later.

In the early 1920s, Hungarian Jewry ignored the significance of "restricted numbers." It drew much encouragement from the fact that this law had been modified in 1928. At the time, Regent Horty and his Prime Minister, Count Bethlen, wished to improve Hungary's economy through loans from the West, which they hoped to encourage by refraining from adopting blatantly anti-semitic policies.

Ten years later, before Austria was annexed to Germany, the then Prime Minister made a speech in one of the country towns in which he voiced all the arguments that had been silenced till then. In essence: The Jews were too prominent in many spheres and did not work for the good of the State. In order to correct these social distortions, it followed that Jewish influence had to be curtailed. In fact, the "Jewish Problem" was being presented in all its severity and urgency; the governing elite was determined to solve the problems that beset the people and the government, by ousting the Jews and transferring their status and property to Hungarians in need of status and income.

Law #15/1938 exposed the weakness of Hungarian Jewry. It was a young Jewish group that believed it had succeeded in blending with the majority. From an organizational point of view, Hungarian Jewry consisted of three separate congregational frameworks. The heads of these organizations fought among themselves to gain the most titles and honors in the Hungarian public. The bourgeois was dominant on congregational committees and the presence of the small merchants, clerks and tradesmen, who were the majority among Hungarian Jews, had a disproportionate effect. But it should not be assumed that, even if the Jewish representation had been drawn from circles with personal and trade connections with their Hungarian colleagues, it would have succeeded in preventing the approaching catastrophes.

Due to the first anti-Jewish law, some 20,000 Jews, mainly in the free professions, lost their income. In 1938, the country's High Court decreed that Judaism was not a religion, but a race. The Hungarian Parliament authorized the new definition by an absolute majority. Only a few social-democrats and liberals opposed it. The gist of the decrees — active Jewish participation in the economy — was limited to twenty percent.

The second anti-Jewish law (#2/1939) was already founded on racism. However, it contained certain concessions for those who had converted till the collapse of the short-lived communist regime on August 1, 1919. The Jews lost what they had achieved in three generations on Hungarian territory. Their contribution to the progress of the country and people since the Middle Ages brought them nothing but extreme anti-semitic discrimination, whose crude expression penetrated and won the support of all levels of the Hungarian population. Antisemitism became official government policy. The new law cut active Jewish participation in the economy from twenty to six percent.

Among the tens of thousands of Polish refugees flowing into Hungary at the beginning of WW II, were thousands of Jews seeking asylum. They were not the first Jewish refugees fleeing from the Nazis. They were preceded by Jews moving eastward after the annexation of Austria and the end of Czechoslovakia's independence. Hungarian Jewry's welfare institutions, which were already receiving aid from JOINT, cared for them against their will. The new antisemitic laws hit Hungarian Jewry hard. Hundreds of thousands were left without means of sustenance. The welfare institutions toiled to provide aid. No countries were prepared to absorb Jewish immigrants — and the gates of Palestine were locked.

In September 1940, and then in April 1941, Hungary annexed more territories. The second Arbitration Agreement in Vienna (with the participation of Germany and Italy) granted Hungary the northern sector of Transylvania. With the Nazi invasion of Yugoslavia, Hungary expanded its borders southwards as well. As the population grew, the number of Jews rose to 725,000. Another 150,000 Hungarians of Jewish origin were considered to be subject — by reason of race — to the new anti-Jewish law (#15/1941) based on the Nuremberg Laws. This time an official protest, though weak, was made by the Christian Churches: the new decrees hurt their flock too.

But in spite of all this, the status of Hungarian Jewry until 1941 — compared to Jews in other countries under direct or indirect German rule — was relatively good: after all, their lives were still not in danger.

On June 27, 1941, the Hungarians joined the Nazi invasion of the USSR. Its forces penetrated territories in the East, together with the Germans. After only three weeks, the Hungarian Aliens Police (KEOKH) initiated and organized the first deportations — behind the back of the Minister of the Interior. Jewish refugees in concentration camps, waiting in vain for immigration permits, were rounded up together with other Jews, who did not have documents to prove Hungarian citizenship. Jews from various communities were arrested in a totally arbitrary manner. Some 20,000 were deported to occupied Galicia, where they were put into ghettos together with the local Jews. With the beginning of the destruction of these ghettos, the first of the Hungarian Jews in the environs of Kamenetz-Podolsk were annihilated. This was just the beginning of what was to take place with greater intensity over the next three years.

As early as 1940, Jews aged between twenty and forty were being enlisted in special units in the Hungarian army. They were swiftly sent to the forced labor units. The enlisted men were subjected to military discipline which grew stricter all the time. Until Hungary entered the war, these units were made to work all over Hungary at various jobs: roadwork and laying railway tracks, fortifications, and so forth. Scores of such labor units were attached to the Hungarian forces in conquered USSR territories. Here, close to the front and far from the homeland, Hungarian soldiers and officers abused Jews attached to their units. They did everything in their power to destroy those placed in their hands. They were explicitly told by their commanders — mainly senior officers of German extraction — that they would return home only when the last Jew in their unit had been destroyed.

In 1942, a senior Hungarian army officer, also of German extraction, initiated a "sweep" to "purify" a broad area that had been under Yugoslav rule until a few months before. The security forces executed, without trial, about a thousand Jews, as well as thousands of Serbs and others. This took place near Novi-Sad (Újvidék). To cover the traces of this mass murder, the victims' corpses were thrown into the Danube. Their possessions were stolen. The event became known within a few days throughout the country and abroad. Some parliamentarians protested emphatically, not so much because of what had transpired to the Jews, but because of the terrible injury done to the Yugoslav population.

Until 1942, attacks on the lives of Jews were carried out in remote places, hundreds of kilometers from the main centers. In the heart of the country, in Budapest and the country towns, the Jews did not believe such attacks were systematic. Furthermore, in 1942-1943, at the height of the annihilation of the Jews in all the countries bordering on Hungary, it seemed that Hungarian Jewry would not share this fate. Refugees who made their way to Hungary continued to find asylum. Their descriptions of the horrors and the flow of information about the dreadful fate of the men of the forced labor units at the front, taking the lives of some 40,000, further substantiated the danger. But at this stage, the focus of destruction was far from the borders of Hungary. In the meantime, the

Regent appointed a new Prime Minister. Outwardly, Kallay took a consistently anti-Jewish stand; he was an antisemite, like most of his class. Nevertheless, he was not bloodthirsty, he didn't hate the Jew "more than was necessary." His government's legislation added limitations — mainly of an economic nature. Gradually, the Prime Minister began to adopt a more cautious approach, particularly after the Nazi defeat at Stalingrad and the Allied landing in Africa. Kallay summoned the Jewish leaders and confided to them that he and the Regent no longer believed in an Axis victory. He promised that he would do whatever he could to gain time. The fate of the Jews also depended on the race against time.

In April 1943, Horthy visited Hitler at his headquarters, where his hosts unequivocally informed him that they intended to annihilate all Jews. Hitler and Ribbentrop demanded that the Jews be held in concentration camps until they were "exterminated like germs and pests!..." Horthy refused. It can therefore be established with certainty that: the deeds of the Nazis were known to Hungary's top political echelons and to the Jewish leadership. The latter did nothing to forestall the approaching evil; it is difficult to say that they were psychologically ready to do so. They all had blind faith in Horthy's political sagacity and in Kallay's maneuvering skills.

However, Hungarian Jewry had a sort of "alternative-leadership" which included the Zionist based Rescue and Aid Committees that had been operating since 1941, and the religious congregational organizations, but of course they did not win "official recognition." Jews arriving in the capital from Transylvania and as refugees slipping over the Slovakian border contributed a valuable Jewish-national human resource. They also displayed a far greater willingness to endanger themselves for their fellow men than did the official conservative Jewish establishment. It could account for the fact that until the end of 1943, no more than seven to eight percent of the whole of Hungarian Jewry was lost! Compared to what became known regarding the Jews of Germany, Poland and even Romania, the small numerical loss increased confidence and optimism.

These statistics appeared to justify the majority of Hungarian Jewry's complete faith in the Hungarian ruling institutions. The Nazis were absorbing blow after blow and the Jews felt that any rational person had to see that the war could end any day, that Germany's defeat was imminent. The table of laws imposed on the Jews robbed them of sources of livelihood, but there was no direct threat against their physical existence. Therefore, very few Jews strayed from the rules of behavior suitable to a law-abiding community. Only a few hundred refugees and deserters from forced labor battalions obtained forged documents. Nobody considered "going underground."

The Germans did not miss any opportunity to put pressure on the Regent and his government to start applying the "Final Solution" to the Jews of his country, too. The Hungarians were told that it was the Fuhrer's wish that they cooperate in the "Solution of the Jewish Problem." His representatives in Hungary knew their allies very well and that Jewish property had been promised to the Hungarians. The German envoy intervened with the Foreign Ministry again and again, demanding "the removal of Jewish influence" from the Hungarian economy and culture. He also insisted on the wearing of the Yellow Star as a prelude to deportation. But to no avail; the intense pressure was fruitless. Nobody knew how weak the opposition had been. It was known only that masses of Hungarians on all levels had already had a taste of plundered Jewish property. Antisemitism was on the increase among all classes, thanks to the unbridled anti-Jewish propaganda of the Kállay government. The high ranking officers, the state administration, the economy and trade were full of Germans of Hungarian birth who identified heart and soul with the "ideological homeland." The Hungarian extreme right, which was split into many conflicting parties, aided Nazi pressure with all its might. The only common denominator among these parties was hatred of Jews. Hundreds of thousands of those under the umbrella of the extreme right listened with pleasure to Hitler's speeches. Unlike the Governor and Prime Minister, the majority of the Hungarian people was ready to help the Fuhrer, or at least to observe from the sidelines.

On March 19, 1944, all illusions were shattered. Among the various elements that tipped the scale in favor of occupying Hungary, the German Foreign Ministry mentioned Hitler's determination to implement the Final Solution in Hungary, too. The Germans forced the formation of a new government. Kállay fled to the Turkish Legation. The Regent gave his government a free hand in carrying out policy regarding the Jews. All the important people in whom the Jewish leadership had placed their hopes disappeared, were arrested, or silenced. Eichmann and his Hungarian henchmen set the pace, relying on accumulated experience. Eichmann was assisted by his experts, who were transferred from the annihilation operations in other European countries.

Even now, the Jews continued to hope that "it still couldn't happen here!" and "Horthy won't allow it!" Not many days passed before it was proven that, actually, everything is possible.

New orders of clearly evil intent were published: the Yellow Star, the concentration in country towns, the special arrangements, generally at railway sidings, pointed to the final phase of being handed over to the Germans at border stations.

The Nazis appointed a Judenrat. Actually, the same people who had been the community leaders served on it. We can only assume what the Judenrat thought. The archives were lost, but from testimony given after the Holocaust by its members, it is difficult to give a definite answer as to whether they really thought they could disobey the Nazis. Hungarian Jewry, stunned by the swift and cruel reversal in their fortunes showed no organized resistance to the oppressors. Not one of their admired leaders called on them to disobey the government rulings. The community was perfectly disciplined. Scores of young men, who could have raised some resistance were not with their loved ones! They were serving, as mentioned, in the forced labor battalions. In the spring of 1944, tens of thousands of them were no longer alive. Against the old, women and children, the Germans pitted the Hungarian gendarmerie. Even in peaceful times they instilled fear, how much more so now, with German encouragement and the conviction that purifying Hungary of its Jews would be for the personal welfare of genuine Hungarians. In certain places, the Jews embarked on the trains with a sense of relief, because they believed that the Germans, known for being "businesslike," would be less pedantic than the Hungarians!

The pace of deportations was stepped up: perhaps Eichmann's men were afraid they would encounter armed resistance as in the ghetto uprisings, or other difficulties as in Bulgaria or Romania. On the other hand, Eichmann could be fairly certain that rescue of the Jews, in the manner of Denmark, was out of the question in Hungary.

The Judenrat tried to enlist the intervention of the Christian churches and diplomatic representatives after the courageous emissaries of the Halutz movement, risking their own lives, brought them verified information about the annihilation of the ghettos in the districts. Furthermore, taking a rare step, they even made an illegal appeal to the Hungarian people asking for their support. Since this was an illegal act, only the representatives of neutral countries tried to help. It was 1944, and they all wanted to prove their good intentions to the Allies who were going from victory to victory in the war. But the Hungarian churches hesitated for a long time, until most of the Jews had been deported, while the Hungarian masses offered heartfelt thanks to their government for freeing them from the "Jewish blood-suckers".... In this Sodom, there were some exceptions, but too few to have any effect.

The Jewish Rescue and Aid Committee began discussions with the Germans. Intuitively, the leaders knew that what lay behind the cynical and dreadful offer of "goods for blood" was the intention of a high-ranking Nazi to exploit Hungarian Jewish lives in order to establish contact with the western Allies. Himmler had come to the conclusion that the war was lost. He was conniving to create a split in the Allied camp by conducting negotiations with the British and the Americans via the Jews. It should be noted that other echelons in the Berlin regime knew nothing — officially at least — of the plan to exchange Jews for goods.

Zionism, including the pioneer youth movements, was an almost marginal movement in the Hungarian Jewish community. The organized youth chose the right way in producing Aryan documentation and in smuggling members into Romania and Slovakia, where a relatively calm mood now prevailed. Obviously, for the time being, it was impossible to help the masses by such means. Even if the central council would have taken the risk of alarming the Jews by portraying the whole truth about what was awaiting them, the number of escapees to neighboring countries would not have risen much. Bound to children and the elderly, with no knowledge of languages, their chances of rescue were weak. A few thousand fled, most of whom were saved.

Also, there were no helpful auxiliary factors for partisan warfare. There was no Hungarian resistance movement with which to cooperate. In the spring of 1944, there was no chance and maybe no point in fighting Germans and their henchmen on the outskirts of Budapest and other cities.

Nevertheless, they tried to discover rescue opportunities of one kind or another. However, by the time these ways were discovered and they had actually dared to use them, the deportation of most of Hungarian Jewry, apart from the population of the capital, was an established fact.

The first way was multi-faceted: The Central Judenrat continued to employ all the accepted means of intercession. They appealed to every government factor willing to lend an ear to their pleas: the Regent, the nobility and members of parliament, a few ministers (of the government that had fully agreed to the deportations). Special appeals were made to the Christian churches, who did respond, at first in defense of their own flock of Jewish origins and a little later, after much hesitation, for the rest of Jewry. After the Allied occupation of Rome, at the beginning of 1944, the emissary of the Holy See even urged the Hungarian Archbishop to raise his voice in protest!... Judenrat circles, the heads of the Orthodox congregations and the pioneer movements distributed the "Auschwitz Protocols," which had reached Hungary in mid-May. Judenrat activities became desperate and frantic when all that remained were the Jews of Budapest and a few batches of forced laborers throughout the country and at the front. Shmuel Stern, President of the Judenrat, and his intimates knew that this time they were directly engaged in a life and death struggle for their own lives, too. With the constantly worsening situation of the Germans at the front after the successful landing in the west and the Soviet onslaught in the east, and because of the behavior of the occupying forces in Hungary, there was growing bitterness against the Nazis in certain circles of the general public. The "Hungarian way" of rescue, which the Judenrat now adopted, however inexcusably late — and without abandoning their efforts with the representatives of neutral states — suddenly seemed wise.

The second way — which one could call "rescue through direct contact with the Germans" — was much broader in scope. The heads of the Rescue and Aid Committee negotiated with the S.S. concerning what they defined as the "Europe Plan." For known reasons, this program did not bear fruit. Eichmann followed Himmler's orders regarding the conduct of the negotiations as though possessed by the devil. When it became clear that Yoel Brand's mission had failed, he was very pleased. The pace of transports was stepped up again. Eighty, and sometimes more, people were squeezed into each boxcar. The deportees were misled. They were not told of the trains' final destination.

This way resulted in the rescue of 1,600 Jews on the "Kastner-train." Possibly, it also helped to rescue the 15,000 deportees to Austria who, in Eichmann's words, were kept there "on ice" — to serve as a kind of deposit in proof of the seriousness of S.S. intentions. It is more likely that Kaltenbrunner, Eichmann's superior officer, in response to a request from his friend, the Mayor of Vienna, had ordered several transports from Hungary to be diverted there to restore the ruins around the city. He hoped thus to lay the infrastructure for the south-eastern lines of defense. To Kastner, Eichmann described compliance with Kaltenbrunner's orders as "keeping the Jews on ice...."

The third way was the one used by the pioneer youth movements. They did not want contact with official elements, whether Hungarians or Nazis. They did not mind dealing with the rescue of small numbers. In the summer of 1944, the tools and methods that made such a decisive contribution in the autumn and early winter of that year, were prepared and tested.

Ultimately, at the beginning of July, a strange blend of circumstances worked to stop the deportations:

1. Diplomatic pressure from the Allies;
2. Pressure from the neutral legations and the International Red Cross;
3. A failed attempt by the extreme right to rebel against the Regent;
4. The stunning influence of the truth about Auschwitz, with the distribution of the Protocols;
5. The Nazi's unwillingness to quarrel with Horthy — who had issued absolute orders to halt the transport of Jews from Hungary — because of the Jews of Budapest.

By the second half of July 1944, some 450,000 Hungarian Jews had been deported and there was a certain respite. Eichmann, who did not want to submit to the Regent's orders, managed to annihilate a few more concentration camps — by misleading the Judenrat. Together with the Nazi faithful in government circles and the Hungarian security forces, his operations division prepared to renew the deportations in the second half of August.

During this period, a number of plans were raised for the emigration of the country's remaining Jews. The representatives of Sweden and Switzerland handled the relative contacts. It is doubtful whether anyone honestly believed that it was possible, in the second half of 1944, to move tens of thousands of people over borders and constantly bombarded roads. Whatever the case, the Hungarian government presented these plans as a reason for the halt in deportations.

Eichmann might possibly have succeeded in "getting his hands" on Budapest's Jews as well — had Romania not deserted the Axis on August 23, 1944. Hungary's Minister of Internal Affairs informed Eichmann of his government's willingness to arrest the capital's Jews on August 25. The tyrant, impatient as always, demanded that this be moved forward to August 20, for "transport reasons." All the preparations had already been made. But Horthy disagreed with his government, which still firmly insisted on August 25, as the date for the start of the operation. The Regent made the counter proposal that the Jews be concentrated in camps in the districts ("Bulgarian style") from where they would be used in the war effort.

Meanwhile, Himmler forbade the renewal of the deportations; the confrontation with Horthy at the same time as the crisis with Romania, only added to Germany's serious difficulties. Eichmann wanted to bypass the order from the "S.S. Reichsfuhrer." He conveyed the Hungarian government's agreement and ignored Horthy, "the stubborn old man." The Regent however, got to know about Himmler's order when one of Eichmann's aides leaked it to the central Judenrat who, in turn, hurried to inform Horthy, reinforcing his opposition to the deportations. Fear of committing another crime, pressure from the Christian churches and neutral diplomats, together with the West's indirect intervention, all had their influence on Horthy.

But what really prompted Himmler to forbid further deportations? We have only assumptions. Perhaps Himmler thought that Brand's mission was continuing, in spite of the announcement by the B.B.C, and that negotiations were at an advanced stage. Perhaps precisely the fact that Brand had not returned, led Himmler to conclude that something was going on....

Within a week of Romania's surrender, the Eastern front had come hundreds of kilometers closer to the heart of Hungary. The Germans were busy with the establishment of improvised front lines, at first on sovereign Hungarian territory in eastern Transylvania. A few days later, the Hungarian government was sacked and Horthy appointed General Lakatos, whom he trusted, as Prime Minister. The General was ordered to hasten the process of Hungary's withdrawal from the war. In view of the Soviet army's rapid and deepening penetration into Hungary, the "Jewish Question" was temporarily neglected. Eichmann had been "insulted" and wanted to withdraw his operations unit which was disbanded on August 28, 1944. Its senior officers stayed in Budapest for about a week longer in the hope that their services would still be required.

Regent Horthy and General Lakatos could not keep secret their activities for a truce. The Nazis received reliable information. Their senior agents served as Ministers in the Hungarian government. In the framework of the governor's preparations, it was even suggested that the Jewish forced labor units be armed to reinforce the military elements faithful to him. After failed attempts in the West, Horthy's representatives signed a truce agreement in Moscow on October 11th 1944. In the course of the Hungarian government's contacts with the Kremlin, Molotov showed a certain interest in the Jews of Budapest, too. From the end of June, the Jews had been concentrated in special houses marked with the Yellow Star. These houses were scattered over almost all the city's districts; no ghetto was established, because of the fear that the Allies would bomb districts of Budapest that contained no Jews....

On the afternoon of October 15, Horthy, without preparing public opinion in advance, announced Hungary's surrender. In a manifesto to the nation, he also related to what had befallen Hungarian Jewry: "...Under the aegis of the German occupation, the Gestapo took control of the handling of the Jewish Question, employing methods that they had used before, elsewhere, in a manner that went against the principles of humanity...." This was Hungary's sole public statement in this spirit, from the time the Germans entered Hungary, seven months earlier.

The Nazis went into action with forces they had on standby. Horthy was arrested and the government handed over to the Arrow Cross Party, which unified all the extreme right streams under the "Leader of the Nation" Szalasi. This party had always combined extremist social slogans with absolute, extreme hatred of Jews. From October 16, 1944, organized mass rioting against the Jews of Budapest began. The rabble was organized into armed, party-controlled squads. They contained trigger-happy youths, who trampled, robbed and shot without mercy as they broke into Jewish houses.

The new regime announced that it was annulling all concessions made by Horthy and his people to hundreds of Jews for special services rendered to Hungary. They also canceled passports issued to hundreds of other Jews who had been granted travel documents to Sweden before the overthrow of Horthy. Eichmann returned to Budapest on October 17 and began to organize the new phase of the deportations. This time it was without means of transport, because the railway lines were congested and partly destroyed. The death march to the German border had begun. In the beginning, males aged between sixteen and sixty were mobilized, but not them alone. Three days later, females aged between eighteen and forty were also mobilized. For a time, these Jews were used to building fortifications outside Budapest. Two weeks later, in early November, the "foot march" of men and women in the direction of the border began. Eichmann's original intention was to send 50,000 Jewish men westwards. Once these were on the way to the border, he wanted to get permission from the Szalasi government to send a further 50,000 of both sexes and in this way, more or less conclude the "Final Solution." Hungarian soldiers escorted the marching Jews. The retarded were shot, the sick were left by the roadside to die of weakness and exposure to the hard weather. Many soldiers would rather have gone to the front than witness what they saw. On November 21, Himmler issued an order, backed by the "Leader of the Nation" Szalasi, putting an end to the "march." The Jews who reached the border were not fit for any kind of work....

Pressure from the neutral legations, who warned all non-Axis nations against recognizing Szalasi, achieved a certain alleviation of extremist policies against the Jews. The Hungarian Minister of the Interior announced that they would recognize the "protection passes" issued by the neutral legations to those Jews whose immigration would be "arranged" with their help, after the war. A quota would be fixed for each legation: the Swedish, Swiss, Spanish and Portuguese, the Vatican and also for the International Red Cross, which worked independently. Suitable arrangements were made to house all those who did not receive "protection passes" in the central ghetto that was established in a limited area in the seventh District. All those who were "protected" by the various documents they held, were ordered to congregate in a separate area in the fifth district, known as the "international ghetto."

In fact, the protection form was an invention with no cover. Within days, thousands of protection forms were prepared by the Zionist youth movements: their members had decided to make it possible for every Jew to get the document that in most cases meant: life. It was a unique, most successful rescue campaign. Its greatness lay in the simplicity of the idea and its adaptation to the circumstances of the time and place. While the operation was run by a handful of people, tens of thousands of Hungarian Jews were rescued.

If there were some German and Hungarian elements who did not recognize the protection forms — they were in the minority. Generally, these documents were recognized. Many even managed to be rescued by them from the "death marches." The protection forms also increased the chaos that confused the Arrow Cross squads. Other documents — also the product of the Halutz underground — helped the general Hungarian underground which was beginning to raise its head, at last. Their assistance was far smaller than that of Raoul Wallenberg, Secretary of the Swedish legation, who devoted all his energy to rescue. He gave countless examples of courage in confrontations with the armed gangs and their government. The race against time was in its final stage. From the beginning of November, the thunder of canons advancing on Budapest could be clearly heard. But Eichmann and his men deported 40,000-50,000 Jews who were concentrated in Budapest — including scores of the forced labor battalions from the Soviet occupied east of the country.

There were changes in the leadership of the Central Judenrat. President Stern, who had been the outstanding leader of Hungarian Jewry over the last decade, stepped down. His successor as acting chairman, Stockler, was a man who differed from him in every respect. He was much younger and also a courageous man. He had no illusions about the Hungarians who were expected to rescue them. By now, everyone was aware that the remnant of the capital's Jews could be saved only by extensive illegal activity, sabotage and fraud, reliance on neutral legations and mobilizing the daring members of the Halutz movements and others (disguised as Arrow Cross members, for example) for rescue and defense operations in the central ghetto.

On December 24, 1944, the Soviets surrounded Budapest. By then, the government had fled from the capital. Fierce street fighting continued for weeks. In the midst of the siege, the Arrow Cross began removing the Jews holding protection forms from the international ghetto. There were hundreds of casualties during their transfer to the central ghetto. One of the architects of the rescue activity, the president of the Hungarian Zionist Federation, was kidnapped from a hotel and killed.

The "international ghetto" was liberated on January 16, 1945. Within two days, the walls of the central ghetto also came down. The Germans held out until February 13 on the right bank of the river. Jewish institutions, hospitals and homes for the aged were attacked and those who had taken refuge in them were murdered.

With the fall of Budapest into Soviet hands, the fascist Hungarian government continued to "defend" the west of the country. Scores of forced labor battalions and many thousands of Budapest deportees toiled in the hard winter, almost without rest, suffering at the hands of their hard taskmasters, constructing fortifications along the German border. Starvation, plagues and the many executions gradually decreased the number of Jews. Those who were left were deported to Germany at the end of March. Even prior to this, in February 1945, the Szalasi government had canceled the "exemption" granted to Jews married to non-Jews. Consequently, a few more hundreds of people were sent to the crowded concentration camps in shriveling Germany. The whole of Hungary was liberated on April 4, 1945.

Of the 875,000 people considered to be Jews, close to 600,000 were annihilated. The generation whose blood was drained is still living. The generation that showed resistance when the Jews were led to the slaughter — is also still alive. In the Holocaust blood-balance, the losses of the Hungarian tribe of our people amount to some ten percent. Since most of them were taken to the last of the "death factories" so close to the end of the war, when their chances for remaining alive seemed so good, the pain is felt even more deeply.

There was Holocaust and there was heroism. The rescue operations of the Pioneer Youth movements present a chapter of unique bravery in Jewish resistance during the years of the annihilation.

Names of Cities and Streets

in Hungary and in neighboring countries in 1944 and in 2001,
with English pronunciation (where necessary):

Hungarian	English
Budapest	
Buda	
Pest	
Andrássy út	Andrashy Street
Apponyi tér.	Apponyi Circus
Balaton	
Barcsai utca.	Barchai Street
Baross utca.	Barosh Street
Bethlen Gábor utca	Bethlen Gabor Street
Bethlen tér.	Bethlen Circus
Békásmegyer	
Békéscsaba	
Bocskai utca	Bochkai Street
Budakeszi	Budakesi
Budakeszi út	Budakesi Street
Csóványos	Chovanosh
Debrecen	
Dob utca	Dob Street
Duna.	Danube
Eger	

Hungarian	English
Erzsébet hid	Erzabat Bridge
Erzsébet körút	Erzabat Boulevard
Ezüst hegy	Esusht Hill
Farkasrét	Farkashret — a quarter in Budapest
Ferencváros	Ferenzvarosh — a quarter in Budapest
Fő utca	Fo Street
Garany	
Gyarmati utca	Garmaty Street
Győr	
Hegyeshalom	
Hungária körút	Hungary Boulevard
Igmándi	
Izabella utca	Isabella Street
József körút	Joseph Boulevard
Józsefvárosi pályaudvar	Railway station at Josephvarosh
Kálmán utca	Kalman Street
Kistarcsa	Kistarcha
Kisvárda	
Kohányi utca	Kohanyi Street
Kolumbusz utca	Columbus Street
Kőbánya	Kobanya — a quarter in Budapest
Lánc hid	Lanz Bridge
Lipótváros	Lipotvarosh — a quarter in Budapest
Majestic szálló	Majestic Hotel
Margit hid	Margit Bridge
Margit körút (Martírok utja)	Margit Boulevard (via Martirok)
Markó utca	Marko Street
Mátészalka	
Mérleg utca	Merleg Street
Miskolc	
Moson utca	Moshon Street
Mosonmagyaróvár	

Hungarian	English
Nádor utca	Nador Street
Népszinház utca	
Nyiregyháza	
Ó utca	O Street
Óbuda	
Orsó utca	Orsho Street
Pannonia szálló	Pannonia Hotel
Percel Mór utca	Percel Mor Street
Pestszentlőrinc	
Pécs	
Pozsonyi út	
Retek utca	Retek Street
Rózsadomb	
Rózsa utca	Rosa Street
Royal szálló	Royal Hotel
Rumbach utca	Rumbach Street
Sárvár	
Sip utca	Ship Street
Sopronkőhida	
Svábhegy	
Szabadság tér	Sabadshag Circus
Szeged	
Szent István körút	Saint Ishtvan Boulevard
Székesfehérvár	
Szolnok	
Teleki Pál utca	
Teleki tér	Teleki Circus
Tolonc	
Vác	
Váci utca	Vac Street
Vadász utca	Vadas Street
Városház utca	

Hungarian	English
Városliget	
Vésztő	
Wekerle Sándor utca	Wekerle Shandor Boulevard
Zöldmáli utca	Zoldmali Street
Zugló	

Slovakia (Czecholslovakia) 1991	Hungary 1938-1945
Dunajská Streda	Dunaszerdahely
Nové Zámky	Érsekújvár
Košice	Kassa
Komárno	Komárom
Lučenec	Losonc
Samorin	Somorja

Transylvania (Romania) 1991	Hungary 1939-1945
Ditró	
Transylvania	Erdély
Baile Felix	Félix Fürdő
Cluj	Kolozsvár
Nagyilonda	
Oradea	Nagyvárad
Sighethul Marmatiei	Mármarossziget
Sfintu Gheorghe	Sepsiszentgyörgy
Satu Mare	Szatmárnémeti

Vojvodina Province (Yugoslavia) 1991	Hungary 1941-1945
Bačka	Bácska
Subotica	Szabadka
Topolja, Bactopolja	Topolya, Bácstopolya
Novi Sad	Újvidék

Notes

Chapter 1

1. A town in eastern Slovakia (in Hungarian: Kassa). Annexed by Hungary between the years 1938-1944).
2. Aaron Rosenfeld, a Hashomer Hatza'ir leader in Poland, fell during the Slovakian uprising in autumn 1944.
3. One of the main railway stations in the Hungarian capital.
4. The office was located in the Seventh Quarter, on Erzsébet Boulevard 26.
5. A village in central Slovakia.
6. The largest of Slovakia's cities. During 1938-1945, it was the capital of "independent" Slovakia.
7. The Jewish center, Ústredna Židov in Slovakian, or U.Z., was established in accordance with an order issued by the independent Slovak authorities from September 26, 1940.
8. Yoshko (József) Baumer, today a member of Kibbutz Ha'ogen.
9. Until the Nazi occupation, it had been permitted to send out fifty children, accompanied by one or two adults!
10. The movement's club was located on József Blvd. in the capital's Seventh Quarter.
11. A town in Transylvania (Western Romania).
12. Miklós Kállay was Prime Minister of Hungary during the years 1942-1944. From the middle of 1943 — that is following the fall of Stalingrad and the landing of the Allied Forces in North Africa — he had been trying to get close to the Allies, in an attempt to save Hungary from Soviet occupation. The Nazis were aware of Kállay's programs; two of his cabinet ministers regularly supplied the Germans with a detailed report on all government discussions. His memoirs constitute a kind of document of defense: M. Kállay, Hungarian Premier (New York, 1954).
13. At the end of December 1943, the Hungarian government permitted the legal and open activity of Zionists all over Hungary. The indefatigable efforts on the part of Chairman of the Zionist Federation in Hungary, Nathan Komoly were crowned with success — since it was necessary for the authorities to ingratiate themselves with the west. For this purpose, everything including Zionism, was acceptable.
14. Nathan (Otto) Komoly (1892-1945), an engineer by profession, one of the leaders

of the Zionist Federation in Hungary. He served as Federation Chairman in 1944. As one of the leaders of the rescue operation, he was murdered just a few days before the liberation of Budapest from the Nazis and their helpers. For information on the man and his activity, see: Arielli, Mordekhai; Nathan (Otto) Komoly (Tel Aviv, 1970).

15. Cvi (Ernö) Szilágyi, one of the leaders of Hashomer Hatza'ir in Hungary from the mid 1930s, until 1944. As opposed to other Zionist youth movements, the Hashomer Hatza'ir in Hungary during the 1940s was not close to a group of adults. Cvi Szilágyi joined the movement as an older member and for various reasons did not emigrate to Israel when his turn came to do so, and his work on forming a group of older members was reflected repeatedly: he enjoyed distinction and a great deal of moral authority, and thus also represented the movement. His success was also due to his very charismatic personality, which captured the intellectual circles in which he moved. A copy of the memo remains with the Fürst family, Ramat Gan.

16. Novi Sad, a city in Vojvodina, northern Yugoslavia (annexed by the Hungarians during the years 1941-1944). At the end of January 1942, the commander of the security forces in the region initiated a "cleaning up operation" against the partisans. In this operation, thousands of ordinary, law-abiding citizens were slaughtered. It is not known to this day, the exact number of dead. It is assumed that some 5,000 people were killed, including 1,000 Jews and the remainder were Serbs and others.

17. This, of course, is a mistake. The third anti-Jewish law, which was passed in 1941 (no. 1941/15) implemented in Hungary the racist principles of the Nuremberg laws.

18. The official 'line.'

19. The Hungarian Nation, a liberal Hungarian daily, read to this day in Hungarian intellectual circles.

20. See "The Book of the Hashomer Hatza'ir" (Merhavia, 1956), Vol. A, pp. 395-402. At the end of the 1930s, Zionism was identified with communism; it was determined that the Zionist movement was part of the international socialist movement. Colonel Gábor Ugrai was entrusted with the task of depressing the Zionists and the communists, including Hashomer Hatza'ir. see pp.118 and 166: E. Hollós, Rendőrség, Csendőrség, Vkf. 2 (Budapest, 1971).

21. A concentration camp in southeast Slovakia, a region annexed by Hungary. The camp was meant to hold "suspects," communists, mercenaries, Jews and gypsies.

22. Anyone under constant police surveillance in Hungary was obliged to report to the local police station two or three times a day. He was forbidden to leave home after dusk.

23. Concentration camps in eastern Hungary.

24. The camps were named for the Budapest streets in which they were located. These camps usually housed Jewish refugees from the countries neighboring Hungary.

25. The National Authority for Foreigners' Control.

26. An underground word meaning "one of the lads."

27. Rut Lorand (in Czechia), Feiegenbaum (Endre) Avri — now in Prague.

28. Itzhac Herbst, Hashomer Hatza'ir member, deceased in Tel Aviv.

29. Compared with the Nuremberg system of laws, the anti-Jewish legislation in

Hungary was relatively moderate. But the two laws, 1938/15 and 1939/4 had a devastating effect on thousands of Jews, who lost their sources of livelihood as a result of these laws.

30. Law 1920/25 restricted members of the "religion of Moses" to six percent of the total number of higher education students in Hungary. But *numerus clausus* meant that there were still Jewish students to be found in Hungary.
31. In Hungarian: OMZSA, or Pártfogó Iroda. The Office's activity claimed "charity begins at home."
32. Hungarian currency. In 1944, twelve to twenty Pengös were worth one US dollar.
33. A nickname for Toloncház.
34. In Hungarian: Betyár-becsület, a much accepted term in the underworld of many countries.
35. The only nation of among Hungary's neighbors, with whom there had never been any conflict was the Polish nation. There is real admiration among the Hungarians for the Poles. The Hungary of the tyrant Horthy and various heads of government gave generous asylum to many Polish war refugees, including thousands of Jews, who pretended to be born and raised as Poles...and in Budapest, until the German invasion, there was a recognized and distinguished representation of the exiled Polish government in London. Furthermore, the Hungarian government hoped to use these, in their search for a listening ear in the West.
36. Three years previously, in the summer of 1941, the "KEOKH" were very active in locating Jews who had — according to the Hungarian authorities — doubtful citizenship, and rounding them up prior to deporting them to the eastern occupied territories.
37. Unlike other countries, Romania for example — the Hungarian administration was strict with regard to the term "anonymous donation." Instead it was possible to use good connections, Christian patrons, or crafty lawyers, who often managed to influence the authorities, including the foreigners' police.
38. Encouraged by Prime Minister Kállay, there was a fruitful period for all the different ideologies and their representatives, who wanted to point out that Hungary was struggling "only" against the Soviet Union, while not taking part in any fight against the western allies. Semi-official government publications repeatedly stressed the fact that Hungary was seeking peace. In a new year editorial, it was asserted in one of the papers that Hungary could not accept the Casablanca surrender conditions for the simple reason that there are no allied military units in the region, to whom to surrender.... At the same time, the fringe satirical theaters (a typical Hungarian phenomenon), were an outspoken sounding board for the people's weariness of the war. These preached in favor of detachment from Germany, and were very popular among the audiences, most of whom were Budapest Jews. On the other hand the Nazis and their servants were keeping a close watch on these expressions.
39. Until March 19, 1944, some 6,000 Jews immigrated into Hungary during the war years. See: Y.Z. Zahavi, "From Integration to Zionism" (Jerusalem, 1972), pp. 419, henceforth, Zahavi.
40. In Hungarian: Gordon-kör. It was the name of the adult sector of Hashomer Hatza'ir. After 1945, the name was changed to "Borochov Circle."

41. Haika Klinger (1917-1958), after taking part in the underground in the Benedin ghetto, she came to Hungary, via Slovakia at the beginning of 1944. She emigrated to Palestine even before the German invasion, following a brief stay in Hungary. Exerpts of her experiences were published in "A Ghetto Journal" (Merhavia 1959).
42. Jenő Kolb (1898-1959), later became manager of the Tel Aviv Museum.
43. The nickname "Uncle" in Hungarian relates more to a fondness than to a blood relationship. Uncle Frisch's restaurant was located on Csengeri Street in the capital's Sixth Quarter.
44. These moneys were sent from two places: Menahem Bader, member of the Jewish Agency Redemption Mission, sent sums of money from Istanbul; Heini Bornstein, who spent the war in Switzerland, sent money from there. See: Menahem Bader, "Sad Missions," (Merhavia, 1954).
45. The first refugees from Slovakia started arriving in Hungary during the second half of 1942.
46. Dan Zimmerman, now living in Raanana, was a senior researcher at the Technion and manager of the association for rubber research.
47. The residence was called after the street Zöldmáli in which it was located. A students' residence was also located at Bácskay, in the city's fourteenth Quarter. There was another one on the main street of the city's third Quarter.
48. Pil (Elephant) — the movement nickname of Moshe Alpan (now in Tel Aviv).
49. At this time, the population of the Hungarian capital was a little over one million people. What seemed natural and significant to someone who was raised and grew up in the big city, is not necessary to someone who came from a small place, especially the remote provinces.
50. These doormen were representatives of the authorities. As well as being entrusted with the maintenance of a building, they were also required to see to closing the gate at a regular hour each evening. They also managed the "tenants' roster," in which every one was obliged to register, who planned to stay in the building for more than twenty-four hours.
51. In Hungarian: Rendőri Bejelentö. According to a law from the revolutionary restrictions of 1849, anyone who plans to stay in a certain place for longer than twenty-four hours is required to inform the regional police or gendarme station of this intention. These would then issue a stamped authorization. These documents, which served as an identity card in every way, were valid until official identity cards began to be issued, a gradual and irregular process which did not include the entire population up until the end of the war.
52. Avri Fisher who perished in the Holocaust.
53. Michael Berger who perished in the Holocaust.
54. This camp was situated in an ordinary apartment building in the center of town. At that time it was not overly guarded.
55. February 1944.
56. One of the capital's quarters, the third, on the right side bank of the Danube.
57. A para-military organization for the education of Hungarian youth.
58. A method was devised of "washing" documents.
59. The gates of houses or entrances to houses in Budapest displayed the occupiers'

names in full. Anyone entering the house could know exactly who lived in the house and whereabouts.
60. According to the law, the authorities were obliged to supply a copy of or the original birth certificate to anyone who asked for it (if the person in question was born after 1895), since these details were kept in registers which were "open to public perusal." This arrangement was the result of the civil registry of all births notwithstanding the demands of the church authorities, who never allowed access to their registers.
61. Yoheved Barmath, who was arrested later, imprisoned in the "Workers' Prison" and later disappeared without a trace.
62. In 1944 Budapest had fourteen quarters, each with its own census office.

Chapter 2

1. A town in the county of Zaglambia, Poland.
2. The distance between Bendin and Auschwitz is thirty-six kilometers as the crow flies.
3. Hungary's musical tradition was famous, both because of the country's artists and because the audiences, many of whom — in both cases — were Jewish.
4. A royal castle on one of the hills overlooking the river's right bank.
5. See the "Hashomer Hatza'ir Book" (Merhavia, 1956, vol. a, pp. 439-472).
6. Herman-Zvi Federit, for many years one of the central activists of the Hungarian football league, M.L.Sz. He was one of the few who were unafraid to deal openly with the refugee mercenaries. He emigrated to Israel and died some years ago in Kibbutz Kfar Szold.
7. VAC, initials of the Hungarian Athletics and Fencing Club, a well known Jewish sports team in Hungary, between the two world wars.
8. Moshe Rosenberg, engineer, architect, headed the *Haganah* headquarters in Hungary. He emigrated to Israel and died some years ago in Ramat Gan.
9. One of Hungary's largest publishers, it was housed on one of the capital's main streets, Andrássy út.
10. This good woman also kept forbidden scientific literature among the books in her library, which, like her heart, was open to all. She now lives in Canada.
11. The "Yavne" publishing house was responsible for publishing books of Jewish interest in Hungary.
12. At that time the twelfth quarter of the capital, on the right bank of the Danube.
13. The offices were on Király Street in the Seventh Quarter.
14. A typical Hungarian name.
15. For many years, Cvi Szilágyi had been a member of the top leadership of the "Hashomer Hatza'ir" in Hungary (see note 15, chapter one).
16. Herbert Spencer (1820-1903), the British intellectual and philosopher. His ideas were called "Utilitariansm."
17. Georgeone (Barbarelli) (1477-1510), an Italian painter from the Renaissance period.
18. Zoltán Weiner, a wealthy furrier, had connections with the illegal Communist Party.

19. Tibor Barabás was born in 1911, a journalist and writer, of Jewish origin. He was recruited (as a Jew) into the forced labor platoons. He published several books on Jewish issues, including one on Uriel De'Costa. He was a member of Rákosi's establishment after 1945. He was secretary of the Hungary Writers' Guild during 1946-1949. He wrote a number of screenplays as well as a regular column in the Communist paper, "Szabad Nép." He was awarded the Lajos Kossuth Prize.
20. The late Moshe Krausz, Mizrahi member, one of the key Zionist activists in Hungary, deceased in Tel Aviv.
21. The second largest city in Yugoslavia. During the years 1941-1945 it was the capital of "independent" Croatia, under the Nazis.
22. In the year 1939, 4650 Shekalim were sold in Hungary. They took part in the elections. They consisted of less than one percent of Hungarian Jewry at that time.
23. Joel Brand (1906-1964), one of the Mapai leaders in Hungary. He published his own version of the events in Mission to the Condemned (Tel Aviv 1957). See also, Joel and Hanzi Brand, The Devil and the Soul (Tel Aviv, 1960).
24. Dr. Rezső (Rudolf) Israel Kastner (1906-1957), one of the Mapai leaders in Romania (Transylvania), later in Hungary. Secretery of the Aid and Rescue Committee in Budapest (1944). His activity was controversial and was the cause of a lengthy court case against him in the later half of the 1950's in Israel. In March 1957, he was murdered on a Tel Aviv street. See: Dr. Rudolf Kastner, Die Budapest Waadat Ezra We-Hazala (Basl, 1946), which was republished as: Ernst Landau, Der Kastner-Bericht (Munich, 1961). On the trial see: Shalom Rosenfeld, Criminal File 124, Greenwald-Kastner Trial (Tel Aviv 1955).
25. The late Shmuel Springman (b. 1905), a key figure with Mapai in Hungary. He was active with the Aid and Rescue Committee, and its bursar. In fact, he was responsible for helping refugees since 1939. He left Hungary in January 1944, first for Turkey, then he emigrated to Israel.
26. A member of a youth movement was expected to maintain different kinds of norms.
27. The late Dr. Moshe Bar-Zvi (Schweiger) was a member of the central committee of Yugoslav Zionists, prior to his arrival in Hungary. He died a few years ago in Israel.
28. Ivo Davidovitch, now lives in Israel.
29. This cafe was located on one of the city's main streets, named for Kaiser Wilhelm II (Vilmos Császár).
30. Dr. Yehezkel Ernő Marton, member of the Romanian Parliament, representing the Jewish party in Transylvania. Founder and first editor of the Hungarian Zionist paper "Új Kelet" (A New East), first in the Transylvanian capital, Cluj, then, to his death, in Tel Aviv.
31. The largest city in Transylvania and its historic capital since the Middle Ages.
32. The stalls in which King Aegeas of Elis kept 3,000 oxen. They had not been cleaned out for years and Hercules had to do it as one of his labors. He did the job in one day, by diverting the river Alpheus to sluice out the stalls.

Chapter 3

1. The German army occupied Prague, without a fight or any resistance on the part of the local inhabitants, on March 15, 1939. Hitler liked to set out on his various operations on Sundays: "The Night of Long Knives," in June 1934, the annexation of Austria, the invasion of Norway and Denmark, the attack on Yugoslavia, the invasion of the Soviet Union — all these took place on Sundays.
2. Leon Blatt was a Jewish refugee from Poland and one of the leaders of "Zionist Youth" in Hungary. He is living in Israel.
3. Eli Sajó, former secretary of Maccabi Hatza'ir in Slovakia. We lost trace of him during his attempt to cross the Hungarian-Romanian border.
4. The Zionist leadership, which consisted of older people, was by nature, less dynamic than the younger people, which they saw — at least until the German invasion of Hungary — as "playing at boy-scouts." Now it was becoming clear that these kids had a wealth of experience, especially in everything regarding resistance to the Nazis and their accomplices.
5. The first announcement — regarding the appointment of a new Hungarian government — easier to handle for the Germans — and about the arrival of the German armies, in the spirit of the Hungarian-German Union was officially published only on the evening of March 22, 1944.
6. Miklós Horthy, the ruler, was called on March 15, to a meeting with Hitler, near Salzbourg. It was there that the Führer informed him of the occupation of Hungary. After lengthy negotiations, Horty agreed not to resign. Budapest was rife with rumors regarding the ruler's fate, on the arrival of the Germans. Anyway, he remained a free man, because the Nazis were interested in the continuation of his administration in order to keep matters calm in Hungary.
7. The occupation of Hungary had been prepared at the end of 1943. Hitler signed the order for the operation in March 1944. A chapter of the order related to "security arrangements," which included, among other things, the arrest of all those who spoke out against the Nazis.
8. A Swiss illustrated magazine, popular in Major, which had a large German-speaking population.
9. See the memoirs of the Jewish Council chairman, Shmuel Stern, Heritage Files, books sixteen and eighteen (Tel Aviv, 1973-1974).
10. Rightly or not — the Jews of Budapest enjoyed great prestige, especially among the Jews of the provinces, for being wise and intelligent. There is no doubt that this reflected the feelings of inferiority of the provincials in the presence of their brethren from the big city.
11. A concentration camp east of Budapest.
12. This department included A. Kolb, Yehuda Weiss, Moshe Rosenberg and others.
13. Menahem Klein of Macabbi Hatza'ir from Slovakia was the first one responsible for the production of forged documents. He was lost during an attempt to cross the border to Romania.
14. A Shapiograph
15. In the capital's Sixth Quarter.
16. Avri Fischer

17. Nesher Adler, member of the main Hashomer Hatza'ir leadership in Hungary. He was lost during an attempt to cross the Hungarian-Romanian border in June 1944.
18. Uri Herman, perished in the Holocaust.
19. Efra Teichman-Agmon, now in Jerusalem and Ephra Nadav (Löwinger), now in Tel Aviv.
20. Many thousands of Poland's Jews started escaping to Hungary in 1939. The numbers decreased until the occupation of Hungary and accelerated annihilation of Polish Jewry. It ceased entirely in 1944.
21. Robert Weltsch in the paper Jüdische Rundschau, Berlin, April 4, 1943.
22. The original sentence in German was: 'Tragt ihn mit Stolz den gelben Fleck!'
23. Vilmos Császár Boulevard, in the capital's Fifth Quarter.
24. The film with the French comedian had been made before the war. The mere fact of showing French films, when the only officially permitted foreign films in Hungary were produced by Nazi Germany, was seen as something of a demonstration. It was shown for many months, until being removed due to German disapproval.

Chapter 4

1. The appointment was handed over on behalf of the Jewish Agency Delegation, which was stationed at Istanbul.
2. Dov Avrahamchik was a refugee from Poland and a representative of the youth movement "Tora and Work."
3. The money arrived from the Jewish Agency delegation at Istanbul. It is hard to define its real value since the Hungarian currency — the Pengö — was undergoing a process of speedy inflation. It would appear that in April-May 1944, $15,000 would have been worth around half a million Pengös.
4. Arms were obtained mainly due to Mimish's "connections." He had never had to draw courage from his peers...the beginnings of his ties with the black market dealers in Teleki Square, near the capital's "flea market," were connected to the purchase of documentation. After a while, Mimish was able to buy food cards, too. His connections had a kind of "dynamics" which led to the purchase of several weapons. Later on, additional sources were opened. It seems that the number of weapons obtained was between twelve and sixteen; see: The Attorney General versus Adolph Eichmann, (Jerusalem, 1974), henceforth, 'the Attorney General.'
5. In the city's Twelfth Quarter.
6. In his testimony at the Eichmann trial, Moshe Rosenberg claimed that his mother in law had been smuggled in by an SS officer and not this Hungarian officer. See: Attorney General, pp. 945.
7. From April 3, 1944, the allied forces started a systematic bombing of Budapest. As well as military targets — factories and railway stations, thousands of apartments were also destroyed, especially in those quarters which were in the vicinity of the factories.
8. A mountain range surrounding historical Hungary, from the north-west, north, north-east, east and for hundreds of kilometers, to the south as well. In 1918-1920 Hungary lost control of this range, although during the years 1939-1940, certain parts of the mountain range were returned for a period of four years.

9. Szatmárnémeti in Hungarian. A city in Transylvaina, some 150 km from the Carpathians. A short while later, use was made of the bunker in Satu-Mare, by the time the city was already empty of Jews. People who were on the way to Romania, spent the night at the bunker and crossed the border at dawn.
10. The ghetto was set up during the third week of May.
11. Two or three pistols (at that time the underground had no more than thirty pistols, one sub-machine gun and a few grenades).

Chapter 5

1. Transportation of Jews from Slovakia had ceased in September 1942 (after more than 50,000 of them had been transported to concentration camps). Transportation was renewed after the Slovakian uprising in September-October 1944. In the spring and early summer of 1944, the situation in Slovakia was immeasurably better than in occupied Hungary.
2. Now living in London.
3. Korona, the Slovakian currency.
4. And which we called *"Retiyul."*
5. "Recontra-*tiyul*," in the semantics of those days.
6. The partisan activity had been increasing since the second half of 1943, although the general uprising took place only a year later.
7. Yoshko (Josef) Weiser — Hashomer Hatza'ir member in Slovakia — joined the Communist Party and was the editor of the Slovakian "Pravda." He lives today in Czechia.
8. A large village in south-west Slovakia.
9. A town in Transylvania, occupied by Hungary 1940-1944.
10. David Stern, Hashomer Hatza'ir member, perished in the Holocaust.
11. At the end of April 1944, the Jews of Košice and its vicinity were concentrated in a closed ghetto. The deportations began during the third week of May 1944.
12. There is no certainty if this was indeed the man's name. Zachar is a common family name.
13. A common enough name among Hungarians. It was natural for people involved in this kind of activity to divulge as little personal information as possible.
14. Partisan activity in Slovakia was concentrated in the country's east. On the Hashomer Hatza'ir's connections with the partisans, see: Akiva Nir, Paths in the Circle of Fire (Tel Aviv, 1967).
15. A mining town in the hear of Slovakia. From August 29, this was the capital of the anti-Nazi resistance.
16. Egon Roth, member of the management committee of Hashomer Hatza'ir in Slovakia.
17. Haviva Reick (Martonovitz). On her activity and fateful mission, see D. Ben Nahum: As a Mother, She Came to Rescue (Tel Aviv, 1965); A Shadmi, Without Finding and Without Surrendering (Tel Aviv 1973).
18. On October 10, 1944, news arrived that the uprising had been quashed. The Nazis held their victory march on October 30, 1944 in Bánkska-Bystrica.

19. With the entry of German forces into "independent" Slovakia, in order to quash the uprising, there began a deportation of the country's remaining Jewish population.
20. It is hard to say that masses of Hungarians flowed to join Tito's battalion. On the other hand, in an effort to make contact with the partisans, János Kádár (who was later leader of the governing party in Hungary) tried to smuggle across the border to Croatia, where Tito's forces were active, in the spring of 1944. He was unsuccessful and arrested on the Hungarian side, far away from the border. The Hungarian security authorities were still horribly efficient!
21. Member of the Hashomer Hatza'ir leadership in Hungary, today in Hungary.
22. A hill in the capital's Twelfth Quarter. Its hotels — with the occupation of Hungary — accommodated various German offices. Among other, Eichmann stayed there. Zvi Szilágyi was called to the Gestapo.
23. Avri Lissauer was deported, but remained alive. At the writing of this chapter, his whereabouts were still unknown.
24. A town in western Hungary, close to the Austria-Germany border.
25. Metuka Cseh — today: Anna Klein in Holon (at that time she was eighteen years old!).
26. Called by the Hungarians Munkács, until 1938, a town in Carpatho-Russ in Czechoslovakia; between the years 1938-1944 — under Hungarian control; later in Soviet sub-Carpathan Ukraine.
27. A nickname. The real name was Anton.
28. A town in Transdanubia, in western Hungary.
29. Milan Grigorjevic.
30. Israel Harari — member of Kibbutz Ein Dor.
31. On the forced labor units of the Hungary army, see: Moshe Zandberg (Zanbar), A Year Without End (Jerusalem, 1966); Hillel Danzig, In the Shadow of Horses (Tel Aviv, 1976).
32. The contacts in those neutral countries were not able to fulfill a leading role — from afar. They received letters with information on events in the German-occupied countries. However, developments were so quick and the situation so dynamic, that by the time a response from Genev or Istanbal arrived in Budapest, the situation had undergone fundamental change. Anyway, neither the Jewish Agency delegation, nor the representatives in Geneva, recommended crossing over to Romania. It was an intuitive idea on the part of the experienced refugees, who raised the hypothesis that on the "fringes" of the German-occupied zone, the situation might be improved than nearer to the Reich zone. This assumption turned out to be correct.
33. A town in western Romania (Transylvania), which remained under Romanian jurisdiction, on the partition of Transylvania — between Romania and Hungary in 1940. Heading the rescue activity was Aaron-David Finklestein, who describes this in his book: Fénysugár a borzalmak éjszakájában (Hungarian, Tel Aviv, 1958).
34. Oradea-Mare, or Nagyvárad, in Hungary, the second largest town in western Transylvania, very close to the Hungarian border. Between 1940 and 1944, it was under Hungarian control.
35. Immediately following March 19, the Romanian Antonescu regime published a decree, whereby any Jew crossing into Romania illegally would be shot!

Nonetheless, the Romanians did not shoot immediately, because they knew that hundreds of Jewish refugees captured by them were handed back to the Hungarians...or, at best, were "redeemed" by them according to methods acceptable to Jewish communities in southern Transylvania and sent on in the direction of Bucharest.

36. Meir Löwinger was a member of Hashomer Hatza'ir in Slovakia.
37. Misho (Michael) Neumann was a member of Maccabi Hatza'ir. He and his girlfriend were lost trying to smuggle across the border to Romania.
38. Uri Meir was a member of Maccabi Hatza'ir in Hungary.
39. The late Hana Ganz had been a member of "Habonim" in Transylvania, deceased in Israel.
40. Yirmiyahu Weiss, member of the Hashomer Hatza'ir in Slovakia.
41. The military prison of the Budapest region was located on Margit Bulevard in the capital's Second Quarter. The mere mention of the place was enough to instill fear...following liberation, the town elders renamed the street "Saints' Way" (Martírok útja), with the objective of commemorating the hundreds who had been executed there (including the emissary-paratroops, Hana Szenes).
42. In the capital's Seventh Quarter.
43. Shraga Weil, member of Kibbutz Ha'ogen.
44. I.e. the Polish National Committee, which was connected to the representatives of the Polish government in exile in London. The Shikorsky government maintained constant "ties" with Hungary. Horty's Hungary never recognized(!) the disappearance of the Polish state. Notwithstanding the demands of the Germans, a diplomatic representative of the exiled government acted with near freedom in Hungary (the representative, Edmund Feitowicz was arrested on March 19, 1944). The Polish Committee worked in a semi-free manner. Hundreds of Jews, masquerading as Poles in order to escape, were taken care of by this committee.
45. Miko Weiss was born in the town of Popard in north-western Slovakia.
46. David Gur (Gross), now living in Ramat Gan.
47. The Jews of Oradea were cramped into the ghetto in the second week of May 1944. The cadet division of the Hungarian Gendarmerie was entrusted with concentration and deportation, which commenced at the end of May and ended at the beginning of June. These cadets competed among themselves over acts of cruelty toward the Jews, encouraged by their officers. Scenes from the deportation were filmed by the Germans and presented — several weeks later — in Switzerland, in order to prove to the neutral public that the cruelty of the Hungarian police forces was far greater than that of the Nazis!
48. Hava (Auslaender) Ben Porat, now in Kibbutz Ga'aton.
49. The river that crosses Oradea.
50. I.e. David Gur.
51. Yaffa Burger-Krausz, now a member of Kibbutz Kfar Masaryk.
52. Meira Mosesh, sent to the border so advantage could be made of her knowledge of Romanian, and she was lost.
53. The late Moshe Kilon (Klein), deported to Auschwitz, was a member of Kibbutz Yas'ur.

54. Eta Berger, Survived Auschwitz, now in Israel.
55. Moshe Shapira, now a member of Kibbutz Yas'ur.
56. Nomi Livne (Engel), deported to Auschwitz, now in Israel.
57. Hedi Federweiss-Shapira, now a member of Kibbutz Yas'ur.
58. Lea Adler-Stern, deported to Auschwitz, now in Jerusalem.
59. Yutzi (then Yutza) Herbst, wife of Mimish (Yitzhak) Herbst. She died in 1974 in Israel.
60. Ferencváros, a team at the top of the Hungarian first league for dozens of years.
61. Hungarian initials for The Nagyvárad Athletics Club (Oradea).
62. An Ihud member from Poland.
63. A holiday resort some ten kilometers out of Oradea.
64. Leu (pl, Lei), the Romanian currency. This was worth around $120 at the time.
65. The border was some eight kilometers from town.
66. "Mr. Szabó." Szabó is a very common Hungarian family name, one of the names used by Pil.
67. A large town in southern Hungary. In 1944, it was the second largest town in Hungary.
68. A large town in south west Romania (Transylvania).
69. There were several categories in Hungary which deferred antisemitism, at its peak — deportation, and allowed exemption for certain people belonging to these categories. People with national decorations from the first world war, people who did special service for the Hungarian nation, etc. including their families. Altogether, about 5,000 people all over the country were granted the status of "exceptional person" and allowed to remain in their places.
70. Tamar Benshalom, the author's wife, now a member of Kibbutz Ha'ogen.
71. Ben-Eretz (Alexander) Grossman was arrested early on the morning of June 15, 1944 in Oradea. He was transferred immediately to the ghetto which still existed in Cluj. From there, he and his friends were taken by the Gestapo to the Nazi concentration camp in Budapest.
72. The hat was brown and beige — the colors of the well-known hunting hats in Hungary. Such a hat, decorated with a bunch of pig bristles, was characteristic of Hungarian hunters. Jews simply did not wear such a hat…. Pil was convinced that for this very reason, the hat had special qualities. For him, it was a king of lucky charm, looking after him, even if its wearer did not have a truly Aryan face.
73. A town on the river Tisza, south east of Budapest.
74. A railway crossing south of Solnok.
75. "Jew."
76. It is worth pointing out that the Hungarian people's admiration of the Poles was deeper even than their admiration for the Germans. Even people who were addicted with their souls to the Nazis, considered the extending of assistance to the Poles — Christian Catholics! — as clear proof of the traditional Hungarian gallantry.
77. In the capital's Fifth Quarter.
78. In Hungary: Hadviseltek Bizottsága (Retired Soldiers' Committee). Founded in 1938, with the expulsion of the Jews from the general organization of "Battlefront Fighters." This organization encompassed thousands of Jewish officers and men

who had fought in World War I. The organization's leaders often tried — sometimes with some success — to pull strings in order to make life easier for the people in forced labor units. Many of them — led by Béla Fábián, member of the Hungarian parliament — thought they could engender the sympathy of their Hungarian brother-officers by demonstrating their patriotic feelings....
79. With all our negative feelings against the "Battlefront Fighters," their activity pales in comparison with the units of stewards and Jewish police in the Polish ghettos.
80. One of the firmest opposers of the proposal that every activity which seemed to him in breach of the law, should be carried out from the Judenrat building!
81. The late Neshka Goldfarb, one of the leaders of the Dror movement in Hungary, was a member of Kibbutz Farod.
82. In the capital's Fifth Quarter.
83. According to the basic rules of international diplomacy, a house in which a foreign representative is situated and works is without the general territory of the country in which it is located, including its judicial authorities.
84. The news of Romania's resignation from the war on the side of Germany, was made known during the evening of August 23, 1944. Pil was awoken, therefore, in the early morning of August 24.
85. This does not refer to the followers of Shabtai Zvi, but to a special cult which formed in the seventeenth century in Transylvania, whose people were called "Shabtais," or "people of the tribe." Over the generations, many of them became close to Judaism and even integrated into it. On the other hand, there were those who belonged superficially to one of the Christian religions, while maintaining their own religion in secret.

Chapter 6

1. A small town in the Vojvodina province of north Yugoslavia, under Hungarian rule during 1941-1944. The Hungarians built a concentration camp on the outskirts of the town.
2. Hans Fogel, member of Hano'ar Hatzioni from Poland.
3. Zipporah Agmon (Schechter), former member of Kibbutz Ha'ogen. She died in 1967.
4. The "transport," organised by the *Va'ad ezra vehatzala* (Aid and Rescue Committee).
5. A large city in eastern Germany.
6. A village in the vicinity of Austria's capital city.
7. The original objective — according to Eichmann — had been "to keep some 30,000 Hungarian on ice..." in return for $200 a head and their board and lodgings in a special camp. See: G. Reitlinger, The Final Solution, London, 1971 (henceforth: Reitlinger), pp. 475. The Aid and Rescue Committee was supposed to raise this money. It did not succeed in this endeavor. In the end, some 15,000 Hungarian Jews were expelled to the vicinity of Vienna, instead of to Auschwitz. In his report, Dr. Kastner mentioned a larger number, 18,000. One of Eichmann's aides reckoned it was only 9,000, in his testimony at the tribunal in Bratislava.

8. In the city's First Quarter. This was the Pest county prison and served the Germans after March 19, 1955, who held their prisoners there.
9. The nickname of Hana Stern, Hashomer Hatza'ir member from Košice, who was lost in the Holocaust.
10. The illegal-immigrant ship "Mefkora" set sail from the Romanian port of Konstanza in the Black Sea, on August 3, 1944, with hundreds of emigrants on board. She was accompanied by another illegal immigrant ship, the "Bulbul." On the night of August 5, the Mefkora was torpedoed, without warning, by a submarine. Only five of her passengers survived and were picked up by "Bulbul."
11. Renka Kellerman was one of the victims of Mefkora.

Chapter 7

1. The first deportation trains set out in this order: a) from the concentration camp at Kistarcsa, b) from the concentration camp at Topolja, c) from the military operations region in south west Hungary — all at the end of April, before the deportations organized by Hungarian establishment.
2. Secret consultations took place in the Hungarian Ministry of the Interior on April 4, 1944, the subject: Purifying the country of Jews. But official orders were issued only on April 27.
3. The guards belonging to the National Catholic Party in Slovakia, named after the priest Andre Halinka, founder of the party.
4. "Rising up" in Croatian. Members of the Croatian National Party militia, which had been organized as a storm troops, in emulation of the Nazis.
5. A nickname. She perished in Auschwitz.
6. One of the main leaders of Hungarian Jewry since the early 1930s and up to 1944. For many, Jews and non-Jews alike, this man was the symbol of Hungarian Jewry. It was of course, too simple an assumption. Still it was a fact that the "advisor to the court" — President of the largest and wealthiest community in the country and Chairman of the Jewish council — had a hand in many shortcomings, which determined the lives of Hungary's Jews for good or for bad.
7. Most of these couriers belonged to the Wehrmacht's Abwehr. They did not particularly sympathize with the SS. Being originally from Vienna did not automatically guarantee sympathy for the Jews. It would seem that after 1943 they began to feel the approaching downfall and wanted to ensure themselves a few "good points" for the post-Reich period.
8. Sonder-Einsatz-Kommandos.
9. At the time of writing this chapter, there was no knowledge of Eichmann's real background. He himself spread the story of his knowledge of Hebrew.
10. The late Nathan Schvalb, (Dror) member of Kibbutz Hulda, who spent World War II in Switzerland as an emissary for Halutz.
11. The nickname of Dieter von Wisliceny, who was Eichmann's right hand man at the rank of Hauptsturmführer with the SS (captain). He was caught at the end of the war, sentenced to death and executed in July 1948 in Bratislava. He was active in Greece and Slovakia also, and the Slovak refugees remembered him from there.

12. Kurt Becher was an SS Obersturmbanführer (colonel). He was responsible for economic issues in several of the Nazi occupied countries, including Hungary.
13. On the eastern front, the German forces had been in constant retreat since 1943. The retreat was escalated because of Soviet pressure. On the western front, which opened only with the allied invasion in June 1944, retreat began after six weeks. Two additional fronts — the Balkan and the Italian — were more or less stable, compared with the main fronts.
14. He set off for Vienna on May 17, 1944 and two days later flew to Istanbul.
15. This assumption is unfounded. The German authorities had connections for the purpose of feeling out a possible peace (indeed such connections were available to all the important elements in the Reich, separately). They did not need Joel Brand for this.
16. Between 1938 and 1941, Hungary was returned several areas which had been Hungarian historically, but had been lost in the 1920 peace agreements. Deportations were organized in such a way that the Jews would be expelled from these regions before their brethren in "Hungary proper" were dealt with.
17. According to Hungarian political definition from between the two world wars, the "mother country" weeps for her sons who were torn away....
18. In Hungarian: "Nagy vonal."
19. Most of the Jews, apart from those who were residents of Budapest, were saved from the ghetto in Cluj, birthplace of Dr. Kastner. This in itself turned public opinion against him.... 1,600 souls were a mere drop in the ocean of so much suffering. The removal of Jews from ghettos in the satellite towns which had already been sealed, aroused the wonder of the Hungarians, especially as these removals were carried out by the Nazis themselves!... Eichmann "revealed" to the dumbfounded Hungarian authorities that a "dangerous Zionist conspiracy" had been uncovered, connected to the imprisoned conspirators who were being taken to Budapest for further investigation. (See Reitlinger, pp. 476).
20. The larger the number of people arrested in the wake of the occupation of Hungary, the more people there were to become expert "rescue activists," mostly Hungarians with good connections. This was mainly in return for large sums of money — rarely from humane motives — these succeeded in getting a few prisoners released.
21. The Hungarian press and politicians had spent the two months preceding the March 19, 1944 in unrestrained incitement against the Jews. This wall of hatred seemed to have no cracks.
22. The synagogue on that street in the city's Eighth Quarter, served as an assembly camp.
23. During April-June, there were an average of two or three air attacks a week in Budapest. In July-September, this increased significantly. In September, the city was also bombed by Soviet planes and after October, until the siege of the city, air attacks became a daily routine.
24. Judith Hartman, a member of Kibbutz Ha'ogen.
25. In the end the group was deported, but some of them managed to stay alive.

Chapter 8

1. Chairman of the Palestine Committee was Nathan (Otto) Komoly. Members of the presidency were: Shalom Offenbach (who was also treasurer of the Aid Committee) and Cvi Szilágyi. They all arrived at the presidency meeting hoping to be included — or their loved ones — in the list. People who were paralyzed with fear, offered all that was dear to them — money, valuables, etc. It was a terrible spectacle: hundreds were weeping, shouting, threatening and begging — all together and in a cacophony of voices. Members of the Jewish Council had no compunctions about recommending their own dear ones. The lists, which kept changing, included several Christian converts who for years had distanced themselves from Judaism. These were now causing a furor because of the means they had placed at Dr. Kastner's disposal which allowed them to be taken into consideration.... Others accused Dr. Kastner of never having produced a report on the delegation's financial system. The commotion, tension and emotional upheaval of the people made any kind of detailed list impossible.
2. There were plenty of rumors about this kind of trick on the part of the Nazis. No emigration transport had ever been organized that ended up in the death camps.
3. In the national congress of the Jewish Hungarian communities in Hungary in 1868, there was a split between the ultra-Orthodoxy and the majority stream which strove for assimilation. (In actuality, several dozen communities continued to maintain the situation as it was before the split and as for the two major streams, they too had a national organization.) Relations between the two major streams — the Neologists and the ultra-Orthodox — up to the Holocaust, were tense, and that's putting it mildly.
4. "External" elements were also of influence: there were days on which hundreds of Jews came to ask to be included in the transport — while the next day, many of them waived their inclusion. The reason for this was that encouraging news from the battlefronts were raising their hopes....
5. Unlike in the suburbs and provinces, no central ghetto was built in Budapest. Rumors spread that in the event of a ghetto being formed, the allies would increase their bombing of those regions of the city in which no Jews lived...thus "Jewish houses" were established all over the city and Jews were forced to move into these houses, which had a large Yellow Star on a black background fluttered at their entrance. The move had to end by midnight on June 24, 1944. The following morning an announcement was posted on each of the Jewish houses, that the movement of Jews in the city's streets was restricted to three hours a day. Later this was extended to six hours.
6. In the capital's Sixth Quarter. The "camp" was located in a synagogue. In Bocskai Street, too, a synagogue served as a "camp." Moshe Rosenberg, an engineer, converted these synagogues into temporary camps to accommodate hundreds of people.
7. Yehuda Weiss, Deceased in the United States.
8. It was on a Sabbath eve, June 30, 1944. There had been a lengthy air raid warning that day: for over three hours the allied planes were active in Hungary's air space. The transport train waited from six to eleven o' clock in the evening in one of the

capital's external stations...groups of travelers arrived there on foot. They numbered 1,684.

9. A town in north-west Hungary, close to the Austrian (German) border. The Germans claimed that the Hungarian authorities had not agreed to the train's departure across the border and turned it back to Komarno (Komáron, in Hungarian), a town on the banks of the Danube, some eighty kilometers west of Budapest. From here the train was turned to Slovakia and the transport arrived at Bratislava.

10. One of the worst of Germany's death camps. The transfer was removed to a special camp, "Vorzuglager."

11. Auspitz bei Brünn. In Bratislava the travel papers had been checked and the passengers were horrified to discover that their destination had been determined as Auschwitz! Telegrams were despatched forthwith to the Aid and Rescue Committee and the Jewish Council (the daughter, son-in-law and grandson of the council's president, Shmuel Stern, were among the train's passengers). Armed with the telegrams, Dr. Kastner made his way quickly to Eichmann's HQ. Eichmann smiled and reassured Kastner. He claimed that, since Camp Strasshof had filled up, he had directed the train to Auspitz, and it turned out that his clerks were guilty of misspelling!

12. A large town in western Austria, on the banks of the Danube.

13. "The Protocols of Auschwitz" — testimonies of two Slovak Jews who had succeeded in escaping from the death camp and return to Slovakia, had been smuggled into Hungary. See: Zvi Erez, "Six Days in July 1944 in Hungary" (Hebrew) in Yalkut Moreshet, vol. 20, pp. 165, ref. 23. These "Protocols" had been translated by a group of Zionists: Dr. P. Herschkovitz, Dr. A. Kurz, A. Kinori, L. Komoly (the daughter of the president of the Zionist Federation) and S. Friedland, on June 14, 1944. The group also made sure the translation received widespread distribution. At the end of June, beginning of July 1944, it may be assumed that most of the remaining Jews of Hungary were well aware of the hidden meaning of "showers at Auschwitz."

14. On July 8, 1944, the transport arrived at Bergen Belsen. On August 21, the first 318 members arrived at Montreux (see Reitling, pp. 47). It seems that the Germans' objective regarding this transport, was to "create a comfortable climate"...and to continue negotiations, not with Joel Brand, who had been arrested by the British, but with Sally Mayer, representative of the JDA in Switzerland. The Swiss immigration authorities were annoyed that the members of the transport had not come equipped with entry permits, as demanded by law...the remaining 1,368 members of the "Kastner transport" arrived in Switzerland on December 6, 1944. The number of deaths should be deducted from the original number and the births added.

15. Several months before its collapse, Portugal and Turkey declared war on Germany, in order to be included among the founder nations of the United Nations.

16. Dr. Kastner did indeed publish his report immediately after the war ended. Dr. R. Kastner: "Der Bericht des Jüdischen Rettungskomitees aus Budapest 1942-1945."

17. In return for each of the passengers on the transport, the Germans had originally

demanded $1,000. It is not known exactly what sum was ultimately paid. Anyway, all the partners in the "deal" were aware that the Nazis did not get the full amount.

Chapter 9

1. As a non-aligned country, the Swiss consulate in Hungary represented a large number of countries with whom Hungary was in a state of war. These included Britain and the United States.
2. Travel documents issued by the British Mandatory authorities in Palestine. Switzerland represented British interests, thus according to international law, Switzerland was able to handle British documents in Hungary, since there was no British consulate there. The idea was simple enough; implementing it was far more complex.
3. Charles Lutz. During 1939-1941, he had served as Swiss Consul to Palestine.
4. Arthur Weiss was the leading glass wholesaler in Hungary. His home in Vadász Street was probably the best possible advertisement for his merchandise: many of the building's walls, including its roof, were made of special glass. From an architectural point of view, the building was a unique specimen. A. Weiss, the successful wholesaler, was one of the leaders of Budapest's Neologue community. He had excellent organizational ability, was firm, decisive, resourceful and had foresight.
5. Unfortunately, it is not possible, in a discussion of the dissent between Dr. Kastner and M. Krausz, to ignore their political backgrounds: Moshe Krausz belonged to Mizrahi, while Dr. Kastner, was one of the leaders of Mapai.
6. In other words, after August 23, 1944. It appears that German bureaucracy sometimes moved at a slow and inefficient pace, too.
7. The concepts, ideology, and mode of behavior sported by Arthur Weiss and Moshe Krausz were totally different from those of the youth movements. The age gap was also a contributing factor to the creation of personal tensions, in addition to the general world-view.
8. The Hungarian authorities under Nazi occupation, had no reason to quarrel with the Swiss consulate. At this time it was looking out for Hungarian interests in many countries. It was one of the few neutral foreign consulates from which national leaders in Budapest extracted maximum effect. It was because of this effect that the authorities chose to turn a blind eye to the activity in Vadász Street, of which they were well aware.
9. In August and September 1944, with the easing up of tension, the Regent of Hungary and his Interior Minister decided to allow several hundred Jews, who had done much for Hungary in various fields, to remove their Yellow Stars. Due to their father's financial achievements, the Weiss family was one of them.
10. The name Dr. Rafai has a distinctly Hungarian ring to it.
11. He disappeared after the liberation.
12. On August 12, 1944, Jewish Council member P. de Freudiger (the title was granted to his grandfather by Franz-Josef) set out in a sleeping compartment for Bucharest, thanks to the Romanian passports smuggled to him by a courier of the Romanian consulate in Budapest. About seventy of his friends, all members of the ultra-

Orthodox community, went with him. de Freudiger claimed that Wisliceny — from Eichmann's office — had warned him of the imminent deportation of the capital's Jews.
13. Two weeks after the escape — August 23 — Romania experienced a dramatic turn of events. M. Krausz could not, of course, have anticipated it....
14. The last two consignments had left Hungary opposed to the orders of the ruler: one from the concentration camp at Kistarcsa, on July 19, 1944; the second from the Sárvár concentration camp on July 24, 1944. Deportations stopped after this date, until October 1944.
15. The Hungarian senior officials knew that the Regent had forbidden the continuation of transports. At that time(!), no-one dared defy him. Horthy's wishes underwent a kind of seeped down to the lower government levels. The failed attempt on Hitler's life on the one hand, the success of the allied forces and the constant advance of the Russian army on the eastern front, on the other, and perhaps even more, the behavior of the German occupying forces, caused even more Hungarians to open their eyes.
16. This prison remained under the control of the Nazis and was not returned to the Hungarian authorities.
17. Dr. Kotarba's brother, who died in 1957 in Israel.
18. One of the leaders of "Zionist Youth"; one of the leaders of the World Zionist Congress in London, where he deceased.
19. Miklós Frenkel, one of the Hungarian "Mizrahi" leaders; today in Israel.
20. In the prison on Fő Street, Ben-Eretz Grossman found an SS man who was willing to cooperate with the prisoners without asking for any financial reward! Via this man, Ben-Eretz was able to make contact with the author. He also made friends with the former General Manager of the Hungarian National Bank. This man had connections with the wife of the Regent. Prolonged Hungarian pressure proved fruitful: on September 14 1944, all the prisoners of the Nazis were removed to the concentration camp at Kistarcsa — into the hands of the Hungarians. Many of these, including Ben-Eretz Grossman, were released on September 29 1944.
21. By that time the battle-front was inside Hungary.
22. During the morning, the Regent's son had been kidnapped by Nazi agents, who masqueraded as supporters of Tito...this caused the leader to lose control of events which had been planned in advance, and were supposed to take place a few days hence: the announcement on Hungary's withdrawal from the war and the alliance with Germany. At 13:10, the Budapest radio station announced — in accordance with the Regent — that Hungary had called for an armistice. The Regent's manifesto was read out immediately after this, together with two repeats of the order of the day. The news spread like wildfire.

Chapter 10

1. The Royal Hotel served as the German High Command. The nervous guards shot a few rounds and it was a wonder that no-one in Budapest raised a hand against the Germans on October 15....
2. Two "Tiger" tanks, on their way to take control of the radio station. At 15:50 they

took control of the station, without any resistance. The Germans and their lackeys, members of the Arrow Cross, were much better organized than the ruler and his government (which included two ministers, who served as informers to the Germans).

3. The International Red Cross, Department A, headed by Nathan Komoly, president of the Zionist Federation in Hungary. The office was located in the city's Fifth Quarter.
4. Dr. Kastner's name in Hungarian.
5. At that moment, probably less than ten people in Budapest knew that as part of Hungary's plan to withdraw from the Axis forces, the Soviet army had stopped — in accordance with the Hungarian leader — its advance toward Budapest. The iron fists of the Soviet armored divisions were eighty to a hundred kilometers from the capital.
6. Radio broadcasts were resumed at 17:25. Until then, following two announcements of the Regent's charter and his order of the day, broadcasting ceased for fear of an air attack. Broadcasting was resumed and rousing German and Hungarian marches were played(!), after the Chief of Staff's order of the day was read out, calling for continued fighting on the side of the Germans.
7. Károly Beregfy (Berger), of Serb-German origin, was the highest ranking Hungarian officer to support the Arrow Cross overthrow. He was appointed Minister of Defense after October 16. No-one understood the call, while it was being made over the radio. But quite simply, Beregfy was stuck in his car outside Budapest and his fellow-broadcasters as well as the Germans did not know his whereabouts.
8. In order to put pressure on the Regent, who had lost most of his military power, the Germans fired several rounds of ammunition toward the royal palace — in which he resided — on the morning of October 16. A few minutes later, they burst into the palace.
9. A sea port on the Barentz Sea (the frozen northern sea). There are nickel mines in the vicinity of the town, which until 1940, had been a part of Finland, who lost it to the Soviets in the war of 1939-1940. From 1941-1944, it was under Finnish control once again. In wake of Finland's withdrawal from the war on the German side, the withdrawal of German troops from northern Finland to Norway, the Soviets occupied the town once again on October 15, 1944. Today the town is known as Pechenga.
10. Ferenc Szálasi, a retired army officer, leader of the extreme right wing Arrow Cross Party in Hungary. From October 16 until April 4, 1945, when the Nazis and their Hungarian helpers were chased out of Hungary, he served as "leader of the Hungarian nation." He was executed for war crimes in 1946.
11. Within three weeks, at the beginning of November 1944, all those who had been exempt under the previous administration were exempt once again by the Arrow Cross administration.
12. Doumier Honore (1808-1879), a well-known French artist and caricaturist.
13. Line in other countries, the railways were under the control of the Hungarian government. Railway workers wore special uniform and had a hierarchy of their own.

14. From October 15, 1944, German and Hungarian guards were placed alongside all the bridges which joined both parts of the capital, Buda to the west and Pest to the east. These guards made a constant check of the documents held by the passersby. It was very dangerous, therefore, for Jews to cross these bridges.
15. Died in Kibbutz Ga'aton, Israel.
16. Betzalel Adler, diedn in Western Germany.
17. Willy Eisikovitz, now living in Austria.
18. With the arrival of the forced labor units which had begun congregating in Budapest, the number of guns in our possession arose. The new arrivals had managed to obtain and bring large numbers of weapons and not only small ones.
19. The man, Rossi, sold out later in December 1944, when he dishonestly captured a hiding place belonging to the Rózsadomb underground movement, took their emergency arsenal and disappeared. The Italians disowned him.
20. Miky Langer was born in Popard in north-east Slovakia.
21. Following the Arrow Cross revolution, battle continued on Hungarian soil. About half of the country was already in the hands of the Soviets. Hundreds of people escaped westwards from this territory. The state of anarchy increased together with the paralysis of the authorities. These too, were mostly in a state of transfer to western Hungary. The greater the danger, the greater the chance of survival, because anyone who had the nerve to contribute his own modest effort toward increasing the chaos — by not wearing the Yellow Star — managed to stay alive.
22. The couriers continued to operate until about the middle of December 1944.
23. In spite of the letters and large quantities of information being passed on by various means to Switzerland and Turkey, and thence to the Jewish organizations in the allied countries, the situation in Hungary was never fully understood. Not only Swiss birth certificates were delayed. A further example of miscomprehension — which had no justification anywhere — was the unsuccessful briefing supplied to the paratroopers from Palestine who were supposed to be in Hungary. On the other hand, even if there was a constant stream of information, it very soon became out of date.
24. In the autumn of 1944, the states occupied by the Nazis were also closed to citizens of the unaligned countries, so that even if someone bearing a Spanish passport had tried to enter, he would not have received permission from the Germans. On the other hand, let us not forget that Menahem Bader was about to come to Hungary in the summer of 1944 — as a representative of the Jewish Agency — to deal with the "merchandise for blood" deal. His journey never materialized because of opposition by the British.

Chapter 11

1. The order was published on October 20, 1944. Some 50,000 men were drafted. They were organized into digging-units and sent out to conduct hasty trenching operations in the vicinity of Budapest.
2. On October 23, Jewish women aged between eighteen to forty, were also drafted and sent to the trenching. Groups of women and men were sent out later, with the renewed expulsions to the Romanian border.

3. For the first time, the official newspaper, Budapesti Közlöny, dated October 21, 1944, announced that anyone with a letter of protection issued by a non-aligned state, was exempt from trench-digging units. Nonetheless, the security forces did not always honor these letters. On the other hand, many Jews were subsequently released, having been recruited for this work, as soon as they managed to prove that they were the owners of a letter of protection.
4. The Swiss "Letter of Protection" bears the date October 23, 1944.
5. See photograph of the "Letter of Protection" issued in the name of Sándor (Simha) Hunwald.
6. There were disagreements and endless arguments as to whether a quota of 7,800 **families** had been promised letters, or 7,800 **people**.
7. At that time there was a promise to the Swedish consulate of 4,500 "passports" (in German: Schutzpasse).
8. Figaro chocolate was the name of an unsuccessful product with which the German company "Stimmer" tried to compete with the superior product made by the Jerbo company, whose owner was Swiss born. Hence the play on words.
9. In the capital's Fifth Quarter. The Swiss consulate, which inherited the building from the American consulate, was located twenty meters from the false consulate.
10. According to Hungarian custom (and not only in Hungary), the doors of offices and various official institutes, were always open to people in high places…. Moreover, it was the custom for officers in the security forces not to be obliged to stand in line. The widespread and sophisticated use made by the Jews of the "letters of patronage" aroused the Nazis' wrath. The Head of the Security Ministry protested to his counterpart in the Nazi Foreign Ministry on November 11, 1944, that entire military companies had vanished from the roads leading to Germany as a result of the Hungarians' recognition of the "letter of patronage."
11. Efra's testimony.
12. Dr. Kotarba-Osterweil escaped in 1942 to Hungary, established a hostel for the young refugees from Poland, including many Jewish children, under Polish identity. He died some years ago, after a long term of service at the hospital at Be'er Ya'akov.
13. In the capital's Seventh Quarter.
14. The order was issued on November 12, 1944, demanding the concentration of all "letter" holding Jews in a given number of houses, in which some 4,000 Jews had lived until then. Those who were not equipped with the "letters" were later expelled to one of the brick factories and from there went on a "march of death" toward the German border. The authorities reckoned that this accounted for some 4,500 people sheltering in the shadow of the Swedish consulate; 2,500 under the auspices of the Vatican delegation; 100 under the protection of the Spanish consulate; 698 under protection of the Portuguese consulate and 7,800 under the protection of the Swiss consulate. Seventy-two houses were defined for the holders of Swiss "letters" except that it then transpired that thousands of Jews were already crowded into these houses, instead of the official quota; it should be pointed out that from the beginning of November, it was possible to hear clearly the sound of the approaching battle front. The Jews felt they were reaching the final stages of the race — the race with death. On November 2, several Soviet tanks penetrated Pest,

but were dispelled temporarily. A further Soviet attack, whose aim it was to capture Budapest in honor of November 7, was also stopped.
15. All the "protected houses" were located in the capital's Fifth Quarter.
16. In the capital's Fifth Quarter.
17. Another source has it that the Betar leader died after liberation, in January 1945.

Chapter 12

1. In other words, after Romania joined the anti-Nazi coalition.
2. An island on the Danube, in the south of the city, which housed a large concentration of heavy industry: the Manfred Weiss factories and others connected with this conglomeration. This was one of the strongholds of the Hungarian Labor Movement. The Nazis and the Arrow Cross wanted to disband the factories and take their machinery westwards. Opposition on the part of the laborers prevented this, but the factories continued producing for the Nazi war machine — until the Soviet occupation.
3. In 1942, the Garany concentration camp housed about 150 communists and 380 Jews, including eight members of Hashomer Hatza'ir. One of these young people was able to gain the confidence of the other prisoners and took care of both the communists and observant Jews who needed kosher food — due to his connections with the camp commander, who was relatively liberal.
4. Haim Gnud, who was shot by the Arrow Cross on a Budapest street before the liberation.
5. Following the fall of the councils in Hungary in 1919 and until the Soviet occupation in 1944/45, the Communist Party in Hungary was divided and disunited, full of warring factions. Until 1941, when Hungary entered the war against the Soviet Union, there was still some kind of bond with Moscow, which was severed during the war years. Although it was called a "Party," it did not boast many members. All the factions together did not amount to more than a few hundred. The faction loyal to Moscow was known as the 'line' (in Hungarian: Vonal), or the Hungarian Communist Party (in Hungarian: Kommunistak Magyaroszagi Pártja, or KMP). On the dissolution of the Komintern in 1943, and in face of the burning animosity toward communists, which had been nourished with such devotion by twenty-five years of a "National Christian" administration, the members of this faction preferred to be known under the name "Peace Party" (in Hungarian: Békepárt). Another faction, to which the Kovács belonged, called itself the "Communist Party" (in Hungarian: Kommunista Part, or KP). Current Hungarian historiography sees the KP as a deviation, and its members have been hounded since 1945. Most of them were arrested, some being executed for "Trotskyism," cooperation with the Horthy administration and other accusations. Only after 1956 was their status gradually re-instated.
6. The nickname of Sándor Futó-Galambos.
7. Iván Kádár.
8. In David Gur's testimony.
9. The Hungarian National Independent Front (in Hungarian: Magyar Nemzeti Függetlenségi Front, or MNFF), which brought together all the underground

democratic political forces. On November 23, 1944, all the officers in the military department of the "Front" were arrested, as a result of espionage. On the other hand, many of the Front's civilian leaders succeeded in evading arrest. Many of them had in their pockets papers produced by the workshop for the production of forged documentation belonging to the Zionist Youth Movements, but probably did not know who it was who had made it possible for them to stay alive.

10. Pál Demény was a veteran activist with the Hungarian communist movement, of Jewish extraction. He had spent many years behind bars in Hungarian jails. In the autumn of 1944, he was head of one of the communist factions, whose members planned to impose a proletarian dictatorship with the arrival of the Soviets...in contradiction to the policies of Moscow, about which they knew nothing. Due to the "wide front" tendency (which included the rest of the democratic parties, in addition to the communists), "Demény's factions" activity was considered provocative and destructive with regard to all the labor movement and the anti-Nazi underground, as was claimed after 1945. The sentence against him for "conspiring against national democracy" was revoked in 1957 and from a legal point of view, he was reinstated. Anyway, all official information on the man pointed to the fact that: "He was not worthy of reinstating the national honor, because of his previous factional activity...."
11. A heavy industry conglomerate, located in various places in Budapest's northern quarters.
12. Those present from Hashomer Hatza'ir were Rafi, Pil, Efra and Yoshka M. Most of them had doubts as to the man's reliability; Efra was the only one who refused to believe the informers and maligners and was convinced that Kovács-Demény was indeed telling the truth. It would be only right to point out that a considered guess would place "Demény's faction" with three times as many members (1,500!) as the 'Line faction'!
13. He meant the Communist Party, of course, which, following the overthrow of the republic in 1919, was proclaimed illegal. The General Labor Party — of the Social Democrats and the Trades Unions — was legal, under Horthy's rule. Several delegates from the Social-Democrat Party sat in Parliament.
14. The underground Hungarian Communist Party held several congresses — outside of Hungary. In this respect, Demény is inaccurate.
15. Josef Sombor-Schweinitzer was a senior police officer, one of the heads of the police political department, from the thirties and until his arrest and exile by the Nazis. Schweinitzer was of German extraction (born in 1895 and apparently married to a Jewish woman), was the brains behind the war of the Horthy administration against all the political movements — from the right and even more so, from the left, which the powers-that-be considered a danger to the administration and their continued rule.
16. At the beginning of September 1944, the "Peace Party" announced it was changing its name and would be called from then on the "Hungarian Communist Party" (in Hungarian: Magyar Kommunista Part, or MKP). The change of name drew new members to the party, who had been involved with other factions or opponents.
17. 'A Free Nation,' the leading Communist paper in Hungary, came into existence in 1942, in the underground. In 1945 it came out and ceased publication during the

Hungarian Rebellion in October 1956, when the party disintegrated. Some time later, the daily re-appeared under the name Népszabadság (Freedom of the Nation).
18. Until the first days of liberty, there was no clear picture of expected political developments. It was only through the activity of the democratic parties, which the Soviets used all available means to activate, that it became gradually clear that — for the time being, anyway — the Soviet Union was not planning to impose its social government on Hungary and the other occupied countries.
19. In all these meetings, the Hashomer Hatza'ir representatives presented the stand that after the fall of the Nazis, the Jews must be recognized as a national minority, as had been the custom in a series of countries bordering on Hungary between the two world wars. All the documentation on these meetings was lost in 1949, when it became known that the man who would be testifying at a show trial was one of the underground communist leaders, László Rajk, who held extremely senior positions after 1945, and was very familiar with Ben-Eretz Grossman and his colleagues.
20. Mostly, contact was maintained with people who later held key-positions with the top leadership in the "Small Holders' Party" (Független Kisgazda Párt, or the FKGP), including Zoltán Tildi, who was President of Hungary 1946-1949. Nathan Komoly, President of the Zionist Federation, also met him often. There were also talks with Lajos Dénes and Ferenc Nagy, both of whom would serve as Hungarian Prime Ministers. Also Professor Dezső Keresztúri (today a highly acclaimed professor of Hungarian literature at the University of Budapest), met representatives of the Hashomer Hatza'ir. Dr. István Pesti, editor of the most audacious satirical journal at the time and today a member of the Hungarian parliament, was an underground activist with whom we had connections.
21. Several dozen British prisoners of war had found refuge in Hungary, after escaping from Germany. There was no state of war between Hungary and Holland.
22. Joel Palgi. See: Joel Palgi, "A Great Wind Come" (Tel Aviv, 1946), pp. 347, (henceforth: Palgi).
23. Tim Barker, a British flying officer whose plane was shot down over Germany and he was taken prisoner. He escaped to Hungary, where he was hidden by senior Hungarian circles, who were sympathetic to the allied forces. See: Palgi, pp. 344.

Chapter 13

1. JDC = Joint Distribution Committee.
2. In the capital's Seventh Quarter. There was hardly any trouble involved in renting apartments and even entire houses, for the needs of an institution with a meaningful sign post over the door or gate, proclaiming the "International Red Cross." Many property owners believed, and were right to a degree, that in the increasing anarchy, the prestige of an international organization would impart some protection for their assets.
3. Zvi Goldfarb was a refugee from Poland. In 1942, he left the Warsaw Ghetto and made his way to Slovakia. From there he moved to Hungary and became the leader of Dror in 1944 in Budapest. Zvi and Neshka lived and deceased in Kibbutz Farod.
4. "Young Soldier" was the name of the Hungarian pre-military educational organization until 1945. Membership in this organization was mandatory for

sixteen to eighteen year-olds. In 1944 several age groups were recruited from the "Levente" for active service as an emergency force, with no practical use. Members of "Levente" took part in acts of cruelty against Jews. On the other hand, members of the organization enjoyed freedom of movement.

5. Marek Gut, a refugee from Slovakia. He was caught by the Arrow Cross and executed on the banks of the Danube.
6. Josef Meir (member of Hashomer Hatza'ir), who maintained connections with various aspects of the Hungarian political spectrum. He was drafted into the forced labor units. With the help of forged documents, he deserted on October 13, 1944 and returned to Budapest.
7. György Nonn was one of Hungary's communist leaders, of German-Transylvanian origin. After coming out of the underground he became chief of the party's youth movement. He also filled senior government positions. He was later pushed out of the front line and serves as manager of the state book publishers.
8. This was a volunteer unit formed in November 1944 by the Arrow Cross, for fighting in "dangerous" places (or so they said!). There were not many volunteers for the Legion and most of these preferred to "fight" the defenseless Jews than the Soviet tanks. The Legion was such a failure that it was disbanded very quickly in western Hungary.
9. The Security Aid Division (Kisegítő Karhatalmi Alakulat, or KISKA). Several such battalions were recruited, most of them from Budapest. The original trend had been to secure the hinterland. Hundreds of army deserters on the one hand and Jews on the other, filled the ranks of the Division. The Germans and their helpers found the Division a serious nuisance.
10. The book shop belonging to the Arrow Cross was blown up. Grenades were thrown at a German car and in several places around Budapest, useless sabotage was done to the railroad. The one who took part in these activities, later a colonel in the security police, Gábor Csillik, mentioned them all in his book: Gábor Csillik, Budapesten harcoltunk (Budapest, 1964) — henceforth: Csillik.
11. András Kállay, son of the former Prime Minister of Hungary, Miklós Kállay.
12. This is probably a mistake. The fathers of these soldier-guards belonged in the past to the Hungarian political elite.
13. The capital's entertainment quarter.
14. In the capital's Thirteenth Quarter. A Dror member was killed in the course of the attack on the bunker; the rest, together with their leader, Eli Shlamovitz (was Chairman of the Merom Galil Regional Council), were taken prisoner by the Hungarian authorities.
15. He now lives in Haifa.
16. A military and civilian prison in western Hungary, where the main political prisoners were held, during the middle of December 1944. Zvi Goldfarb and his wife Neshka were among them. Zvi withstood terrible torture and remained faithful to his version, that he was an Italian called Mario Marchezi. Fortunately for them, they were returned to Budapest after a few days, several hours before the Soviets managed to cut off the Hungarian capital.
17. The central prison in Budapest (in the Fifth Quarter), which had a reputation all over Hungary.

18. In Hungarian "testvér": this is how members of the Arrow Cross referred to each other.
19. Napoleon III. All over Europe, many people kept their assets in the form of these, and similar, gold coins.
20. December 26, 1944.
21. There is no way to accurately assess the number of people who were shot on the banks of the Danube, but it is believed that these were several thousands.
22. Csillik, who had been arrested earlier and was imprisoned together with the Zionist prisoners described in his book (pp. 242) the escape of the David Gur-Zvi Goldfarb group from the point of view of those who remained in prison. He recalled his fury when he was informed that same day — so he said — that the Jews who had dared, succeeded. He and his friend (a Jewish communist) had no-one who would worry about them.... The prisoners were transferred on December 26, 1944 to a prison that was "further away" from the front, to Fö Street. The following day the officer came with his men, armed from head to toe, in order to execute an additional one hundred prisoners.... This time Csillik's Jewish friend was also taken and he himself, remained in jail. The book hints at the weaknesses of the communists in everything connected with getting their colleagues released from jail, as compared with the audacity of the Jews.
23. All trace of the informer disappeared after the liberation.
24. After taking over the administration, the Arrow Cross only dared to organize one public meeting in Budapest. Two members of the communist underground placed two bombs in that meeting. There were not many casualties, but the commotion was most impressive, as was the fear.... The armed forces investigated the incident enthusiastically. The press reported that the culprit had been arrested — a member of the Zionist organization, Betar! His picture was published in one of the illustrated newspapers. But, according to reliable information, the meeting was blown up by communists. The meeting convened not in the cultural center, but in the capital's largest theater building.
25. This was an "accepted" method of interrogation. It did not leave any signs of torture on the victim, which could be relied upon in court.
26. Starting with the arrest of Moshe Shapira and his friends in June 1944, the files gradually thickened against members of the main leadership of Hashomer Hatza'ir: Rafi Ben Shalom, Pil (Moshe Alpan), Dan Zimmerman (who was by then in Romania), Mimish (Yitzhak Herbst, who was know by the police under another name, Imre Hranyó).

Chapter 14

1. This is a well known mistake. The truth is that on December 24, 1944, the Soviets attacked west of the capital blocking several of the roads leading to it. Two routes remained open. On December 25, therefore, these routes were used by anyone who wanted to run for their lives (including some of the guards at the Margit Boulevard military prison, who tried their luck). But in the early afternoon, the Soviets arrived at a point north west of Budapest, on the River Danube. Thus the city was cut off. To the west of the city, in the region of the hills bordering on Buda, the Soviets had

reached a point about 1,500-1,800 meters — as the crow flied — from the prison and blocked the road there for hours on end.
2. It is unclear whether there were any plans to demolish the two ghettos: the large one in which most of the Jews were accommodated (in the Seventh Quarter) and the "Protected Houses" region (in the Fifth Quarter). Remnants of the Arrow Cross in the west have been claiming that it was they who thwarted the SS plans to demolish the ghettos. Nazi commanders made the same claim, with a small difference: it was they who prevented the Arrow Cross from carrying out the demolition.
3. On December 31, 1944, an armed company of Arrow Cross men under the command of a monk of the Order of Minorities, attacked the "glass building." They hurled a number of grenades into the building and there were several casualties. The inhabitants were taken out into the street, and then Arthur Weiss intervened. He had previous experience with troops who stormed Vadász Street (on one occasion a gendarme unit came to do a check-up. Weiss invited the officers in for a drink and when they were less than sober, he "bought" their goodwill with a large sum of money). This time he went up to the commander of the Arrow Cross and protested loudly at the attack on the building which was ex-territorial.
4. Several authorities were acting within the besieged city, often in conflict with each other, and who occasionally canceled an order published by an opposing authority....
5. Arthur Weiss was called for "friendly" consultations — so said the Arrow Cross on the evening of January 1, 1945. Everyone tried to prevent him from going, but his successes had convinced him of his strength so he took the risk. The circumstances of his death are unclear.
6. In the capital's Fourth Quarter.
7. A non-commissioned officer. The man died during the siege.
8. January 1, 1945.
9. The hotel — one of the most distinguished in the capital — was located in the Fourth Quarter.
10. Rata, Soviet fighter planes.
11. It was known that political prisoners, taken after the siege of Budapest, were transferred to the royal palace, which was well protected by the Germans and the Hungarians. The Hungarian democratic authorities imprisoned several dozen Arrow Cross activists, with the intention of exchanging these for those prisoners being held by the other side.
12. On January 20, 1945 — two days after the expulsion of the Nazis and their henchmen from the left bank of the Danube — several hundred political prisoners were executed in Buda.
13. In November 1944, the German/Hungarian front collapsed, one of whose branches had been supported until then by the Carpathian mountains.
14. For many years, Simha Hunwald had been a member of the higher leadership of Hashomer Hatza'ir in Hungary. For this reason, his emigration to Palestine had been postponed. Due to the aid administered by the movement, under his supervision — to refugees from Slovakia, he was arrested and held in a concentration camp for many months. He was later drafed into the forced labor

units and sent to the occupied territories in Russia and Ukraine. He was one of the few to remain alive after the great retreat from the River Don. Simha Hunwald learned Russian as a result of the split in the Hungarian front in January 1943, near Voronez. His knowledge of the language allowed him, after recovering from typhoid fever, to wear Hungarian uniform and serve as assistant manager of the hospital. In this guise, he was able to help all the Jews who came his way. During the final months of 1944, he did all he could — under the guise of János Kűhne, "clerk of the Swiss consulate" — to save lives. His great misfortune was to arrive, in a car bearing diplomatic corps number plates, at the courtyard in front of the "Glass building" only minutes after the runner was shot and killed. The Arrow Cross coveted the diplomatic corps car. The car, and its two passengers subsequently disappeared. Simha Hunwald's life and death engulf the great tragedy of the Hashomer Hatza'ir movement in Hungary.
15. "Protector of the motherland," the name given to a Hungarian soldier.

Josef (Joshka) Meir's Testimony

1. When the Communist underground movement in Transylvania was eliminated, and contact was established between Hashomer Hatza'ir and the Communists, Josef Meir's name became known to counter espionage interrogators of the Second Branch of the Hungarian High Command. As a result, he was brought back from the Forced Labor Brigade in West Hungary to the interrogation center at Szamosfalva; but his interrogators did not succeed in discovering anything, in spite of their tough interrogation.
2. Efra Teichman and Cipi Schachter were members of the Hashomer Hatzair movement. Josef Scheffer (who later became a member of Kibbutz Kfar Hahoresh) and Josef Meir were first to escape. They later organized the escape of other members of the Forced Labor Brigade who were also members of the Halutz movements.
3. These were mainly personal contacts. Josef Meir, who had come from Transylvania to Budapest in 1940 and had lived in the underground for two years, did not want to join the Forced Labor Brigade. Taking advantage of his completely Aryan appearance, and regional dialect, which was absolutely different from that spoken in the capital and common among Jews, he worked as a metal worker. He renewed and reinforced the connections he had established in Transylvania with trade union functionaries. He did this — with the knowledge and consent of the movement — by joining the activities of the young workers of the metalworkers' union.
4. This was one of the extreme right wing parties whose leaders and members had left the Arrow Cross Party, not for ideological reasons, but against a background of disagreements in the top echelons.
5. One of the right wing movement's eccentric figures. A retired cavalry colonel who, in the mid-1930s, was one of the important recipients of the funds funneled into Hungary by Nazi Germany for the purpose of organizing and consolidating sympathizers. Rátz hated the designated "Leader of the People," Ferenc Szálasi, who was beneath him in rank, being only a (ret.) major. As a member of the Hungarian gentry, he was nervous of the rabble that had rallied to his original party.

From 1940, he began to "turn left." Soon he claimed to have made contact with the Soviets!... In any case, after 1943, he made several blunt speeches in the Hungarian parliament in favor of returning the Hungarian troops to their homeland and against the harsh attitude to the Jews. He died in 1952.

6. Certain extreme right wing groups, and more than a few of the bodies accepted into the Arrow Cross Party, were in the semi-underground until 1944 because of their hostility to the regime of Regent Horthy. At the same time, to avoid complications, they issued member cards with personal code names. Josef Meir acquired such a card in the beginning of 1943, to reinforce his identity, since he too was in the underground, although for completely different reasons.

7. The people of the Arrow Cross Party's "service-units" were equipped with arms in October 1944, and wore the party symbol on their arms (See the photograph of Josef Meir in uniform). They performed policing duties and were among the main persecutors of Jews, killing thousands in cold blood.

8. In the Eighth District of the Capital.

9. "Tiger" the German army's major campaign tank in Word War II.

10. The excuse for the attack on the "Jews' houses" in Népszinház Street and Teleki Square was miserable: some Polish Jewish refugees who were living in one of the houses and had weapons celebrated the news of Hungary's surrender by firing some shots at an Arrow Cross patrol (the refugees had not yet heard about the coup!) The Nazis and their helpers carried out a massacre on the spot.

11. Thousands of Jews from surrounding areas were taken from their houses, marched with raised arms to the central city garage and allowed to return to their homes only after a few hours.

12. In the Seventh District of the capital.

13. Efra's hometown. The Jewish population was well-known to its Hungarian neighbors, whereas a Jew could easily conceal himself in the big city.

14. In the Sixth District of the capital. This was where the Arrow Cross Party center was located. After the liberation it became the State Police headquarters...

15. In the Sixth District of the Capital.

16. In the Sixth District of the capital. The incident lasted for 2.2 Km!

17. The intention was for them to actively participate in rescuing Jews, while armed and wearing actual Arrow Cross uniforms. Of course, anyone of obviously Jewish appearance would soon be caught pretending to be one of the thousands of armed people filling the streets.

18. Mainly in a chemical and a metal plant, both in the fourteenth district of the capital.

19. This was an opposition communist group that was active at the end of the '20s, mainly among the workers in the armament industry on Csepel Island. Its members were persecuted by both the underground Communist Party and the secret police. They provided samples of documents for forgery, contacts with factories and hiding places (for most of this period, Josef Meir lived in a villa situated outside the capital in Vitéz Telep, a suburb of the nationalistic minor aristocracy, placed at his disposal by this group). They also supplied explosives prepared by them in a chemicals factory that served as one of their centers. The group's special activity was smuggling and hiding soviet prisoners who had escaped from German captivity. Josef Meir provided them with escorts, civilian clothes and forged documents.

20. Sándor Futó-Galambos, a veteran communist, was close to the 'hardline' underground central committee. He supplied many samples of official forms for forgery. Great quantities of ready documents produced by the workshop were handed to him. He was one of those behind the idea of rousing the industrial workers in the capital and its environs against the idea of dismantling machines for despatch to Germany. The central committee hardliners tried to organize active resistance to this. The results were disappointing, apart from one or two places. After 1945, Futó Galambos became one of the directors of the nationalized coal industry.
21. The capital's tenth district, which had industrial plants and workers' housing in abundance.
22. In the capital's eighth district
23. This refers to György Prinz. By law, the Civil Defense was an official authority and, therefore, many possibilities were open to the officers of such a body. In emergencies, Prinz also hid soviet prisoners of war in the hospital.
24. The warehouse belonged to the family of a member of Hashomer Hatza'ir, Magda Fülöp.
25. One of the main activists in this group was the late Moshe Klein, who was an instructor in the movement.
26. From mid-December 1944, the Hungarian capital was gradually vacated. The government, government and cultural institutions, and entire plants complete with equipment and workers were transferred to west Hungary. Many military units were concentrated over the River Danube, in Transdanubia, with the intention of being closer to the Austrian (German) border in their flight from the Soviet army. Quite a few Hungarian soldiers chose to desert from the crumbling ranks of the army as they passed close to their homes, where they could obtain civilian clothes and go into hiding with the help of their families, until the Soviets arrived.
27. East of the capital. Contact was made with the help of Gyorgy Prinz. The unit commander was an officer by the name of Walz.
28. In the fifth district of the capital.
29. In the fourth district of the capital. The meeting took place in the waiting room of a dentist who was close to the military branch of the Hungarian underground — Magyar Nemzeti Függetenségi Front — which was the underground's roof organization that was promptly blown up by the detectives and inspectors of the National Prosecution Seat.
30. In fact, Tartsay was the campaign officer head of the military branch. The plan was for a special unit to take over the broadcasting station. A password would be broadcast on the radio and all the units with whom the underground had established contact would mobilize to open the front for the Soviet army, thus facilitating conquest of the capital. The plan was leaked and never went into operation. Tartsay was caught and hanged at the end of November, 1944.
31. In the eighth district of the capital.
32. Not only the general underground was weak; the Communists' battle units were also of extremely limited power and initiative.
33. In the thirteenth district of the capital.

34. "Moustache"; his real name was Béla Hajós. After 1945, he became a senior member of the Hungarian Communist Party Executive Committee.
35. Most probably this partisan commander was Lajos Fehér, who became Minister of Agriculture and Vice Premier of Hungary.
36. In addition to the supplies 'obtained' from military and Arrow Cross stores by means of forged documents, Josef Meir organized, with Efra Agmon, the transfer of food and civilian clothing from the International Red Cross, or Bureau of Economics stores, for which he was responsible.
37. Josef Meir recalled that he gave orders to seek contacts with the people of the National Prosecution Seat the day they received news of the disappearance of David Gur and his comrades, in response to a request from Rafi Benshalom and Moshe Alpan. Through the same contacts, news was received that they had been held at the Erzsébet Circle Party headquarters, but were taken to a place unknown to our informants. An additional detail was known: the Arrow Cross had burned corpses in the furnaces of the building that day.
38. In the growing disarray, relations between the various military and party units were strained. Each of them was interested in proving to the Arrow Cross-based Hungarian government, which was no longer in its capital, and perhaps even more to the German Command, that it and only it was the sole Hungarian support they could rely on…. Therefore, they all wanted large units. Anyone who wished — and, specially, dared — could enlist and be armed.
39. In the fourth district of the capital.
40. A member of the German minority in Hungary. Josef Meir knew him from the days of the metalworkers' union. A deep friendship formed between them. Zircz was connected with many factors in the anti-Nazi underground and was a great help. After the liberation, he served in the State Defense Authority. In 1956 he defected to become a journalist in West Germany.
41. This was the underground name of Hashomer Hatza'ir member Jaakov Markovics-Meron, now a member of Kibbutz Ein Dor.
42. The peaked caps of the military gendarmerie were decorated with black cock feathers, similar to the 'regular' gendarmerie. The military gendarmerie was a dreaded unit; its soldiers knew that if they were to fall into captivity, there chances of survival were nil.
43. "Halt!" in Russian.

Efra Teichmann-Agmon's Testimony

1. A town in North Eastern Hungary.
2. He was a member of Kibbutz Ma'anit.
3. Owing to the approach of the Soviet army, the whole of North-Eastern Hungary, including Munkács, was declared a Military Zone and the whole population was placed under military rule.
4. A large village in central Hungary.
5. A railway crossing town about sixty kilometers east of the capital.
6. Only the senior levels of the movements participated in this group. Only those

seniors who were capable of physical effort and of keeping secrets were invited to join the training exercises.

7. In the third district of the capital. The training included physical fitness, swimming, assembly and dismantling revolvers. A little later, we would also learn the use of the sub-machine gun used by the Hungarian army. The Senior group possessed one such sub-machine gun at the time.
8. Hungarian Jews, as honest citizens, believed that the rule of law and order would protect them as long as they were faithful to it. In their blindness they did not comprehend that those who sought to destroy them had, in fact, placed them outside of the law.
9. The largest of the Hungarian congregations. All the rest "rallied" to the stands taken by the Pest congregation (on the western bank of the river) in Buda, there was an independent congregation that was much smaller than the one on the east bank.
10. Shmuel Stern, Chairman of the National Office of the Neologue Community.
11. The assimilated Hungarian Jews gave the name "Sidelocks" to the orthodox Jews who had settled mainly in the northern and eastern districts of the country.
12. In the seventh district of the capital. A crowded community of Jews lived in this street; for this reason the street, actually a long section of it, was incorporated in the ghetto in December, 1944.
13. Hundreds of thousands of Hungarian Jews fought shoulder to shoulder with their non-Jewish neighbors in World War I. Some ten thousand fell in battle. This wartime partnership aroused great hopes — most or all of them false.
14. Without exception, the men at the top were elderly men in their sixties. They had many years of private and public activity behind them. Their spiritual strength and ability to progress failed in the face of the cruel, swift initiative of the Nazis and their Hungarian supporters. The Jewish leadership was unable to withstand a category of criminals on whom the lives of hundreds of thousands depended.
15. This was the sad conclusion of Béla Zsolt, himself one of the forced labor men.
16. The Polish refugee Halutzim brought to Hungary their accumulated "experience" from 1942-1943. This experience, which was suited to Poland and the time, did not apply to conditions in Hungary in 1944. In Poland nobody could know how long German rule would last, and therefore it was better to dive deep into the bunkers. A year or two later, in 1944 in Hungary, there was a race against time, when the light at the end of the tunnel was growing brighter; the Soviets were drawing closer day by day.
17. Ester Vardi-Schechter, today of Kibbutz Ha'ogen.
18. Hayim Fettman, who became a senior officer in the IDF.
19. The third biggest city in Hungary, in the east.
20. Now Moshe Golan of Tel Aviv.
21. A town in north-eastern Hungary.
22. Now of Tel Aviv.
23. Now of Nahariya.
24. In Pécs, in the center of the country over the Danube, there was a forced labor unit in which the three comrades served. Efra Agmon supplied them with suitable

documents with which later in 1944, they escaped from where the battalion was stationed.
25. Dr. László Somogyi was a General Zionist and one of the few Jewish clerks employed by the Hungarian Railways, owing to his outstanding service at the Front in World War I.
26. "Magyar Államvasútak."
27. Owing to the crush, we had to engage some "bouncers." We also had to have announcers to read out the names of those who had received Protection Passes.
28. The second biggest river in Hungary, in the east.
29. This was an emotionally difficult decision, both necessary and risky. In the end, it was shown to be clever and successful. Instead of the limited quota, tens of thousands of Jews were rescued.
30. In the fourteenth district of the capital.
31. Like the rest of the senior officials of the International Red Cross, Friedrich Born was a Swiss citizen. He did much for the rescue of Jews from the capital.
32. To obtain the longed-for slip of paper — and with it the hoped-for rescue — the Jews took risks in openly breaking the order against being in the city after the permitted hours.
33. Without the Pioneer Youth Movements' application of the ideas conceived by Zionist personalities, the brilliant idea of the rescue could never have taken on flesh and bone.
34. The Arrow Cross attacked the home in Munkácsi Mihály Street where there were many casualties. Other homes were abandoned by the adult staff and the children, who, unable to take care of themselves, suffered from malnutrition during the weeks of the siege.
35. Now Dr. Vera Friedman of the USA.
36. He died in Hungary after the war.
37. Today a member of Kibbutz Ga'aton.
38. Today Jaakov Hollander of Rehovot.
39. The soldiers and Arrow Cross men came to "supplement their needs"...from the "Jews' storerooms," that is, they came to rob.
40. Rudolf Weisz, died in Tel Aviv after the war.
41. In the seventh district of the capital; one of the ghetto bakeries.

David Gur's Testimony

1. Referring to houses where Jews with Protection Passes from one of the Vatican legations or the Swedish Red Cross were concentrated.
2. Details of these anti-Jewish laws can be found in "Yalkut Moreshet," issue 20, p.165, Note 21.
3. This, of course, is a generalization. Nevertheless, there is no doubt that Hungarian Jewry, both as an organized body and as the individuals that comprised it, could have done more for their refugee brethren from surrounding countries.
4. From the day of its inception, the Zionist movement was a small minority among Hungarian Jewry and the Halutz movement was hounded most of the time by the

security services, while even "official" factors of Zionism did nothing to ease the way for the Hungarian Halutzim.
5. "Police Residential Report." See photograph.
6. The pre-military Levente organization's I.D. cards were issued to youth only.
7. In the seventh district.
8. In the sixth district.
9. There were stamps bearing the Hungarian state emblem — two angels. On others, the state emblem was accompanied by oak branches. All these "decorations" only added to the difficulties.
10. The Aliens Control Authority (KEOKH) changed the residence permits at frequent intervals.
11. From April 5, 1944, every Jew had to wear the Yellow Star.
12. It is reasonable to suppose that their protest was not motivated by Jewish pride, but rather by the fear of disobeying the rulers' explicit orders. At later stages, when many leaders were freed of the obligation to wear the Yellow Star (in recognition of their deeds for the Hungarian homeland...) not one of them continued to preach for "martyrdom," or "Sanctification of God's Name."
13. In the fourth district.
14. That is, the second half of May 1944.
15. In the sixth district.
16. In the third district.
17. 30 June, 1944; the meeting with Yoel Palgi took place on 24 June, 1944.
18. In the tenth district.
19. In the second district.
20. Several corps of security reinforcements were mobilized. These only added to the growing chaos.
21. According to Hungarian military terminology the "direct orders" were meant to indicate execution of a certain — not secret — operation which needed the help of military and civilian factors; for example, in moving from one place to another. To prove that the operation was by a military authority, a "direct order" had to be presented at all inspections etc. At first, only officers were authorized to sign such orders; later servicemen with the rank of sergeant were also allowed to sign. As a result, these military papers did not have a uniform appearance, which made forging them somewhat easier.
22. Referring to the building at 2, Percel Mór, mentioned in an earlier chapter, in the fifth district.
23. A border station between Hungary and Germany (Austria). From the first week of November 1944, many thousands of Budapest's Jews were brought here. They arrived at the end of their strength, after a crushing enforced march of close to 250 kilometers, under conditions of starvation, cold, and debasement. Many of the marchers fell by the way, others were shot by their army escorts. In Hegyeshalom itself, and all along the way, courageous bands of neutral legation clerks and the Halutz underground worked to produce protection passes for the marchers and on quite a few occasions the bearer of such a pass was taken out of the march and returned to Budapest.

24. In the seventh district.
25. In the seventh district.
26. In general, it can be said that Italy was more highly valued than Germany in Hungary, maybe because of its support of Hungary (under the oppressive peace agreement) in the 1920s.
27. British and Dutch officers were hidden by a senior clerk in the Hungarian Interior Ministry, Dr. Josef Antall, one of the prominent figures in the small Hungarian civilian underground.
28. One of the central activists of the Communist Party. After the war he served as external affairs liaison and was a member of the Presidential Council of the Hungarian Republic.
29. He was a student before being conscripted to the army.
30. Retired officer of the Hungarian army. Among the leaders of the planned uprising against the Arrow Cross regime, in order to open the front to the Soviet army. He was caught, together with many of the plotters, and hanged on December 8, 1944.
31. Retired officer of the Hungarian army, from which he retired in protest against its growing Nazi tendencies. One of the commanders of the underground communist 'military line.' After 1945, Police Superintendent in the capital. In 1947, Commander in Chief of the new Hungarian army. Executed in 1950, after a false trial. His honor was restored in 1956.
32. Already in the early 1940s, György Nonn was sentenced to eight years in prison for communist activities in Transylvania (whose northern area was annexed by Hungary in 1940). This son of prosperous farmers of German origin, who was also a law student (and married to a Jewess...) got the job of prison clerk, usually given to one of the intellectual prisoners. He exploited his position to escape in 1944.
33. The military prison on Margit Avenue was known to be one of the toughest of these institutions, because of the military discipline that prevailed there.
34. A lower clerk whose promises did not always live up to the reality.
35. As the lowest rank of aristocrats were called. Their children were unable to earn a living from the income of their "estates" and therefore, in great numbers, they filled government posts, mainly in administration of outlying districts. In general the "gentry" were extremely anti-semitic.
36. One of Hungary's greatest writers in our times; of Jewish origins, he spent many years in Western Europe. He was in prison after his return, together with Pál Demény; their association dates from this period. He was one of the outstanding idealistic leaders of the "Hungarian October" in 1956. He was sentenced for his activities and served some two years in prison until he was granted a pardon. He achieved great national and international prestige. Since all his works have been translated into European languages, his countrymen hoped that Tibor Déry would be given the Nobel Prize — before he died. He died in 1977.
37. Hungarian writer and journalist; of Jewish origins. As a member of the Hungarian civilian underground he was one of the distributors of the "Auschwitz Protocols" in the summer of 1944. He was caught on November 22, 1944, but managed to escape. A total and courageous supporter of the State of Israel.
38. A member of the communist underground, faithful to the 'line.' Held central positions after 1945.

39. A member of the Demény faction, from Csepel. Also active in the underground in other industrial zones. After 1945, he headed the workers council in heavy industry's greatest industrial stronghold — Csepel. He later moved into diplomatic circles and became Hungary's ambassador in Warsaw.
40. A member of the Demeny faction. Conducted research into geographic economy. Caught by the Nazis and deported to Germany. On his return, he became a professor at the University of Budapest. Was again persecuted in the Stalinist period. He was re-instated in 1956. From then until his death in 1976, he continued his scientific activity.
41. Secretary of the central committee of the Underground Line. Was caught and deported to Germany. After 1945, he became Deputy Secretary General of the Communist Party, Minister of the Interior, and Foreign Minister until he was subjected to a false trial in 1949 and was executed for the "transgression" of Titoism. Reinstated in 1956.
42. Veteran Soviet agent between the two World Wars. In the last few months of the Holocaust, he took refuge in one of the children's homes. After 1945, he became "Head of the State Defense Authority." Arrested in 1952, he was to be the main activist accused in an anti-Zionist trial!...Later received a pension from the Comunist Party.
43. In the early years of 1970, he was Vice-Premier and Finance Minister of Hungary.
44. Past member of Demény faction. Director of textile plants after 1945. Later served as Deputy Foreign Minister and Hungarian Ambassador to Greece and India.
45. Past member of Demény faction. After 1945 was secreatary of the Communist Party in one of the industrial districts and, later, Minister of Heavy Industry.
46. Member of Demény faction. Arrested by the Soviets in 1945 and returned to Hungary only in 1946. One of the few who dared testify in favor of Pal Demeny at his trial. Accepted into the ruling party only in 1956.
47. The daughter of the famous writer, Zsigmond Móric. She was also a writer.
48. In the seventh district.
49. (1879-1942). He was founder of the "Critical Realism" school of writing in Hungary. There were many sympathetically portrayed Jewish characters in his works. He fought against antisemitism with his pen and his reputation.
50. In the fifth district.
51. A right wing, nationalist student organization, named after one of the Atilla the Hun's imaginary sons. This office became a sort of military rallying point when the students were enlisted in the "University Storm-troopers," in November 1944.
52. So named for the unit's commander, László Vajnay. Originally intended for policing and security for the Nazi and Hungarian forces at the front.
53. At a certain stage, after the Arrow Cross was overthrown, it would be one of the Hungarian S.S. units, to be formed in the spring of 1945.
54. Named after the commander of the unit, Pál Prónay. Originally intended for light warfare against the Soviet Army.
55. These were three girls belonging to the Hungarian Hashomer Hatza'ir, who had Aryan papers and shared an apartment: Erzsi Goldstein, Hava Barmat (now a member of Kibbutz Ein-Dor) and Bruhi (Braha) Hőnig.

56. In the fourteenth district. This referred to a chemical factory on the Mogyoródi Road and a metal factory on A'lmos Vezér Street.
57. In the seventh district.
58. The second President of the Czechoslov Republic, Edvard Benes, was particularly hated by the Hungarian people, whose youth were taught to hate him while still at school!... The reason for this hatred: the thousand-year-old occupation of Hungarian lands, together with the ethnic Hungarian population, who were oppressed, seemingly, by the Benes regime. When some of the territory was returned and re-annexed by Hungary in 1938/39, the Jews of the territory were accused of collaborating with the Czech regime. The false accusation that the Jews had contributed funds to the Czech air force, for the purchase of planes, was an important element in the anti-Jewish incitement.
59. A town in southwest Slovakia. Its Hungarian name — Érsekújvar. Between the two world wars, quite a number of Jews were members of the Hungarian Party, which was one of the parties of the Hungarian minority. It should be noted that the party representative in the "independent" Slovakian "Parliament," Count János Eszterházy, was the only member who dared vote against the Slovakian deportation law. See: Rottkirchen Livia, *Hurban Yahadut Slovakia* — The Destruction of Slovak Jewry — (Jerusalem, 1961) p. 22.
60. This was a kind of official note for sums of different value, contributed to Tito's liberation forces. Many Hungarians were eager to obtain such a note — proving that they were progressive and fought against the Nazis and their helpers....
61. Members of the Arrow Cross Party called one another "brother."
62. Notorious as a bloodthirsty, cruel interrogator.
63. On the December 26, 1944.
64. A common name in Hungary.
65. Because the Soviets were approaching the military prison on Margit Blvd., the prisoners, Jewish and non-Jewish alike, were transferred to the prison in Fo Street. This was done shortly after the group of Jewish prisoners had been removed. The officer from City Command — who remains unidentified to this day — came again on the December 27, 1944. First, he went to Margit Blvd. and then, on being informed that the prisoners he sought had been moved to Fő Street, he went there at the head of his men. It was from here, and not Margit Blvd., as stated, that he led the second group to safety. See: Palgi, p. 352.
66. On the border between the sixth and seventh Quarters.